The Heinemann
Elementary
English Grammar

Digby Beaumont

Heinemann English Language Teaching

A division of Heinemann Publishers (Oxford) Ltd.
Halley Court, Jordan Hill, Oxford, OX2 8EJ

OXFORD MADRID ATHENS
PARIS FLORENCE PRAGUE SÃO PAULO
CHICAGO MELBOURNE AUCKLAND SINGAPORE TOKYO
GABORONE JOHANNESBURG PORTSMOUTH (NH)
IBADAN

ISBN 0 435 28367 7 (with answers)
ISBN 0 435 28368 5 (without answers)

© Digby Beaumont 1993
First published 1993

Designed by Mike Brain

Illustrated by Geoff Jones, Ian Kellas, Kathy Baxendale, John Gilkes,
Peter Kent, Jacky Rough, Paul Russell, Nick Ward, Celia Witchard,
Angela Wood.

Acknowledgements

I would like to acknowledge the invaluable help of Lynn Smart of the
Eurocentre, Brighton, Sussex, who read and commented on various
stages of the manuscript.

I am also very grateful to all the other people whose comments and
suggestions have helped in the preparation of this book, especially
Judith Wilson of the Bell College, Saffron Walden, Hugh Trappes-
Lomax of the University of Edinburgh's Institute of Applied Language
Studies, Helen O'Neill of Godmer House, Oxford, Sally Carpenter and
Jenny Duke.

In addition, I would like to thank Ayşe Güler for her support.

A book such as this could not have been written without the help of the
corpus of published grammar reference books. In this respect, I would like
to acknowledge in particular *A Communicative Grammar of English*, G. Leech,
J. Svartvik (Longman, 1975), *Meaning and the English Verb*, G. Leech
(Longman, 1971), and *Practical English Usage*, M. Swan (OUP, 1980)

Phototypeset by Advanced Filmsetters (Glasgow) Ltd
Printed in Great Britain by The Bath Press, Avon

95 96 97 98 10 9 8 7 6 5

Contents

Introduction   7

A   Nouns and articles

1   **Singular and plural nouns**
(one **chair**, two **chairs**, a **pen**, three **pens**)

2   **A, an**
(**a** house, **an** office, **a** student, **an** engineer)

3   **Possessive 's**
(Mike**'s** camera, your friend**'s** mother)

4   **Countable and uncountable nouns**
(There**'s a cup** on the table. There **are some cups**
on the table. There**'s some coffee** on the table.)

5   **A, an, the**
(There's **a** bank near here. Look, there's Tony
outside **the** bank.)

6   **Talking in general**
(**Houses** are expensive. **The houses** in this street
are very old.)

7   **Proper nouns**
(Are you from **England** or **the United States**?
. My flat is in **Regent Street**, near **the Regent
Hotel**.)

8   **Expressions with and without** the
(We're **going to school**. We're **going to the
cinema**. What**'s on TV**? What**'s on the radio**?)

9   **Review of nouns and articles**

B   Quantity

.10   **Some, any, no**
(We've got **some** milk, but we haven't got **any**
eggs. Are there **any** chairs in the kitchen? There's
no soap in the bathroom.)

11   **Much, many, a lot of, a little, a few, enough**
(How **much** petrol is there in the car? How **many**
brothers and sisters have you got? 'We've got **a lot
of** rice, but only **a little** cheese and **a few**
vegetables.'   'Have we got **enough** coffee?')

12   **Review of quantity**

C   Personal pronouns

13   **Subject pronouns**
(Maria is Italian. **She**'s from Rome. Alex and
Anna aren't at home. **They**'re at the cinema.)

14   **Possessive adjectives**
(Maria is with **her** father. What's **your** name?)

15   **Object pronouns**
(Maria is very nice. I like **her**. Alex and Anna are
late. I'm waiting for **them**.)

16   **Possessive pronouns**
(This isn't Maria's bag. **Hers** is blue. My name is
Tony. What's **yours**?)

17   **Review of personal pronouns**

D   Other pronouns

18   **This, that, these, those**
(Look at **this** photograph. Is **that** your car outside?
Mmm! **These** sandwiches are delicious.)

19   **One, ones**
(My car is the white **one** outside. Who are those
people – the **ones** over there?)

20   **Something, anything, somebody, anybody,
etc**
(There's **somebody** in the office. There isn't
anything good on TV. There's **nowhere** to sit
down in this room.)

Contents

21 Reflexive pronouns
(*My grandfather often talks to* **himself***. Diana hurt* **herself** *when she fell. Do you live by* **yourself***?*)

22 Review of other pronouns

E Talking about the present

23 Present tense of the verb *be*
(*My name* **is** *Gina. I'* **m** *a student. I'* **m not** *a teacher. '* **Are** *you and your friend English?' 'No, we* **aren't***.'*)

24 There is, there are
(**There's** *a stereo in the car.* **There are** *five rooms in the flat. '* **Is there** *a bank near here?' 'No,* **there isn't***.'*)

25 Have got
(*I'* **ve got** *a computer. Madonna* **has got** *blue eyes.* **Have** *you* **got** *any brothers or sisters?*)

26 Imperative
(**Listen***.* **Be** *careful.* **Don't forget** *your umbrella.*)

27 Present simple
(*I* **play** *basketball every Tuesday. '* **Do** *you usually* **work** *on Saturdays?' 'Yes, I* **do***.' Maria* **doesn't live** *in Milan. She* **lives** *in Rome.*)

28 Present continuous
(*I'* **m leaving** *now. Goodbye. Oh, no! Look outside. It'* **s raining***. '* **Are** *you* **working** *at the moment?' 'Yes, I* **am***.'*)

29 Present continuous and present simple
(*I'* **m leaving** *now. Goodbye. I usually* **leave** *work at 5.30. Look! It'* **s snowing** *outside. It often* **snows** *in Britain in the winter.*)

30 Verbs not normally used in the continuous
(*I* **know** *your brother.* **Do** *you* **understand** *this word? Monica* **has** *long blonde hair.*)

31 Review of talking about the present

F Talking about the past

32 Past tense of the verb *be*
(*I* **was** *at home yesterday. I* **wasn't** *at work.* **'Were** *you and Julia at the cinema last night?' 'Yes, we* **were***.'*)

33 Past simple
(*We* **played** *tennis yesterday. Tony* **stayed** *at home last night. He* **didn't go** *out. 'I* **went** *to Canada in 1990.' '* **Did** *you* **go** *to Ottawa?'*)

34 Past continuous
(*'What* **were** *you* **doing** *at 3 o'clock yesterday?' 'I* **was cleaning** *my flat.'*)

35 Present perfect simple
(*I'* **ve lived** *here for four years.* **Have** *you ever* **been** *to Australia? Look! Andrew* **has grown** *a beard!*)

36 Present perfect simple and past simple
(*I'* **ve had** *my present job for two years. I* **had** *my old job for five years.* **Have** *you ever* **been** *to Los Angeles?* **Did** *you* **go** *to Los Angeles last summer?*)

37 Review of talking about the past

G Talking about the future

38 Present continuous for the future
(*I'* **m meeting** *a friend this evening. Diana* **is flying** *to Milan next Monday. What* **are** *you* **doing** *on Saturday?*)

39 Going to
(*I'* **m going to write** *some letters this evening. Look at those black clouds. It'* **s going to rain***.*)

40 Will
(*'I'm cold.' 'Are you? I'* **ll close** *the window, then.' I think Brazil* **will win** *the football match tomorrow.*)

41 *Will, going to*
(*I'll clean* my car. *I'm going to clean* my car. He'll *bite* you. He's *going to bite* you.)

42 **Review of talking about the future**

H Modal verbs

43 *Can*
(*Tony can swim*, but he *can't windsurf*. Can you *speak* Chinese?)

44 *Could*
(*Tony could swim* when he was six years old. *Could* you *speak* Japanese before you went to Japan?)

45 *Must*
(*I'm really tired. I must go* home now. You *mustn't be* late for work tomorrow.)

46 *Have to*
(*You have to be* eighteen to vote in Britain. We *don't have to hurry*. We aren't late. I *had to wear* a uniform when I was at school.)

47 *May, might*
(*I may go* to the beach tomorrow. You *might be* rich one day.)

48 *Should*
(*You've got a bad cold. You should go* to bed. Parents *shouldn't hit* their children.)

49 **Requests:** *can, could, may*
(*Can I have* a coffee, please? *Could* you *tell* me the way to East Street? *May I ask* you a question?)

50 **Offers and invitations:** *would like, will, shall*
(*Would you like* a drink? *I'll lend* you some money. *Shall I help* you?)

51 **Suggestions:** *shall, let's, why don't we, how about*
('What *shall* we *do* this evening?' '*Let's stay* at home.' '*Why don't we go* out?' '*How about going* to the cinema?')

52 **Review of modal verbs**

I Questions

53 **Question words**
(*What* . . .? *Who* . . .? *Which* . . .? *Whose* . . .? *Where* . . .? *When* . . .? *Why* . . .? *How* . . .?)

54 **Subject and object questions**
(*Who loves* Tina? *Who does* Tina *love?*)

55 **Question tags**
(*You aren't married, are you?* It's a nice day, *isn't it?*)

56 **Review of questions**

J Infinitive and *-ing* form

57 **Word + infinitive or *-ing* form**
(*I can play* tennis. I want *to play* tennis. I enjoy *playing* tennis.)

58 **Purpose:** *to . . .* and *for . . .*
(*We went to a cafe to have* lunch. We went to a cafe *for* lunch. A lawn mower is a machine *for cutting* grass.)

59 **Review of infinitive and *-ing* form**

K Adjectives and adverbs

60 **Adjectives**
(*That's a good film. I'm happy*. You look *tired*.)

61 Word order with adverbs and adverbial phrases
(*I play basketball in the Sports Centre on Tuesdays. Frank always sings in the bath. He's always happy.*)

62 Comparison of adjectives
(*Today is hotter than yesterday. Which is the hottest country in the world? Greece isn't as hot as Saudi Arabia.*)

63 Adjectives and adverbs
(*She's nervous. She's waiting nervously. I'm a bad dancer. I dance badly.*)

64 Too and enough with adjectives and adverbs
(*I can't go out tonight. I'm too tired. That bed isn't big enough for two people.*)

65 Review of adjectives and adverbs

L Prepositions

66 Place: in, on, at
(*The dictionary is on the desk in my room. Meet me at the airport.*)

67 Time: in, on, at
(*at 8 o'clock, on Monday, in the morning, at night, at the weekend, in October, on 5th October, in 1954, in the winter*)

68 Place and movement
(*on, in, in front of, behind, near, opposite, next to, between, into, out of, onto, off, up, down, along, across, through, over, under, past, round, from, to*)

69 Time: ago, for, since
(*We arrived here three days ago. We've been here for three days. We've been here since Monday.*)

70 Review of prepositions

M Linking words

71 And, but, or, because, so
(*I can surf and windsurf, but I can't water-ski. Do you prefer pop music or classical music? I can't buy a car because I haven't got enough money. I haven't got enough money, so I can't buy a car.*)

72 When, if
(*I'll be at the station when your train arrives. I'll take the driving test again if I fail it the first time.*)

73 Review of linking words

N Days, months, numbers, the time

74 Days, months, numbers
(*Monday, Tuesday . . . January, February . . . one, two, three . . . first, second, third . . .*)

75 The time
(*'What's the time?' 'It's five o'clock.'*)

General information

1	**Short forms** (*I'm, You've*)	216
2	**Pronunciation of endings: -s/-es, -ed** (*books, watches, started, looked*)	217
3	**Spelling of endings: -s/-es, -ing, -ed, -er, -est, -ly** (*cities, driving, used, bigger, biggest, happily*)	218
4	**Irregular verbs**	219
5	**American English**	221

Progress tests	222
Index	238
Answers to the exercises	241
Answers to the progress tests	255

Introduction

Who is the book for?

- This book is for students who want to **understand** and **practise** English **grammar**.

- The book explains and practises all the main grammar points that students need to progress from **beginner** to **upper elementary** level.

- The book is for both **self-study** and **class use**.

What can you find in the book?

- The list of *Contents* on pages 3–6 shows what is in the book.

- There are 14 **sections** in the book, A–N. Each section is about a general area of grammar.

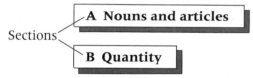

Sections

- There are 75 **units** in the 14 sections. Generally, each unit is about a particular point of grammar.

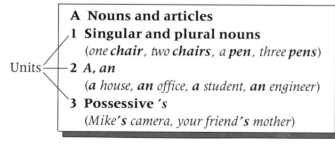

Units

- The units in each section are **graded** – the easiest units come at the beginning of a section and the most difficult units come at the end of the section.

- The units begin with **examples** and **explanations** of grammar points. They then have **exercises** on those points. Answers to the exercises are on pages 241–254.

- Generally, at the end of each section there is a special *Review* unit.

> **9 Review of nouns and articles**

This unit revises the grammar in all the other units in that section. For example, Unit 9 revises the grammar in Units 1–8.

- In *General information* on pages 216–221 there is information about short forms (eg *I'm, isn't*), pronunciation and spelling of endings (eg *-s, -es, -ing, -ed*), irregular verbs and American English.

- There is an *Index* on pages 238–240.

> *a, an* 2, 4–5, 9R
> *a few* 11, 12R

- There are 62 *Progress tests* on pages 222–237. These tests will show how well students have learnt the grammar in the units. Answers to the tests are on pages 255–256.

- *Grammar words* on pages 8–9 explains all the main grammar words in the book.

> **adjective**   eg *old, big*. Adjectives describe nouns eg *an **old** man* or pronouns eg *He's **old**.*

How can you use the book for self-study?

Finding what you want to study

- If you know which grammar point you want to study, use the *Index* on pages 238–240. For example, if you want to study *must*, look up *must* in the *Index* and find the unit number (or numbers) that you need.

- If you do **not** know which grammar point to study, use the *Contents* on pages 3–6. Look at the *Contents* and choose a unit to study.

  Remember! The easiest units come at the beginning of a section and the most difficult units come at the end of the section.

Using the units

- First, study the examples and explanations of the grammar point.
  Remember! If you have a problem with the meaning of a grammar word, look for an explanation of the word in *Grammar words* on pages 8–9.

- Then do the exercise(s).
  You can write most of your answers to the exercises in the book. But when you see ★, it means that you need to write on a piece of paper.
  Remember! The exercises are **not** tests. If you have any problems, study the examples and explanations again.

- Check your answers with the *Answers to the exercises* on pages 241–254.

  Remember! Check your answers with each exercise before you start a new exercise.

Using the tests

- When you finish a unit, you can find the test for that unit in the *Progress tests contents* on pages 222–223.

- Do the test. Write your answers on a piece of paper.

- Then check your answers in the *Answers to the progress tests* on pages 255–256.

Grammar words

Here are explanations of all the main grammar words in the book:

adjective   eg *old, big*. Adjectives describe nouns eg *an **old** man* or pronouns eg *He's **old***.

adverb   eg *I'm leaving **now*** (adverb of time); *Come **here*** (adverb of place); *It **often** rains* (adverb of frequency); *Speak **slowly*** (adverb of manner).

affirmative   eg *We are English* is **affirmative**; *We aren't English* is **negative**.

article   The articles are *a, an* and *the*.

comparative   eg *small**er*** and *cold**er*** are the comparatives of *small* and *cold*.

consonant   See **vowel**.

continuous   *be* + *-ing* eg *I'm **working*** (present continuous); *I **was working*** (past continuous).

countable noun   eg *house, girl*. These nouns have a plural form eg *houses*. We can use these nouns with *a/an* and numbers eg ***a** house, **one** girl*.

formal   We use **formal** language eg in business letters and polite conversations. We use **informal** language eg when we speak or write to friends.

full verb   an ordinary verb eg *play, watch, eat*.

imperative   eg ***Close** the door; **Be** careful; **Don't go** now*.

infinitive   In *I can swim, swim* is the **infinitive without** *to*. In *I want to swim, to swim* is the *to* **infinitive**.

***-ing* form**   verb + *-ing* eg *working*, *playing*.

intonation   Rising intonation is when the voice goes up eg *Are you Italian?* Falling intonation is when the voice goes down eg *I'm Brazilian*.

irregular   See **regular**.

linking word   eg *and, but, so, if*. A linking word joins two ideas eg *I play golf **and** tennis; We'll stay at home **if** it rains*.

modal verb   The modal verbs are *can, could, may, might, will, would, shall, should, must* (and a few other verbs).

negative   See **affirmative**.

noun   the name of a person, thing, etc eg *Jim, car*.

object   See **subject**.

past participle   The past participle of regular verbs ends in *-ed* eg *finished*. Some verbs have irregular past participles eg *go* → **gone**.

perfect   *have* + past participle eg *I'**ve finished*** (present perfect).

phrase   a group of words that we use together eg *at 8 o'clock, in the park*.

plural   more than one eg *book* and *he* are **singular**; *books* and *they* are **plural**.

possessive adjective   The possessive adjectives are *my, your, his, her, its, our, their*.

possessive pronoun   The possessive pronouns are *mine, yours, his, hers, ours, theirs*.

possessive *'s*   eg *Jim**'s** car, my friend**'s** mother*.

preposition   eg *at, in, on, of, for*.

pronoun   eg *he, she, ours, them*. We use pronouns in place of nouns.

question tag   eg *It's late, **isn't it**?*

question word   The question words are *what, who, which, whose, where, when, why, how* (and *how old, how tall, how much*, etc).

reflexive pronoun   The reflexive pronouns are *myself, yourself, himself, herself, itself, ourselves, yourselves, themselves*.

regular   A **regular** form is the usual form eg *girls* is a regular plural (ending in *-s*), but *women* is an **irregular** plural.

short answer   eg *'Are you hot?'*   *'**Yes, I am.**'*

short form   eg *I'm* and *isn't* are **short forms**; *I am* and *is not* are **full forms**.

simple   not continuous eg *I **work*** (present simple); *I **worked*** (past simple); *I'**ve worked*** (present perfect simple).

singular   See **plural**.

stress   In the word *forget*, the stress is on the second syllable *for-* '*get*.

subject   In *Sue saw the man, Sue* is the **subject** and *the man* is the **object**.

superlative   eg *smallest* and *coldest* are the superlatives of *small* and *cold*.

syllable   The word *expensive* has three syllables *ex-pen-sive*.

uncountable noun   eg *rice, petrol*. These nouns have no plural form eg we cannot say ~~rices~~. We do not normally use *a, an* or numbers with these nouns eg we cannot say ~~a rice~~ or ~~one petrol~~.

verb   *Play, work* and *go* are examples of verbs (or full verbs). See also **modal verbs**.

vowel   The letters *a, e, i, o, u* are **vowels**. All the other letters (*b, c, d, f, g, h*, etc) are **consonants**.

1 Singular and plural nouns

one **chair**	two **chairs**
a **pen**	three **pens**

■ SINGULAR (one)   PLURAL (more than one)

a **camera**

two **cameras**

a **watch**   three **watches**

■ Most nouns add -*s* in the plural.

SINGULAR	PLURAL
camera	camera**s**
pen	pen**s**
phone	phone**s**

■ Nouns ending in -*ch*, -*sh*, -*s* or -*x*, add -*es*.

SINGULAR	PLURAL
watch	watch**es**
brush	brush**es**
bus	bus**es**
box	box**es**

Tomato and *potato* also add -*es*: *tomatoes, potatoes*.

■ Nouns ending in a consonant + -*y* (eg -*ty*, -*ly*), take away the -*y* and add -*ies*.

SINGULAR	PLURAL
city	cit**ies**
family	famil**ies**

■ Most nouns ending in -*f* or -*fe*, take away the -*f*/-*fe* and add -*ves*.

SINGULAR	PLURAL
loaf	loa**ves**
wife	wi**ves**

▷ For the -*s*/-*es* pronunciation, see page 217.

■ Some nouns do not add -*s* or -*es* in the plural. For example:

SINGULAR	PLURAL
man	**men**
woman	**women**
child	**children**
person	**people**
tooth	**teeth**
foot	**feet**
mouse	**mice**
sheep	**sheep**
fish	**fish**

a **person**

two **people**

Practice

Exercise 1A

(i) Write the plurals of these words.

1 chair _chairs_   9 dog _____

2 cup _cups_   10 room _____

3 glass _glasses_   11 knife _____

4 book _____   12 dish _____

5 watch _____   13 city _____

6 flat _____   14 office _____

7 pen _____   15 desk _____

8 bed _____   16 box _____

(ii) How do we say the -s/-es endings? Practise saying these words.

/ɪz/	/z/	/s/
churches	cars	shops
brushes	phones	banks
kisses	bags	cats
foxes	arms	
	friends	
	parties	
	wives	

(iii) Now put the plurals from (i) into three groups.

/ɪz/	/z/	/s/
glasses	_chairs_	_cups_
___	___	___
___	___	___
___	___	___
___		
___		

▷ What are the -s/-es pronunciation rules? See page 217.

Exercise 1B

Give the names of these parts of the body.

1 _eyes_ _____

2 _____

3 _____

4 _____

5 _____

6 _____

7 _____

leg	eye	foot	hand
ear	arm	tooth	

Exercise 1C

(i) What are the names of these animals?

| mouse   tiger   chicken   goldfish   zebra   fox |

zebras _____ _____

_____ _____

_____ _____

★ (ii) Now make lists of animals you can find:

in a zoo	on a farm	in a house
zebras	*chickens*	*cats*

Exercise 1D

The names of these things are always plural in English. They all end in *-s* or *-es*. What are the names?

1 (SORTUERS)  2 (TOSHRS)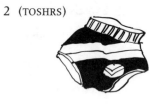

trousers _____ _____

3 (JAMAPSY)  4 (SHTIGT)

_____ _____

5 (ENJAS) 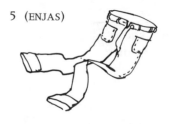 6 (SASGLES)

_____ _____

7 (SOSCSIRS)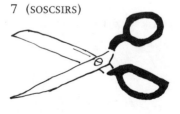

_____

2 A, an

a house	*an* office
a student	*an* engineer

a bicycle

an umbrella

■ Before a singular noun (eg *bicycle, umbrella*), we normally use *a* or *an* (or *one, my, the,* etc).

*Have you got **a** bicycle?* (Not: ~~Have you got bicycle?~~)
*I've got **an** umbrella.* (Not: ~~I've got umbrella.~~)

■ Remember to use *a* or *an* when you talk about someone's job.

*Maria Rossi is **a** journalist.* (Not: ~~Maria Rossi is journalist.~~)
*Tom Cruise is **an** actor.* (Not: ~~Tom Cruise is actor.~~)

■ Compare:

a	*an*
*a **b**icycle*	*an **a**ctor*
*a **c**omputer*	*an **e**nvelope*
*a **d**og*	*an **i**ce cream*
*a **f**ilm*	*an **o**ld man*
*a **g**lass*	*an **u**mbrella*

We use *an* before vowels (*a, e, i, o, u*), and *a* before consonants (all the other letters eg *b, c, d, f, g*).

■ We use *a* before *u* when we pronounce *u* /juː/.
*a **u**niversity* /ə ˌjuːnɪˈvɜːsətɪ/

We use *an* before *h* when we do not pronounce *h*.
*an **h**our* /ən ˈaʊə(r)/

■ We do not use *a* or *an* before a plural noun (eg *bicycles, actors*).

I've got two bicycles.
Al Pacino and Mel Gibson are actors.

■ Compare *a/an* and *one*:

*I've got **a** suitcase.*
*I've only got **one** suitcase. My sister has got two.*

We use *one* to talk about the number—*one,* not *two, three, four,* etc.

Practice

Exercise 2A

What have they got for lunch?

She's got...

1 *a burger*
2 _____
3 _____
4 _____
5 _____

He's got...

6 _____
7 _____
8 _____

ice cream   glass of water   sandwich   apple
milkshake   burger   egg   bar of chocolate

Exercise 2B

(i) What are the jobs? Use *a* or *an*.

electrician   waiter   actor   taxi driver   postman
optician

1 *a postman*
2 _____
3 _____
4 _____
5 _____
6 _____

Practice

Exercise 3A

(i) How do we normally say these things in English?

1 the car of my sister – *my sister's car*

2 the mother of Nick – *Nick's mother*

3 the family of Liz – _____

4 the school of Mike – _____

5 the office of Kurt – _____

6 the TV of Doris – _____

7 the book of Bruce – _____

8 the wife of Tom – _____

9 the beds of the children – _____

_____

10 the house of my parents – _____

_____

(ii) How do we say the *'s/s'* endings? Put the examples from (i) into three groups.

/ɪz/ *Liz's* _____

/z/ *my sister's* _____

/s/ *Nick's* _____

_____

▷ For the *'s/s'* pronunciation rules, see page 217.

Exercise 3B

Charlie Chaplin   **Sherlock Holmes**

Whose are these things?

1

pipe

2

shoes

3

cane

4

hat

5

violin

6

trousers

1 That is *Sherlock Holmes's pipe.* _____

2 Those are *Charlie Chaplin's shoes.* _____

3 That is _____

4 That is _____

5 That is _____

6 Those are _____

Exercise 3C

Nicole   **Shizuo**   **Nancy**

Frank   **Rajah**   **Gina**

Whose is it?

1

2

3

Gina's

4

5

6

Exercise 3D

Ask the questions. Use the possessive *'s* or *of . . .*

1 What is (the name | your teacher)?
2 What is (the name | your school)?
3 When is (the birthday | your teacher)?
4 Who is (the favourite actor | your teacher)?
5 When is (the start | the next school holiday)?
6 What is (the name | your home town)?
7 What is (the number | your house)?

1 *What is your teacher's name?*
2 *What is the name of your school?*
3 _____
4 _____
   _____
5 _____
   _____
6 _____
7 _____

4 Countable and uncountable nouns

> There's **a cup** on the table.
> There **are some cups** on the table.
> There's **some coffee** on the table.

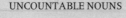

COUNTABLE NOUNS   UNCOUNTABLE NOUNS

*a **cup***

rice

*an **egg***

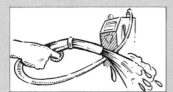

petrol

*a **girl***

snow

■ Countable nouns are the names of things, people, etc that we can count. For example, we can say *one cup, two cups, one egg, six eggs*.

Uncountable nouns are the names of things that we cannot count. For example, we cannot say ~~one rice~~ or ~~two rices~~.

■ Countable nouns have a singular and a plural form eg *cup, cups, egg, eggs*.

Uncountable nouns do not have a plural form. For example, we cannot say ~~rices~~ or ~~petrols~~.

■ Countable nouns can take a singular or a plural verb. Uncountable nouns always take a singular verb.

Where	**is**	the **cup**?	(singular countable)
Where	**are**	the **cups**?	(plural countable)
Where	**is**	the **rice**?	(uncountable)

■ Before a singular countable noun we normally use *a* or *an* (or *one, the, my,* etc).

*I've got **a cup**.* (Not: ~~I've got cup.~~)

■ We use plural countable nouns and uncountable nouns:

□ with *some*

*We've got **some eggs**.*
*There's **some petrol** in the car.*

□ or alone (without *some, the,* etc).

*We've got **eggs**.*
*There's **petrol** in the car.*

We do not normally use these nouns with *a* or *an*. For example, we do not say ~~We've got an eggs~~ or ~~There's a petrol in the car~~.

19

■ These nouns are normally uncountable in English:

| advice bread furniture hair information |
| money news spaghetti weather |

*He's got **some bread**.* (Not: *He's got a bread.*)

*Her **hair is** lovely.* (Not: *Her hairs are lovely.*)

*His **money is** in his hat!* (Not: *His money are in his hat!*)

■ A lot of nouns can be both countable and uncountable.

COUNTABLE	UNCOUNTABLE
Two coffees, please (eg in a cafe)	**Coffee is** expensive.

■ We can count quantities of some uncountable things with *glass, packet, carton, bottle, litre,* etc.

a glass of water

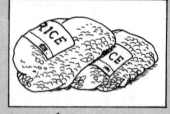

two packets of rice

three cartons of milk

a bottle of oil

two cans of lemonade

a loaf of bread

■ Compare:

UNCOUNTABLE	COUNTABLE
*He's got **some bread**. There **is some milk** in the fridge.*	*He's got **a loaf of bread**. There **are two cartons of milk** in the fridge.*

Practice

Exercise 4A

Put the words with the pictures.

| engine   sugar   glass   oil   rain   shoe |

 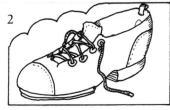

Are these things countable or uncountable here? Make
two lists. Use *a* or *an* where necessary.

COUNTABLE

a shoe (2)
_____

_____

UNCOUNTABLE

rain (1)
_____

_____

Exercise 4B

Complete the sentences. Use *is* or *are*. Add *a* or *an*
where necessary.

1 There __*is a*_____ pen on my desk.
2 There __*is*_____ milk in the fridge.
3 There _____ eggs in the fridge.
4 There _____ old man outside.
5 Those women _____ teachers.
6 That woman _____ doctor.
7 There _____ sugar in this coffee.
8 That _____ expensive radio.

Exercise 4C

What is on the table? Make a list. Use *a, an* or *some.*

Some tomatoes, some meat,
_____

_____

Exercise 4D

There are mistakes in some of these sentences. Find
the mistakes and correct them.

1 There's some oil in the bottle. ✓
2 I've got some informations. *information*
3 We've got a bread.
4 The money is in my room.
5 Furnitures are expensive.
6 Your hairs are lovely today.
7 There's some good news.
8 Are the spaghettis cooked?

Exercise 4E

What can you see in the picture?
Use:

some __

or:

a	box loaf can packet bottle tin carton	of __

Give two answers where possible.

1 some coffee or a packet of coffee

5 *A, an, the*

| *There's **a** bank near here.* | *Look, there's Tony outside **the** bank.* |

■ Compare:

a banana—we do not know which banana

the banana—we know which banana

■ We use *the* when it is clear which thing or person we are talking about.

*It's dark in this room. Switch on **the light**. (=the light in this room)*

*Mr and Mrs Jones have a daughter and two sons. **The daughter** is a doctor. (=the daughter that Mr and Mrs Jones have)*

■ Compare:

*Diana has got **a phone** in her car.*

*Diana is talking on **the phone**. (=the phone in her car)*

Practice

Exercise 5A

What is different in picture B?

A

B

Complete the sentences. Add *a, an* or *the*.

In picture B . . .

1 There's __*a*__ bird in __*the*__ cage.

2 _____ old woman is writing _____ letter.

3 There's _____ cat on _____ sofa.

4 _____ man has got _____ moustache.

5 _____ young woman is reading _____ book.

6 There's _____ glass on _____ table.

7 _____ photograph is on _____ wall.

8 There's _____ alarm clock on _____ TV.

9 _____ goldfish isn't in _____ bowl.

Exercise 5B

Choose the correct answer.

1 (*a shower* or *the shower?*)

a) __*The shower*__ is broken at the moment.

b) There isn't __*a shower*__ in this bathroom.

2 (*a garden* or *the garden?*)

a) Our house hasn't got _____ .

b) Maria is outside in _____ .

3 (*a poster* or *the poster?*)

a) Look at _____ on this wall.

b) I've got _____ of Madonna on my wall.

4 (*a woman* or *the woman?*)

a) I can see two men and _____ in that car.

b) Who is _____ in the corner?

6 Talking in general

Houses are expensive.	**The houses** in this street are very old.

I don't like **carrots**. (=carrots in general)

Money is important. (=money in general)

■ We do not use *the* with plural countable nouns or uncountable nouns to talk about something in general.

Lions are dangerous. (=lions in general)
Life isn't easy. (=life in general)
Do you like **pop music**? (=pop music in general)

■ We use *the* when it is clear which particular thing or person we are talking about.

Pass **the carrots**, please. (=the carrots on this table)

Take **the money**. (=the money in my hands)

■ Compare:

GENERAL	PARTICULAR
I like meeting **people**.	Who are **the people** outside?
Milk is good for you.	**The milk** is in the fridge.

25

Practice

Exercise 6A

What does Diana like?

She likes . . .   **She doesn't like . . .**

1

2

3

(i) Make sentences about what Diana likes and doesn't like. Use these words:

> golf
> opera
> fast-food restaurants
> pop music
> football
> expensive restaurants

1 *She likes opera.*
  She doesn't like pop music.

2 _____

_____

3 _____

_____

_____

★ (ii) What about you? Make sentences about some of these things.

I like I don't like	___.

Example:

> *I like opera.*
> or *I don't like opera.*

(iii)

Ask someone if he or she likes these things.

1 *Do you like computer games?*
2 *Do you like discos?*
3 _____
4 _____
5 _____
6 _____

| classical music   basketball   computer games discos   housework   heavy metal music |

Exercise 6B

Are these ideas general (**G**) or particular (**P**)?

1 Fish is good for you. *G*
2 The fish is in the fridge. *P*
3 Children need love. _____
4 I know the children in that car. _____
5 Young children enjoy playing. _____
6 I like food. _____
7 I like good food. _____
8 I like Chinese food. _____

Exercise 6C

Choose the correct answer.

1 (*The sugar* or *Sugar*?)
a) *Sugar* _____ is bad for you.
b) *The sugar* _____ is in the kitchen.
2 (*the elephants* or *elephants*?)
a) Look at _____ in this photograph.
b) _____ live in Africa and India.
3 (*the bread* or *bread*?)
a) I eat a lot of _____ .
b) I like _____ in that shop.
4 (*the English people* or *English people*?)
a) Who are _____ with Maria?
b) _____ drink a lot of tea.

7 Proper nouns

> Are you from **England** or **the United States?**
> My flat is in **Regent Street**, near **the Regent Hotel**.

■ We do not normally use *the* before 'proper nouns', for example, the names of:

☐ people	**Jim** is my brother. (Not: ~~The Jim~~)
☐ days	Today is **Monday**. (Not: ~~the Monday~~)
☐ months	My birthday is in **May**. (Not: ~~the May~~)
☐ languages	**Italian** is a beautiful language. (Not: ~~The Italian~~)
☐ countries* and continents	What is the capital of **Italy**? (Not: ~~the Italy~~) **India** is in **Asia**. (Not: ~~The India is in the Asia.~~)
☐ cities, towns and villages	**Tokyo** is a big city. (Not: ~~The Tokyo~~) **Toowoomba** is a small town. (Not: ~~The Toowoomba~~)
☐ streets	My office is in **West Street**. (Not: ~~the West Street~~)
☐ cities + buildings	I'm a student at **Chicago University**. How big is **Sydney Zoo**?

*But we say **the** United States and **the** United Kingdom.

■ We normally use *the* with the names of:

☐ hotels, cinemas, theatres and museums	Where is **the Plaza Hotel**? There is a good film on at **the Odeon Cinema**. **The Playhouse Theatre** is near here.
☐ oceans, seas and rivers	Tahiti is in **the Pacific Ocean**. Paris is on **the River Seine**.

■ We use *the* before names with ...*of*...

I'm a student at **the University of Chicago**.
How old is **the Tower of London**?

The Tower of London

Practice

Exercise 7A

Add *the* where necessary.

1 *the* Plaza Hotel
2 / London University
3 _____ University of London
4 _____ February
5 _____ 61st Street
6 _____ Princess Diana
7 _____ President of France
8 _____ Brighton Station
9 _____ United States
10 _____ Atlantic Ocean
11 _____ Australia
12 _____ Hudson River
13 _____ Dallas
14 _____ Odeon Cinema
15 _____ Sunday
16 _____ Bank of Scotland
17 _____ Switzerland
18 _____ Shakespeare Theatre
19 _____ Madison Avenue
20 _____ Museum of Modern Art

Exercise 7B

★ Find the names of three each of these.

1 Countries
2 Continents
3 Capital cities
4 Oceans
5 Seas
6 Rivers
7 Museums
8 Famous hotels

Give the names. Use *the* where necessary.

Example:

| 1 Countries |
| Spain |
| Japan |
| The United States |

Mediterranean

Africa

Waldorf Astoria

Pacific

Rhine	Berne	Caribbean
Ritz	Athens	Tokyo
Louvre	Spain	Atlantic
Danube	Asia	Europe
Prado	Aegean	
Japan	Hilton	
United States	Nile	
Uffizi	Indian	

8 Expressions with and without *the*

*We're **going to school**.* *What's **on TV**?*	*We're **going to the cinema**.* *What's **on the radio**?*

■ We use these expressions without *the*:

(go) to school/college/ *university*	*(be) at school/college/* *university*
(go) to work	*(be) at work*
(go) home	*(be) at home*
(go) to bed	*(be) in bed*
(go) to prison	*(be) in prison*
(go) to hospital	*(be) in hospital*
(go) to church	*(be) at/in church*

(have/eat) breakfast/lunch/dinner
(have/eat/be) for breakfast/lunch/dinner

(go/travel) by car/bus/plane, etc
(go/travel) on foot (=walking)

*What time do you **go to school**?* (Not: ~~go to the school~~)
*Peter **is at work** now.* (Not: ~~is at the work~~)
*Goodbye. I'm **going home**.* (Not: ~~going to the home~~)
*I **go to bed** at about 12.00.* (Not: ~~go to the bed~~)
*Joe is ill **in hospital**.* (Not: ~~is ill in the hospital~~)
*What do you usually **have for breakfast**?*
(Not: ~~have for the breakfast~~)
*Do you like travelling **by train**?* (Not: ~~by the train~~)

■ We often use the expressions *(watch) television/TV* and
(be) on television/TV, without *the*.

*They **watch television** every evening.*
*There's a good programme **on TV**.*

■ We use these expressions with *the*:

(go) to the cinema	*(be) at the cinema*
(go) to the theatre	*(be) at the theatre*
(listen) to the radio	*(be) on the radio*

(play/learn) the guitar/the piano/the violin, etc

*Do you like **going to the cinema**?*
*There's a good programme **on the radio**.*
*Mike can **play the guitar**.*

■ These expressions with *the* have a general meaning:
the town, the country, the sea, the sun, the rain.

*I often swim in **the sea**.*
*Do you like lying in **the sun**?*
*I love walking in **the rain**.*

I prefer the town to the country!

Practice

Exercise 8A

Complete the sentences. Use the words in the box.
Add *the* where necessary.

> violin   university   breakfast   bed   sea   sun
> hospital   church   foot   TV   radio   cinema

1 I usually watch _TV_____ in the evenings.

2 I never go swimming in _____ .

3 I don't usually eat _____ in the
   morning.

4 I'm not tired. I don't want to go to _____ .

5 There are some good films on at _____
   _____ at the moment.

6 I'm always happy when _____ is
   shining.

7 Are you going into _____ for
   an operation?

8 I enjoy listening to _____ in my
   car.

9 Those people are going to _____
   to get married.

10 My sister is a student at _____ .

11 I can't play _____ .

12 I'm lazy. I never go anywhere on _____ .

Exercise 8B

Ask the questions. Add *the* where necessary.

> 1 Do you usually listen to _the___ radio when
>   you're having a shower?
>
> 2 Do you like talking when you're having
>   _/____ breakfast?
>
> 3 Do you sometimes go to _____ school/work
>   on _____ foot?
>
> 4 Do you usually eat much for _____ lunch?
>
> 5 Do you often watch _____ TV in the
>   evenings?
>
> 6 Do you prefer going to _____ cinema or
>   _____ theatre?
>
> 7 Do you sometimes go swimming in _____
>   sea?
>
> 8 Do you like walking in _____ rain?
>
> 9 Do you prefer travelling by _____ car or by
>   _____ train?
>
> 10 Do you play _____ piano?
>
> 11 Do you prefer _____ town or _____ country?
>
> 12 What time do you usually go to _____ bed?

9 Review of nouns and articles

Exercise 9A (▷ Units 1–2, 4)

(i) Are these nouns singular, plural or uncountable?

> tomatoes car bread umbrella music book
> houses men money

Make three lists.

SINGULAR	PLURAL	UNCOUNTABLE
car	tomatoes	bread
_____	_____	_____
_____	_____	_____

(ii) Choose the correct answer. (Sometimes two answers are correct.)

1 Have you got ~~car~~/a car/~~an car~~/~~some car~~?

2 I need *umbrella/a umbrella/an umbrella/some umbrella*.

3 We've got *tomatoes/a tomatoes/an tomatoes/some tomatoes*.

4 We need *bread/a bread/an bread/some bread*.

5 There *is/are* a book on my desk.

6 There *is/are* some men outside.

7 There *is/are* some money on the table.

Exercise 9B (▷ Units 4–6)

Complete the sentences. Use the correct form of the word in brackets. Add *a* or *the* where necessary.

1 (*house*)
a) Ken lives in *a house* _____ in Brighton.
b) *The house* _____ next door is for sale.
c) *Houses* _____ are expensive.

2 (*money*)
a) _____ is important.
b) Take _____ from my wallet.

3 (*teacher*)
a) Who is _____ talking to Mike?
b) _____ work hard.
c) I'm _____ in a language school.

4 (*bed*)
a) That shop sells _____ .
b) _____ in my room is very small.
c) There isn't _____ in that room.

5 (*salt*)
a) _____ isn't very good for you.
b) Can you pass _____ , please?

6 (*car*)
a) There is _____ in the garage.
b) _____ outside is mine.
c) Japan exports _____ .

Exercise 9C (▷ Unit 3)

★ Give examples of these possessive forms.

> 's
> Mike's camera
>
> of...
> the name of my school

When do we use 's? When do we use of...?

Exercise 9D (▷ Unit 7)

We normally use *the* only with the names of some of these:

cinemas cities countries days hotels
languages months museums oceans people
rivers seas streets theatres
names with city+building names with ...of...

★ Make two lists. Give example names.

> without the
> cities – Tokyo, Dallas
> countries – Italy, England

> with the
> cinemas – the Odeon Cinema

Exercise 9E (▷ Unit 8)

Look at these nouns.

> school/college/university cinema work theatre
> radio home bed guitar/piano/violin etc prison
> hospital church town breakfast/lunch/dinner
> country by car/bus/plane etc sea on foot sun
> rain television/TV

★ Which of these nouns do we often use:
– in expressions without *the*?
– in expressions with *the*?

Look back at Unit 8. Make two lists of the expressions.

> without the
> (go) to school/college/university
> (be) at school/college/university

> with the
> (go) to the cinema
> (be) at the cinema

10 Some, any, no

> We've got **some** milk, but we haven't got **any** eggs.
> Are there **any** chairs in the kitchen?
> There's **no** soap in the bathroom.

- We use *some* and *any* to talk about an indefinite quantity. Compare:

There are **some** birds in the tree.

There aren't **any** birds in the tree.

Are there **any** birds in the tree?

- We normally use *some* in affirmative sentences, and *any* in negative sentences and questions.

- But we often use *some*:

  □ in requests

Could I have **some** water, please?

  □ and in offers.

Would you like **some** water?

- We use *some* and *any* before uncountable nouns (eg *water, milk*) and plural countable nouns (eg *birds, eggs, chairs*)

  We also use *some* and *any* without a following noun (instead of repeating the noun).

  'I've got some envelopes. Would you like **some**?' (=some envelopes) 'No, I don't need **any**.' (=any envelopes)

- Compare *not any* and *no*:

There are**n't** any chairs.	There **are no** chairs.
We have**n't** got **any** milk.	We**'ve** got **no** milk.

No is more emphatic than *not any*.

Practice

Exercise 10A

What has this man got in his suitcase?
Put in *some* or *any*.

1 He's got **some** clothes.

2 Has he got _____ cameras?

3 He hasn't got _____ cameras, but he's got

   _____ watches.

4 He hasn't got _____ videos.

5 He's got _____ money.

6 Has he got _____ perfume or cigarettes?

7 He's got _____ perfume, but he hasn't got

   _____ cigarettes.

Exercise 10B

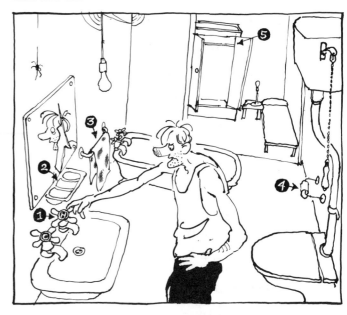

Tony isn't happy with his hotel room. What's wrong
with the room? Make sentences. Use:

There's There are	no ___.

1 *There's no hot water.* _____

2 _____

3 _____

4 _____

5 _____

   _____

clean towels   hangers in the wardrobe   hot water toilet paper   soap

35

Exercise 10C

Re-write the sentences. Use the words in brackets.

1 There isn't any news. *(no)*

   There's no news.

2 We've got no pens. *(any)*

   _____

3 He hasn't got any time. *(no)*

   _____

4 There are no chairs. *(any)*

   _____

5 I've got no bread. *(any)*

   _____

Exercise 10D

What are these people saying? Put in *some*, *any* or *no*.

1

Could I have **some** milk, please?

2

I've got _____ money at all.

3

There isn't _____ more coffee.

4

Would you like _____ stamps?

5

We need _____ petrol.

6

Have you got _____ tomatoes?

11 Much, many, a lot of, a little, a few, enough

> How **much** petrol is there in the car?
> How **many** brothers and sisters have you got?
> 'We've got **a lot of** rice, but only **a little** cheese
> and **a few** vegetables.'   'Have we got **enough** coffee?'

■ We use *much, many, a lot of, a little, a few* and *enough* to talk about quantity:

■ **Much, many, a lot of**

We use *much* and *many*:

□ in questions

How **much** cheese is there. in the fridge?

How **many** tomatoes are there?

□ and in negative sentences

There **isn't much** cheese.

There **aren't many** tomatoes.

■ In affirmative sentences, we normally use *a lot of* (not *much* or *many*) when we speak.

There's **a lot of** milk. (Not: ~~There's much milk.~~)
There are **a lot of** eggs. (Not: ~~There are many eggs.~~)

■ **A little, a few, enough**

We've got **a little** cheese and **a few** tomatoes.
I can't buy a new car. I haven't got **enough** money.
We've got **enough** eggs. We don't need any more.

■ We use:

□ *much* and *a little* + uncountable nouns

much a little	milk cheese

□ *many* and *a few* + plural countable nouns

many a few	eggs tomatoes

□ *a lot of* and *enough* + both uncountable and plural countable nouns

a lot of enough	milk cheese

a lot of enough	eggs tomatoes

■ In affirmative sentences, we do not normally use *much* or *many*, but we often use *too much* and *too many*.

That's **too much** cake for me. (= more cake than I want)
There are **too many** people in this lift. (= more people than is safe)

■ We also use *much, many, a lot, a little, a few* and *enough* without a following noun (instead of repeating the noun).

There's some snow, but not **much**. (= not much snow)
We've got some envelopes, but not **a lot**. (= not a lot of envelopes)
We don't need any more eggs. We've got **enough**. (= enough eggs)

Practice

Exercise 11A

What questions do they ask customers in these places?

1 a post office   2 a theatre
3 a flower shop   4 a bank
5 a petrol station 6 a baker's

Find one question for each place.

How much	bread tickets stamps	do you want?
How many	money petrol roses	

1 *How many stamps do you want?*

2 _____

3 _____

4 _____

5 _____

6 _____

Exercise 11B

Lunch is nearly finished in the snack bar. What food and drink is left? Make sentences.

There's a lot of ____. There's a little ____. There isn't much ____.	There are a lot of ____. There are a few ____. There aren't many ____.

1 *There's a little apple juice.*

2 _____

3 _____

4 _____

_____

5 _____

6 _____

7 _____

8 _____

Exercise 11C

Stanley always feels very tired and unfit. Why?

1

2

3

4

(i) Why does Stanley always feel so tired and unfit?
Look at the pictures. Complete the sentences. Use *too much*, *too many*, or *enough*.

1 He smokes *too much*   .

2 He has _____ late nights.

He doesn't get _____ sleep.

3 He doesn't take _____ exercise.

He doesn't get _____ fresh air.

4 He eats _____ junk food.

He eats _____ sweet things.

★ (ii) Read the sentences in (i) again. Are any of these things true for you?

Example:

> *I don't take enough exercise.*

12 Review of quantity

Exercise 12A (▷ Units 10–11)

Which sentences can you complete with:

☐ a countable noun (**C**) eg *eggs*?

☐ an uncountable noun (**U**) eg *rice*?

☐ a countable noun or an uncountable noun (**C** or **U**)?

1 We've got some _*C or U*_____ .

2 We haven't got any _____ .

3 We've got no _____ .

4 How many _____ are there?

5 How much _____ is there?

6 We've got a lot of _____ .

7 There is a little _____ .

8 There are a few _____ .

9 We've got enough _____ .

Exercise 12B (▷ Unit 10)

There are mistakes in some of these sentences. Find the mistakes and correct them.

1 Have you got any brothers or sisters? ✓

2 Look! I've got ~~any~~ **some** new shoes.

3 I can't make lunch. We haven't got some food.

4 I'm thirsty. Could I have any water, please?

5 Are you thirsty? Would you like some water?

6 We can't go to the concert. We've got any tickets.

7 We can't sit down. There aren't no chairs.

Exercise 12C (▷ Unit 11)

★ Two of these sentences are not usual in spoken English. Tick (✓) the sentences. Write what we normally say.

1 We haven't got much food.

2 Are there many chairs in the room?

3 We've got much food.

4 We've got too much food.

5 There are too many chairs in the room.

6 There are many chairs in the room.

7 Have we got much food?

8 There aren't many chairs in the room.

Exercise 12D (▷ Unit 11)

Choose the correct answer.

1 We've got *a lot of/a little* petrol, but not much.

2 I've got *a lot of/a few* stamps, but not many.

3 He's very rich. He's got *a little/a lot of* money.

4 I can't go out this evening. I've got *enough/too many* things to do.

5 I can't drink this coffee. There's *enough/too much* sugar in it.

6 We can't all get into the car. There isn't *enough/too much* room.

13 Subject pronouns

> *Maria is Italian. **She**'s from Rome.*
> *Alex and Anna aren't at home. **They**'re at the cinema.*

■ The subject pronouns are:

SINGULAR	PLURAL
I	we
you	you
he	
she	they
it	

■ Notice how we use subject pronouns:

> *Tony isn't at home.*   **He**'s   *at work.*
> *Diana hasn't got a motorbike.*   **She**'s got   *a car.*
> *Computers aren't cheap.*   **They**'re   *expensive.*

We use a subject pronoun before a verb (eg *is, has got, are*)

■ Note that we also use *it* to talk about:

- □ the time   ***It**'s 2 o'clock.*
- □ days   ***It**'s Monday today.*
- □ the weather   ***It**'s sunny.*
- □ distances   ***It**'s 4 kilometres to the town centre.*

■ We do not normally leave out subject pronouns.

It's cold today. (Not: ~~Is cold today.~~)
*Maria isn't from Milan. **She**'s from Rome.*
(Not: ~~Is from Rome.~~)

Practice

Exercise 13A

Add *I*, *you*, *he*, *she*, *it*, *we* or *they*.

1 __*You*__ 're hungry!

2 _____ 'm ill.

3 _____ 's angry.

4 _____ 's sad.

5 _____ 're old.

6 _____ 're tired.

7 _____ 's expensive.

8 _____ 's sunny today.

Exercise 13B

Add *he*, *she*, *it*, *we*, or *they*.

1 Judy is very nice. __*She*__ 's my best friend.

2 Judy and I aren't English. _____ 're from Sydney.

3 Sydney is a beautiful city. _____ 's in the south-east of Australia.

4 Paul is my brother. _____ 's 25 years old.

5 Paul and Emma are married. _____ 've got two children.

6 Emma is 22 years old. _____ 's a nurse in a hospital.

14 Possessive adjectives

> *Maria is with **her** father.*
> *What's **your** name?*

■ The possessive adjectives are:

SINGULAR	PLURAL
my	**our**
your	**your**
his	
her	**their**
its	

> *These are our suitcases.*

■ Notice how we use possessive adjectives:

What's	**your**	name?
Alex has got	**his**	camera.
Anna has got	**her**	Walkman.
These are	**our**	suitcases.

We use a possessive adjective before a noun (eg *name*, *camera*) to say who the noun belongs to.

■ Note:

*Julia and **her** brother*
(her brother = Julia's brother)

*Tony and **his** grandmother*
(his grandmother = Tony's grandmother)

*Alex has got **his** camera. Anna has got **her** Walkman.*

Practice

Exercise 14A

What is Mary Adams saying? Add *my, your, his, her, our* or *their*.

<u>My</u> (1) first name is Mary. _____ (2) family name is Adams. What about you? What's _____ (3) first name? And what's _____ (4) family name? I'm married. You can see _____ (5) husband in the picture. _____ (6) name is Arthur. We've got one son and one daughter. _____ (7) son is 20. _____ (8) name is Nick. _____ (9) daughter is 25. _____ (10) name is Emily. Emily is married. _____ (11) husband's name is Bruce. Emily and Bruce have got two children. _____ (12) names are Ken and Eva.

Exercise 14B

Add *my, your, his, her, its, our* or *their*.

1 <u>Your</u> hands are dirty.

2 Are these _____ suitcases?

3 Excuse me, but this is _____ seat.

4 These are _____ seats.

5 What's the cat got in _____ mouth?

6 Mrs Short isn't in _____ office.

7 This is Tom and _____ wife on _____ wedding day.

15 Object pronouns

*Maria is very nice, I like **her**.*
*Alex and Anna are late. I'm waiting for **them**.*

■ The object pronouns are:

SINGULAR	PLURAL
me	us
you	you
him	
her	them
it	

*My wife is repairing the roof. I'm helping **her**.*

■ Notice how we use object pronouns:

There's Joe.	Can you see	**him**?
My wife is repairing the roof.	I'm helping	**her**.
Those people are very nice.	I like	**them**.

Tom is leaving now.	I'm going with	**him**.
Where's Diana?	We're looking for	**her**.
The windows are very dirty.	Look at	**them**.

We use an object pronoun after a verb (eg *see*, *help*, *like*) and after a preposition (eg *with*, *for*, *at*).

■ We do not normally leave out object pronouns.

*There's Joe! Can you see **him**?*

*Peter is horrible. I don't like **him**.* (Not: ~~I don't like.~~)

Practice

Exercise 15A

Put in *me, you, him, her, it, us* or *them*.

Exercise 15B

Answer the questions. Use:

I	like don't like	him/her/it/ them.

Example:

1 How do you feel about tennis?

I like it. _____ *or* **I don't like it.** _____

How do you feel about:

1 tennis?

2 Madonna?

3 discos?

4 jazz?

5 Tom Cruise?

6 pizzas?

Exercise 15C

Complete the pen letter. Add *me, you, him, her, it, us* or *them*.

Dear Tammy,

I'm 16 years old. That's _____ (1) in the photo. I'm a student at Manchester College.

I live at home with my family. I've got one brother and one sister. My sister's name is Tina. She's very nice. Everyone likes _____(2). My brother's name is Dennis. He's sometimes horrible, but I like _____ (3). My grandmother also lives at home with _____ (4).

I'm interested in music. I play the guitar, but I can't play _____ (5) very well. My favourite group at the moment are U2. I like _____(6) very much. What about _____ (7)? What kind of music do you like?

Please write to _____(8) again soon.

With best wishes,

Mike

Exercise 15D

Complete the sentences. Add *I, me, you, he, him, she, her, we, us, they* or *them*.

1

He 's angry with *her*

and _____ 's angry with _____.

2

_____ love _____
Do _____ love _____?

3

_____ can see _____, but _____ can't see _____.

16 Possessive pronouns

> *This isn't Maria's bag. **Hers** is blue.*
> *My name is Tony. What's **yours**?*

■ The possessive pronouns are:

SINGULAR	PLURAL
mine	ours
yours	yours
his	
hers	theirs

Anna has got her tennis racket,
*but Alex hasn't got **his**.*

*This is your coat. That's **mine**.*

■ Notice how we use possessive pronouns:

*This is your coat. That's **mine**.* (= my coat)
*My name is Tony. What's **yours**?* (= your name)
*Anna has got her tennis racket, but Alex hasn't got **his**.*
(= his tennis racket)
*This isn't Maria's bag. **Hers** is blue.* (= Her bag)

We use a possessive pronoun without a following noun (instead of repeating the noun).

Are these your suitcases? — No, these are ours.

Practice

Exercise 16A

Add *mine, yours, his, hers, ours* or *theirs.*

1 This is **mine**. 	2 These are _____ 
3 This is _____ 	4 These are _____ 
5 This is _____ 	6 This is _____ 

Exercise 16B

Add *my, mine, your, yours, his, her, hers,* etc.

That isn't **your** baby.   That's _____.

Tom has got _____ umbrella, but Ron hasn't got _____.

3 This isn't _____ room. _____ is 38, not 28!

4

Doris has got _____ passport, but Julia can't find _____.

5 That isn't _____ pizza.   That's _____

6

Mr and Mrs Short are relaxing in _____ garden.
Mr and Mrs Jones are working hard in _____.

17 Review of personal pronouns

Exercise 17A (▷ Units 13–16)

(i) Complete the table.

SINGULAR			
_I_	_me_	_____	_____
you	_____	_your_	_____
_____	_him_	_____	_____
_____	_____	_____	_hers_
_it_	_____	_____	_/_
PLURAL			
_we_	_____	_____	_____
_____	_you_	_____	_____
_____	_____	_their_	_____

★ (ii) How many ways can you complete these sentences? Use words from the table.

1 That's _____ name.

2 Those books are _____.

3 _____ can swim.

4 Maria likes _____.

Exercise 17B (▷ Units 13–16)

Add words from the table in Exercise 17A.

1 Who's that girl?

– _____ name is Jenny.

2 My office isn't big. _____'s quite small.

3 Look! There's Mike. Can you see _____?

4 I've got my key, but Peter hasn't got _____.

5 Emily is nice. We all like _____.

6 That isn't Diana's house. _____ is next door.

7 Tony isn't here. _____'s at work.

8 My friend and I haven't got a map with _____.

9 Hello. My name is Frank. What's _____?

10 Look. The dog isn't eating _____ food.

11 I've got a problem. Can you help _____?

12 That's Rosie. _____'s Australian.

13 Those people have got their suitcases, but we haven't got _____.

14 Is this your coat?

– No, it isn't _____.

15 Tom and _____ wife have got two children.

18 This, that, these, those

Look at **this** photograph.
Is **that** your car outside?
Mmm! **These** sandwiches are delicious.

■
SINGULAR	PLURAL
this	these
that	those

■ We use *this* and *these* when something or someone is near.

■ We use *that* and *those* when something or someone is not so near.

■ We can use *this, that, these* and *those*:

□ before a noun
(eg *letter, man*)

This letter is for you.
Who is **that** man?
How much are **these**
apples?
Those photographs are
good.

□ without a following noun.

This is for you.
Who is **that**?
How much are **these**?

Those are good.

Practice

Exercise 18A

Add *this*, *that*, *these* or *those*.

1 This is Charles.

2 _____ is Doris.

3 Who are _____ people?

4 _____ sandwiches are delicious.

5 What is _____?

6 Are _____ shoes new?

7 Are _____ your coats?

8 _____ isn't my coat!

19 One, ones

> *My car is the white one outside.*
> *Who are those people — the ones over there?*

■ We can use *one* instead of repeating a singular noun.

I'm making a sandwich. Would you like one? (= Would you like a sandwich?)
Do you want a stamp? Or have you got one? (= Or have you got a stamp?)
My car is the white one outside. (= My car is the white car outside.)

■ We can use *ones* instead of repeating a plural noun.

Do you want large potatoes or small ones? (= small potatoes)
Who are those people – the ones over there? (= the people over there)

■ We only use *one* and *ones* in place of countable nouns.

I'm making a sandwich. Would you like one? (singular countable)
Who are those people – the ones over there? (plural countable)

■ We use *Which one . . . ?* and *Which ones . . . ?* in questions.

Look at these jackets. Which one do you like best? (= Which jacket?)
We've got two kinds of potatoes. Which ones do you want? (= Which potatoes?)

Practice

Exercise 19A

(i) Complete the conversations. Use *one* or *ones*.

1

Man: Which _one_ do you like best?

Woman: Well, the striped _____ is all right, but I really like the white _____.

Man: Oh. Do you? I think I like the checked _____ best.

2

Girl: Those are my videos.

Boy: Which _____? The _____ on the desk?

Girl: No, the other _____. The _____ on the chair.

3

Man: Which of those girls is your sister?

Woman: She's the _____ with dark hair.

Man: The tall _____?

Woman: No. The other _____.

4

Woman: These are our suitcases.

Porter: Which _____, sir? The black _____?

Woman: No. The other _____.

★ (ii) What does *one* or *ones* mean in each conversation?   55

> There's **somebody** in the office.
> There isn't **anything** good on TV.
> There's **nowhere** to sit down in this room.

■

somebody	anybody	nobody	everybody
someone	anyone	no one	everyone
something	anything	nothing	everything
somewhere	anywhere	nowhere	everywhere

■ The difference between **some**body, **some**one, **some**thing, etc and **any**body, **any**one, **any**thing, etc is the same as the difference between *some* and *any*. Compare:

*There's **somebody** at the door.*
*There isn't **anybody** at the door.*
*Is there **anybody** at the door?*

We normally use *somebody, someone, something*, etc in affirmative sentences, and *anybody, anyone, anything*, etc in negative sentences and questions.

■ But we often use *somebody, someone, something*, etc in requests and in offers.

*Can **somebody** help me?*
*Would you like **something** to eat?*

■ We use *-body* or *-one* for people (*-body* and *-one* have the same meaning).

***Nobody** lives in that house.* or ***No one** lives in that house.*
***Everybody** likes Tina.* or ***Everyone** likes Tina.*

■ We use *-thing* for things.

*Look, there's **something** under that chair.*
*You look worried. Is **anything** wrong?*

■ We use *-where* for places.

*Would you like to go **somewhere** for a coffee?*
*We can't go shopping now. **Everywhere** is closed.*

■ Compare:

There isn't anybody here. We haven't got anything for dinner.	There's nobody here. We've got nothing for dinner.

Nobody, nothing, etc are more emphatic than *not anybody, not anything*, etc.

■ We use singular verbs with all these words.

***Everything is** expensive these days.* (Not: ~~Everything are expensive these days.~~)

But we often use *they* (and *their* and *them*) with the words ending in *-body* or *-one*.

*There's **somebody** outside. **They** want to see you.*

■ We can use a *to* infinitive after *something, anybody, nowhere*, etc.

*We're hungry. We'd like **something to eat**.*
*My friend has got **nowhere to live**.*

Practice

Exercise 20A

Complete the sentences. Use the words in the box.

(i)

| somebody anybody nobody everybody |

Woman: Hello. Can I speak to ___somebody___ (1) in the Accounts Office, please?

Man: I'm sorry, madam. It's after 6.00. There isn't _____ (2) in the Accounts Office now. _____ (3) has gone home.

Woman: But I must speak to _____ (4) today.

Man: I'm sorry. There's _____ (5) here. Can you phone back in the morning? There will be _____ (6) here then.

(ii)

| something anything nothing everything |

Mother: Would you like _____ (1) to eat?

Daughter: No, thanks. I don't want _____ (2) at the moment, thank you.

Mother: But you've had _____ (3) to eat all day. Is _____ (4) all right? Are you feeling ill?

Daughter: No. Don't worry. _____ (5) is fine. I'm just not hungry. That's all.

(iii)

| somewhere anywhere nowhere everywhere |

Man: I've got _____ (1) to stay. I need _____ (2) for two nights. I've tried all the hotels near here, but _____ (3) is full. I can't find a room _____ (4).

57

Exercise 20B

Re-write the sentences. Use the words in brackets.

1 There isn't anything in the fridge. *(nothing)*
   There's nothing in the fridge.
   _____

2 I've got nothing to say. *(anything)*
   _____
   _____

3 There's nobody at home. *(anybody)*
   _____
   _____

4 They haven't got anywhere to live. *(nowhere)*
   _____
   _____

5 There isn't anyone outside. *(no one)*
   _____
   _____

6 We've got nowhere to sit down. *(anywhere)*
   _____
   _____

7 I haven't got anything to do today. *(nothing)*
   _____
   _____

Exercise 20C

Complete sentences about these people. Use:

something	anything	to play with	to sleep
nothing	anyone	to listen to	to drink
nowhere	anything	to eat with	to wear

1 She hasn't got *anything to drink*. _____

2 He's got _____

3 She's got _____

4 She hasn't got _____

5 He hasn't got _____

6 He's got _____

21 Reflexive pronouns

> My grandfather often talks to **himself**.
> Diana hurt **herself** when she fell.
> Do you live by **yourself**?

- The reflexive pronouns are:

SINGULAR	PLURAL
myself	**ourselves**
yourself	**yourselves**
himself	
herself	**themselves**
itself	

*He's laughing at **himself**.*

*I saw **myself** on TV last night!*

- We use reflexive pronouns when the subject and the object are the same.

SUBJECT		OBJECT
He	is laughing at	**himself**.
I	saw	**myself** on TV last night.
We	are enjoying	**ourselves**.
Julia	is making	**herself** a cup of tea.
My parents	have bought	**themselves** a new car.

- *By myself, by yourself*, etc = alone or without help.

  *I don't live with anybody. I live **by myself**.*
  *Did anybody help you push the car? Or did you push it **by yourself**?*

- We can use reflexive pronouns for emphasis.

  *Diana repaired the car **herself**.* (Nobody else repaired it.)

- Compare:

  □ *-selves*   □ *each other*

*They're laughing at **themselves**.*

*They're laughing at **each other**.*

59

Practice

Exercise 21A

Add *myself, yourself, himself, herself, itself, ourselves, yourselves* or *themselves*.

Be careful! Don't burn **yourself**

Bob loves looking at

_____

in the mirror!

The cat can open
the door by

_____ .

Susan is teaching

_____

to speak French.

The children cleaned
the kitchen all by

_____ .

We enjoyed

_____

very much last night.

Exercise 21B

Look at the people in the picture. Complete the sentences. Use the words in the box and . . . *each other*.

| know   talk to   seen   waving at |

1 They've just **_seen each other._** _____

2 They're _____

3 They _____

4 They're going to _____

Exercise 21C

What are they doing? Use *themselves* or *each other*.

1 a)    b)

_____   _____

2 a)    b)

_____   _____

22 Review of other pronouns

Put the sentences with the correct pictures. Add *this*, *that*, *these* or *those*.

Look at _____ window.	Who's _____?
Stop _____ men!	Look at _____.

Use *one* or *ones* in place of a word or words in each sentence.

1 You've got a video, but I haven't got a video.
  You've got a video, but I haven't got one.

2 Do you like the brown shoes or the black shoes?

3 Who are those men – the men in the car?

4 My house is the house next door.

5 We'd like to have a holiday in May and another holiday in September.

6 Our children are the children near the tree.

Exercise 22C (▷ Unit 20)

(i) Complete the table.

	some	**any**
–thing	something	_____
–body	_____	_____
–one	_____	anyone
–where	_____	_____

	no	**every**
–thing	_____	_____
–body	nobody	_____
–one	_____	_____
–where	_____	everywhere

(ii) Complete the sentences. Use words from the table in (i).

1 I'm hungry. I'd like __something__ to eat.

2 I haven't got _____ to read.

3 We're bored. We've got _____ to do.

4 The house is empty. _____ lives there.

5 We're going out _____ for lunch.

6 I feel lonely. I haven't got _____ to talk to.

7 The train is full. There's _____ to sit down.

8 You look sad. Is _____ all right?

9 I can't find my pen _____. I've

looked _____ for it.

Exercise 22D (▷ Unit 21)

(i) Add the reflexive pronouns.

SINGULAR

I – _myself_

you – _____

he – _____

she – _____

it – _____

PLURAL

we – _____

you – _____

they – _____

(ii) There are mistakes in some of these sentences. Find the mistakes and correct them.

1 My sister taught himself to swim.   *herself*

2 Anna repaired the chair herself.   ✓

3 The children are making themselves something to eat.

4 I hurt me when I fell down the stairs.

5 We're meeting us at 8.00 this evening.

6 Do you live yourself or with other people?

7 We're enjoying by ourselves very much.

8 We're good friends. We like ourselves very much.

23 Present tense of the verb *be*

*My name **is** Gina.*
*I**'m** a student. I**'m not** a teacher.*
*'**Are** you and your friend English?'   'No, we **aren't**.'*

Use

*I**'m** Maria Rossi. This **is** Bruno Bonetti.*
*'**Are** Maria and Bruno Italian?'   'Yes, they **are**.'*
*Maria **is** a journalist. Bruno **is** a photographer.*

Form

AFFIRMATIVE (+)

FULL FORMS	SHORT FORMS
I **am**	I**'m**
you **are**	you**'re**
he **is**	he**'s**
she **is**	she**'s**
it **is**	it**'s**
we **are**	we**'re**
you **are**	you**'re**
they **are**	they**'re**

NEGATIVE (−)

FULL FORMS	SHORT FORMS
I **am not**	I**'m not**
you **are not**	you **aren't**
he **is not**	he **isn't**
she **is not**	she **isn't**
it **is not**	it **isn't**
we **are not**	we **aren't**
you **are not**	you **aren't**
they **are not**	they **aren't**

QUESTION (?)

QUESTION (?)	SHORT ANSWERS
am I?	Yes, I **am**.
are you?	Yes, he/she/it **is**.
is he?	Yes, you/we/they **are**.
is she?	
is it?	No, I**'m not**.
are we?	No, he/she/it **isn't**.
are you?	No, you/we/they **aren't**.
are they?	

Practice

Exercise 23A

Frank Mancini

Gina Mancini

Paul Mancini

Complete what Frank says. Use *am, is* or *are*.

My name _is_ (1) Frank Mancini. I _____ (2)
23 years old and I _____ (3) a lifeguard. I _____ (4)
from Santa Monica, California. I have one sister and
one brother. Their names _____ (5) Gina and Paul.
Gina _____ (6) 20 years old. She _____ (7) a
student. Paul _____ (8) 28. He _____ (9) a fireman
with the Los Angeles Fire Department.

Exercise 23B

Complete the table. Add *am, is* or *are*. Then write the
short form.

FULL FORMS	SHORT FORMS
I _am_	_I'm_
you _____	_____
he _____	_____
she _____	_____
it _____	_____
we _____	_____
you _____	_____
they _____	_____

Exercise 23C

Make true sentences. Use *'m, 'm not, is, isn't, are* or
aren't.

Example:

1 My teacher _is_ English.
  or My teacher _isn't_ English.

1 My teacher _____ English.

2 I _____ married.

3 My favourite colour _____ blue.

4 My favourite sports _____ tennis and
  windsurfing.

5 My best friend _____ a student.

Exercise 23D

(i) Read about these people.

Mel Gibson, Australian actor

Jodie Foster, American actress and film maker

Gabriela Sabatini, Argentinian tennis player

Steven Spielberg, American film maker

Luciano Pavarotti, Italian singer

Steffi Graf, German tennis player

(ii) Cover (i). What can you remember about these people?

Correct the sentences.

1 Mel Gibson is American.
    He isn't American.
    He's Australian.

2 Steven Spielberg is an actor.
_____
_____

3 Gabriela Sabatini is Italian.
_____
_____

4 Jodie Foster and Steven Spielberg are Australian.
_____
_____

5 Luciano Pavarotti is Argentinian.
_____
_____

6 Mel Gibson is a singer.
_____
_____

7 Gabriela Sabatini and Steffi Graf are actresses.
_____
_____

Exercise 23E

1

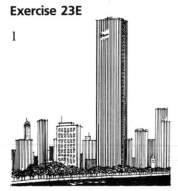

the Sears Tower, Chicago

2

the Parthenon, Athens

3

Brooklyn Bridge, New York

4

the Spanish Steps, Rome

5

Saint Sofia, Istanbul

6

the Pyramids, Egypt

Where are these places? Ask and answer. Use *Is/Are . . .?*

1 the Sears Tower | New York?
2 the Parthenon | Rome?
3 Brooklyn Bridge | Chicago?
4 the Spanish Steps | Athens?
5 Saint Sofia | Istanbul?
6 the Pyramids | Egypt?

1 *Is the Sears Tower in New York?*
– *No, it isn't. It's in Chicago.*

2 _____

_____

3 _____

_____

4 _____

_____

5 _____

_____

6 _____

_____

Exercise 23F

Complete the questions with *is* or *are*. Give true short answers.

1 you | a good singer?
2 your teacher | married?
3 tennis | your favourite sport?
4 your shoes | new?
5 your best friend | English?
6 you | very intelligent?

Example:

1 *Are you a good singer?*
  – *Yes, I am.*   *or* *No, I'm not.*

1 _____
  – _____
2 _____
  – _____
3 _____
  – _____
4 _____
  – _____
5 _____
  – _____
6 _____
  – _____

Exercise 23G

Complete the questions with *is* or *are*. Give true answers.

1 What | your name?
2 Where | you from?
3 How old | you?
4 When | your birthday?
5 What colour | your eyes?
6 Who | your best friend?

Example:

1 *What is your name?*
  – *Carlos Sanchez.*

1 _____
  – _____
2 _____
  – _____
3 _____
  – _____
4 _____
  – _____
5 _____
  – _____
6 _____
  – _____

24 *There is, there are*

> **There's** a stereo in the car.
> **There are** five rooms in the flat.
> '**Is there** a bank near here?'   'No, **there isn't**.'

'**There's** a computer in the car. **There are** two phones.
There isn't a fax machine.'   '**Is there** a TV?'
'Yes, **there is**. **There's** a video too.'

- Note that we normally say, for example, **There's** a
  computer in the car. (Not: ~~A computer is in the car~~.)

SINGULAR	PLURAL
FULL FORMS	FULL FORMS

there is	**there are**
there is not	**there are not**
is there?	**are there**?

SHORT FORMS	SHORT FORMS

there's	
there isn't	**there aren't**

- Note:

- *There is . . .* **and** *It is . . .*:

There's a car outside. **It's** a police car. (*It* = the car
outside)
There's a film on TV. **It's** called 'Sunday in New York'.
(*It* = the film on TV)

- *There are . . .* **and** *They are . . .*:

There are some people at the door. **They're** policemen.
(*They* = the people at the door)
There are some stamps in my room. **They're** on the desk.
(*They* = the stamps in my room)

Practice

Exercise 24A

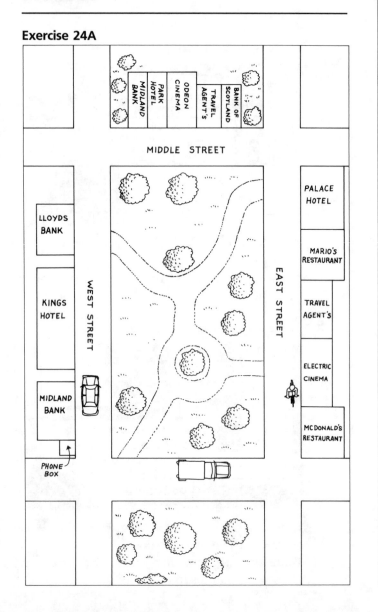

(i) Read about one of the streets in the picture. Which street is it?

> *There is a hotel in this street. There are two banks.*
> *There aren't any restaurants. There isn't a cinema.*
> *There is a telephone box on the corner.*

So which street is it? _____

(ii) Write about the other streets. Add these words:

> There is   There are   There isn't   There aren't

Middle Street

There is (1) a cinema and a hotel in this street.

_____ (2) a travel agent's. _____ (3) a telephone box on the corner. _____ (4) any restaurants. _____ (5) two banks.

East Street

_____ (1) a hotel in this street. _____ (2) a cinema and a travel agent's. _____ (3) any banks. _____ (4) two restaurants _____ (5) telephone box on the corner.

★ (iii) Now write about a street that you know.

> *There is a ____ in the street. There are ____.*
> *There isn't a ____. There aren't any ____.*

Exercise 24B

(i) What's in the room? Use:

Is there __?	Yes, there is./No, there isn't.
Are there __?	Yes, there are./No, there aren't.

1 <u>*Is there*</u> _____ a TV in the room?
   – <u>*Yes, there is.*</u> _____

2 _____ a video recorder?

   – _____

3 _____ any video tapes?

   – _____

4 _____ a photocopier?

   – _____

5 _____ two telephones?

   – _____

6 _____ any photographs?

   – _____

7 _____ a radio?

   – _____

(ii) Where are these things in the room? Use:

Where's _____?	It's _____.
Where are _____?	They're _____.

1 <u>*Where's*</u> _____ the radio?
   – <u>*It's*</u> _____ on the table.

2 _____ the telephone?
   – _____ on the desk.

3 _____ the video tapes?
   – _____ on the shelf.

4 _____ the TV?
   – _____ in the corner.

★ (iii) What's in your room, or your flat or house? Make true sentences.

Example:

> *There's a TV in my room.*
> *There isn't a video.*
> *There are some posters on the wall.*

71

25 Have got

> I**'ve got** a computer.
> Madonna **has got** blue eyes.
> **Have** you **got** any brothers or sisters?

Use

Julia: *Have you got a ticket, Tony?*
Tony: *No. I've only got £5.*

Julia: *Well, we've got three tickets. Here. Take one of these.*

■ We often use *have got* instead of *have* in British English, especially when we speak.

■ We do not use *got* with *have* in short answers.

'Has your brother got a car?'   *'Yes, he **has**.'* (Not: ~~Yes, he has got~~.)

Form

AFFIRMATIVE (+)

FULL FORMS	SHORT FORMS
I **have got**	I**'ve got**
you **have got**	you**'ve got**
he **has got**	he**'s got**
she **has got**	she**'s got**
it **has got**	it**'s got**
we **have got**	we**'ve got**
you **have got**	you**'ve got**
they **have got**	they**'ve got**

NEGATIVE (−)

FULL FORMS	SHORT FORMS
I **have not got**	I **haven't got**
you **have not got**	you **haven't got**
he **has not got**	he **hasn't got**
she **has not got**	she **hasn't got**
it **has not got**	it **hasn't got**
we **have not got**	we **haven't got**
you **have not got**	you **haven't got**
they **have not got**	they **haven't got**

QUESTION (?)

QUESTION	SHORT ANSWERS
have I **got**?	Yes, I/you/we/they **have**.
have you **got**?	Yes, he/she/it **has**.
has he **got**?	
has she **got**?	No, I/you/we/they **haven't**.
has it **got**?	No, he/she/it **hasn't**.
have we **got**?	
have you **got**?	
have they **got**?	

Practice

Exercise 25A

(i) What have the people in the pictures got? Use:

He's/She's They've	got _____.

a bicycle   a dog   a computer a car   a Walkman   a camera

1 *He's got a Walkman.*

2 _____

3 _____

4 _____

5 _____

6 _____

(ii) Have you or your family got the things in (i)?
Make true sentences.

I've/We've I/We haven't	got _____.

Example:

1 *I've got a Walkman.*

or *I haven't got a Walkman.*

1 _____

2 _____

3 _____

4 _____

5 _____

6 _____

Exercise 25B

Complete the table. Add *have got* or *has got*. Then give
the short form.

FULL FORMS   SHORT FORMS

I *have got*   *I've got*

you _____   _____

he _____   _____

she _____   _____

it _____   _____

we _____   _____

you _____   _____

they _____   _____

Exercise 25C

(i) Complete the questions. Use *have got* or *has got*.

1 you | any brothers or sisters?

2 you | any children?

3 How many cousins | you?

4 you | a cat or a dog?

5 your teacher | a car?

6 your house or flat | a garden?

1 *Have you got any brothers or sisters?*

2 _____

3 _____

_____

4 _____

5 _____

6 _____

_____

(ii) Now answer the questions in (i). Give true
answers.

Example:

1 Have you got any brothers or sisters?

– *Yes, I have. I've got two sisters.*

or *No, I haven't.*

1 – _____

2 – _____

3 – _____

4 – _____

5 – _____

6 – _____

26 Imperative

> **Listen.**
> **Be** careful.
> **Don't forget** your umbrella.

Use

■ We use the imperative, for example, in:

□ instructions

□ warnings

Open your books.

Look out!

□ invitations

□ offers

Come in.

Have some more coffee.

□ advice

□ requests

Stay in bed. **Don't go** to work today.

Pass the salt.

■ To make imperatives more polite, we can use *please*.

Pass the salt, **please**.

Form

AFFIRMATIVE (+)

> **Open** the door.
> **Go** to work.
> **Sit** down.

NEGATIVE (−)

FULL FORMS	SHORT FORMS
Do not open the door.	**Don't open** the door.
Do not go to work.	**Don't go** to work.
Do not sit down.	**Don't sit** down.

75

Practice

Exercise 26A

What are these people saying?

Find the sentences for the pictures.

Be careful. Don't drop it.	Close the door, please.
Open your mouth, please.	Don't touch that cake!
Open your suitcase, please.	Put your hands up!
Don't forget your briefcase.	Sit down.

1

Put your hands up!

2

3

4

5

6

7

8

27 Present simple

> I **play** basketball every Tuesday.
> '**Do** you usually **work** on Saturdays?' 'Yes, I **do**.'
> Maria **doesn't live** in Milan. She **lives** in Rome.

Use

How does Julia keep fit?

Julia: *I cycle to work every day. I usually **play** tennis at weekends. I often **go** swimming. I sometimes **go** windsurfing. And I **don't smoke**!*

■ We use the present simple to talk about things that happen repeatedly – for example, *every day, usually, often* or *sometimes*.

■ We also use the present simple to talk about facts that are generally true.
  *Elephants **live** in Africa and India.*
  *A newsagent **sells** newspapers and magazines.*

Form

AFFIRMATIVE (+)

I **work**
you **work**
he **works**
she **works**
it **works**
we **work**
you **work**
they **work**

After *he*, *she* and *it*, verbs end in *-s* or *-es* eg *he works*, *she goes*. ▷ See Exercise 27A.

NEGATIVE (−)

FULL FORMS

I **do not work**
you **do not work**
he **does not work**
she **does not work**
it **does not work**
we **do not work**
you **do not work**
they **do not work**

SHORT FORMS

I **don't work**
you **don't work**
he **doesn't work**
she **doesn't work**
it **doesn't work**
we **don't work**
you **don't work**
they **don't work**

QUESTION (?)

do I **work**?
do you **work**?
does he **work**?
does she **work**?
does it **work**?
do we **work**?
do you **work**?
do they **work**?

SHORT ANSWERS

Yes, I/you/we/they **do**.
Yes, he/she/it **does**.

No, I/you/we/they **don't**.
No, he/she/it **doesn't**.

Practice

Exercise 27A

(i) Write the -*s*/-*es* forms of these words.

1

get _gets_

cook _cooks_

leave _____

use _____

sing _____

stop _____

test _____

read _____

start _____

2

teach _teaches_

finish _____

kiss _____

go _____

3

carry _carries_

study _____

fly _____

▷ What are the -*s*/-*es* spelling rules? See page 218.

(ii) How do we say the -*s*/-*es* endings? Practise saying these words.

/ɪz/	/z/	/s/
closes	lives	puts
watches	brings	works
brushes	sends	rests
passes	snows	helps
	hurries	
	tidies	
	plays	

(iii) Now put the -*s*/-*es* forms from (i) into three groups.

/ɪz/	/z/	/s/
uses	_leaves_	_gets_
_____	_____	_cooks_
_____	_____	_____
_____	_____	_____
_____		
_____		

▷ What are the -*s*/-*es* pronunciation rules? See page 217.

Exercise 27B

(i) Jill is a postwoman. What does she do every day?
Read what she says. Find the examples of the present
simple.

> **Jill:** *I get up at 5.00 every morning. I have*
> *breakfast at 5.30 and leave home at 6.00. I start*
> *work at 6.30 and finish at 2.00. I have dinner at*
> *7.00 and go to bed at about 10.00.*

(ii) What do you do every day? Compare yourself and
Jill. Make true sentences.

Example:

1 Jill <u>*gets up*</u> _____ at 5.00.
  I <u>*get up at 7.00.*</u>

1 Jill _____ at 5.00.
  I _____

2 She _____ breakfast at _____
  I _____

3 She _____ home at _____
  I _____

4 She _____ work at _____
  I _____ work/school at _____

5 She _____ work at _____
  I _____ work/school at _____

6 She _____ dinner at _____
  I _____

7 She _____
  I _____

★ (iii) Now write about a friend or someone in your
family. What does he or she do every day?

Examples:

> *My father gets up at 6.30.*
> *He has breakfast at 7.00.*

Exercise 27C

What do they do in their jobs?

a chef

a swimming instructor

an optician

a pilot

a porter

a fireman

Complete the sentences. Use:

fly   test   teach   put out   cook   carry

1 *A fireman puts out* _____ fires.

2 _____ people's bags.

3 _____ in a restaurant or a hotel.

4 _____ a plane.

5 _____ people's eyes.

6 _____

people to swim.

Exercise 27D

What do you do at weekends? What do your family and friends do? Look at the table.

(I/We/They)	always usually often	play ____. go
(He/She)	sometimes rarely never	plays ____. goes

100% _____ 0%
always usually often sometimes rarely never

Make four (or more) true sentences from the table.

Examples:

I usually go shopping.
I sometimes play tennis.
My father often goes swimming.
My friend and I sometimes go to the cinema.

_____

_____

_____

_____

_____

_____

_____

▷ For *always*, *usually*, *often*, etc, see also Unit 61.

Exercise 27E

Complete the sentences. Use these words:

| do   does   live   lives |

1 *Do* you *live* alone?

   – No, I _____n't. I _____ with two friends.

2 We _____n't _____ in a house. We _____ in a
   flat.

3 Where _____ your parents _____?

   – They _____ in Toronto.

4 _____ your brother _____ with your parents?

   – Yes, he _____.

5 My sister _____n't _____ in Canada. She
   _____ in Mexico.

Exercise 27F

(i) Ask the questions. Use *do* or *does* and these words:

| read   do   drive   wear   rain |

Give true short answers.

1 you | a lot of books?
2 your best friend | a Ferrari?
3 it | a lot in your country?
4 you | yoga?
5 your teacher | glasses?

Example:

1 *Do you read a lot of books?*
   – *Yes, I do.* _or_ *No, I don't.*

1 _____
   – _____

2 _____
   – _____

3 _____
   – _____

4 _____
   – _____

5 _____
   – _____

(ii) Now make true sentences about the things in (i).

Example:

1 I __read_____ a lot of books.

or I __don't read_____ a lot of books.

1 I _____ a lot of books.

2 My best friend _____ a Ferrari.

3 It _____ a lot in my country.

4 I _____ yoga.

5 My teacher _____ glasses.

Exercise 27G

(i) Read what Greg says. Some information is missing.

> **Greg:** *I come from __1__. I'm 19 years old and I'm a college student. What do I do every day? I get up at __2__ and have breakfast. Then I go to college on my __3__. College starts at __4__ and finishes at __5__. I usually have lunch in the __6__. After college I go to the __7__. That's when my day really begins! I __8__ there every day.*

(ii) Ask Greg for the missing information.

1 Where __do you come from?_____

2 What time _____

3 How _____

4 What time _____

5 What time _____

6 Where _____

7 Where _____

8 What _____

(iii) Now find Greg's answers to the questions.

(a) On my motorbike.	(e) It starts at 9.00.
(b) It finishes at 3.00.	(f) From Sydney, Australia.
(c) I surf there.	(g) In the college canteen.
(d) To the beach.	(h) I get up at 7.30.

28 Present continuous

> I'm **leaving** now. Goodbye.
> Oh, no! Look outside. It's **raining**.
> 'Are you **working** at the moment?'   'Yes, I **am**.'

Use

Peter: *What are you **doing**, Diana?*
Diana: *I'm **writing** a letter.*
Peter: *Where's Kurt?*
Diana: *He's **doing** some photocopying.*

- We use the present continuous to talk about something that is happening at the moment we speak.

- We also use the present continuous to talk about something that is happening around now, but not necessarily at the moment we speak.
  *I'm **looking** for a job at the moment.* (But perhaps I'm not looking at the moment I speak.)

▷ We also use the present continuous to talk about the future. See Unit 38.

Form

AFFIRMATIVE (+)

FULL FORMS	SHORT FORMS
I **am working**	I**'m working**
you **are working**	you**'re working**
he **is working**	he**'s working**
she **is working**	she**'s working**
it **is working**	it**'s working**
we **are working**	we**'re working**
you **are working**	you**'re working**
they **are working**	they**'re working**

NEGATIVE (−)

FULL FORMS	SHORT FORMS
I **am not working**	I**'m not working**
you **are not working**	you **aren't working**
he **is not working**	he **isn't working**
she **is not working**	she **isn't working**
it **is not working**	it **isn't working**
we **are not working**	we **aren't working**
you **are not working**	you **aren't working**
they **are not working**	they **aren't working**

QUESTION (?)

am I **working**?
are you **working**?
is he **working**?
is she **working**?
is it **working**?
are we **working**?
are you **working**?
are they **working**?

SHORT ANSWERS

Yes, I **am**.
Yes, he/she/it **is**.
Yes, you/we/they **are**.

No, I**'m not**.
No, he/she/it **isn't**.
No, you/we/they **aren't**.

Practice

Exercise 28A

Write the *-ing* forms of these words.

1

rain *raining*

work *working*

eat _____

read _____

clean _____

do _____

wait _____

look _____

walk _____

3

put *putting*

swim *swimming*

sit _____

stop _____

run _____

jog _____

2

leave *leaving*

smoke *smoking*

shine _____

write _____

come _____

dance _____

make _____

▷ What are the *-ing* spelling rules? See page 218.

Exercise 28B

Picture A

★ (i) What is happening in picture A?

Examples:

A young man is waiting at a bus stop.
He's reading a newspaper.
An old woman is walking across the street.

Picture B

★ (ii) Compare picture B with picture A. What is different in picture B?

In picture B . . .

> The young man isn't reading a newspaper.
> He's reading a book.

Can you find 5 more differences?

Exercise 28C

What are they saying?

I | not | feel | well.	You | not | listen | to me.
We | not | watch | the TV.	You | sit | in my seat.
I | write | a letter.	We | go | out.

I'm writing a letter.

Exercise 28D

(i) Who is who in the office? Read about the people. Write the names in the picture.

> ***Lillian*** *is talking on the phone at the moment, and* ***Sam*** *and* ***Carla*** *are looking at some posters.* ***Benny*** *is reading a report.* ***Bruce*** *and* ***Loretta*** *are working on their computers, and* ***Ed*** *is doing some photocopying.*

(ii) What are they doing in the office? Ask and answer.

1 Benny | work | on his computer?
2 Bruce and Loretta | talk | on the phone?
3 Ed | do | some photocopying?
4 Lillian | read | a report?
5 Sam and Carla | look | at some posters?

1 *Is Benny working on his computer?*
   – No, he isn't. He's reading a report.

2 _____
   – _____

3 _____
   – _____

4 _____
   – _____

5 _____
   – _____

(iii) Cover page 86. What are the people in the office doing? Can you remember?

Ask and answer.

1 What | Bruce and Loretta | do?
2 What | Sam and Carla | look | at?
3 What | Ed | do?
4 What | Lillian | do?
5 What | Benny | read?

1 *What are Bruce and Loretta doing?*
   – *They're working on their computers.*

2 _____
   – _____

3 _____
   – _____

4 _____
   – _____

5 _____
   – _____

Exercise 28E

(i) Where are you now? What is happening? Complete the questions. Give true answers.

1 you | study | at home now?
2 Where | you | sit?
3 What | you | wear?
4 the sun | shine?

Example:

1 *Are you studying at home now?*
   – *Yes, I am.*   or *No, I'm not.*

1 _____
   – _____

2 _____
   – _____

3 _____
   – _____

4 _____
   – _____

★ (ii) What are your family and friends doing now? Write some sentences.

Examples:

My brother and his wife are working.
My friend Astrid is playing tennis.

29 Present continuous and present simple

I'**m leaving** now. Goodbye. Look! It'**s snowing** outside.	I usually **leave** work at 5.30. It often **snows** in Britain in the winter.

*John is a journalist. He **writes** for a newspaper. He isn't at work at the moment. He's at home. He'**s repairing** his car.*

*Michael is a mechanic. He **repairs** cars. He isn't at work at the moment. He's at home. He'**s writing** a letter.*

■ Compare:

PRESENT CONTINUOUS	PRESENT SIMPLE
John **is repairing** his car at the moment. Michael **is writing** a letter at the moment.	Michael is a mechanic. He **repairs** cars. John is a journalist. He **writes** for a newspaper.

□ We use the present continuous for things that are happening at the moment we speak.

*Paul is in the kitchen now, He'**s having** breakfast. Where is Diana? **Is** she **playing** golf?*

□ We use the present simple for things that happen repeatedly – for example, *every day, usually, often* or *sometimes.*

*Paul **has** breakfast at 7.30 every morning. **Does** Diana often **play** golf?*

■ Compare the questions:

What do you do? = *What is your job?*

88

Practice

Exercise 29A

Complete the sentences. Use the present continuous or the present simple.

| teach   have   drive   have   leave |

It's 7.30am. Suzanne Wells is in her kitchen at home.
She **'s having** _____ (1) breakfast. She

_____ (2) breakfast at this time every morning.

She _____ (3) home at 8.30am every day and

_____ (4) to work. Suzanne is a teacher. She

_____ (5) at a school in Canberra,

Australia.

| spend   teach   come   teach   not speak |

It's 10.00 am now and Suzanne is at school. At the

moment she _____ (6) her class

of 8-year-old children. All the children in her class

_____ (7) from Canberra. Many of the children

_____ (8) English at home. So

Suzanne _____ (9) a lot of time

teaching English. She _____ (10) English to

the class now.

89

Exercise 29B

Complete the table. Use the present continuous and the present simple of the verb *work*.

PRESENT CONTINUOUS	PRESENT SIMPLE
I *am working*	I *work*
you _____	_____
he _____	_____
she _____	_____
it _____	_____
we _____	_____
you _____	_____
they _____	_____

Exercise 29C

(i) Complete the questions. Use the present continuous or the present simple. Give true answers.

1 you | often | wear | jeans?
2 you | wear | jeans now?
3 it | rain | now?
4 it | often | rain | in your country?
5 you | study | English every day?
6 you | study | English at the moment?

Example:

1 *Do you often wear jeans?*
– *Yes, I do.*   or *No, I don't.*

1 _____
– _____
2 _____
– _____
3 _____
– _____
4 _____
– _____
5 _____
– _____
6 _____
– _____

(ii) Now make true sentences about the things in (i).

Example:

1 *I often wear jeans.*
  or *I don't often wear jeans.*

1 _____
2 _____
3 _____
4 _____
5 _____
6 _____

30 Verbs not normally used in the continuous

> I **know** your brother.
> **Do** you **understand** this word?
> Monica **has** long blonde hair.

■ We normally use some verbs (eg *want*) only in the simple form (eg *I **want** a drink*), not the continuous (eg Not: *I'm wanting a drink*).

■ Here are some verbs that we do not normally use in the continuous:

hate	like	love	prefer	want	
believe	forget	know	mean	realise	recognise
remember	think (=believe)		understand		
belong to	have (=possess)		need	own	seem

*I **like** that shirt.* (Not: *I'm liking that shirt*.)
*I **don't believe** you.* (Not: *I'm not believing you*.)
***Do** you **think** money can buy happiness?* (Not: *Are you thinking money can buy happiness?*)
*Diana **has** a new car.* (Not: *Diana is having a new car*.)

■ Note that we use the verbs *think* and *have* with more than one meaning. We can use these verbs in the continuous to talk about actions. Compare:

☐ **NOT** AN ACTION	AN ACTION
*I **think** you're right.* (*think*=believe)	*Be quiet! I'**m thinking**.* (*think*=use the mind)

When *think* means 'believe', we can use it only in the simple form. But when *think* means 'use the mind', we can use it in the continuous.

☐ **NOT** AN ACTION	AN ACTION
*Ken **has** a motorbike.* (*have*=possess)	*Ken **is having** dinner now.* (*have*=eat)

When *have* means 'possess', we can use it only in the simple form. But when *have* describes an action such as 'eat', we can use it in the continuous.

We often use *have got* instead of *have* (= possess) eg *Ken **has got** a motorbike*. But we do not use *have got* for actions. For example, we do not say *Ken is having got dinner now*.

■ With verbs such as *see, hear* and *smell*, we often use *can*, not the continuous form.

*I **can see** something under your chair.* (Not: *I'm seeing something under your chair*.)

■ We can use *feel* in the simple or continuous forms.

*I **feel** hot.* or *I'**m feeling** hot.*

Practice

Exercise 30A

Complete the sentences. Use the present simple or the present continuous.

1 I _like_____ (like) this photograph.

2 Emily _____ (watch) TV at the moment.

3 Mrs Reed _____ (own) an export company.

4 My parents _____ (love) their old cat.

5 _____ (you | want) a coffee?

6 _____ (you | go) home now?

7 _____ (you | know) my friend?

8 I can't go out now. I _____ (do) my homework.

Exercise 30B

There are mistakes in some of these sentences. Find the mistakes and correct them.

1 ~~I'm hating~~ cold weather.   *I hate*

2 Are you studying at the moment? ✓

3 Are you believing me?

4 This car isn't belonging to me.

5 What is this word meaning?

6 Tony is waiting outside.

7 I'm preferring jazz to pop music.

8 Are you enjoying yourself?

9 I'm seeing a dog in the garden.

10 You're seeming very happy.

11 How are you feeling?

Exercise 30C

(i) Are these actions (**A**) or not actions (**NA**)?

1 Tony has a good job. _NA___

2 Tony has a shower every morning. _____

3 Tony is having a shower now. _____

4 Tony has a sister. _____

5 I think life is wonderful. _____

6 What are you thinking about? _____

7 I think about you every day. _____

8 They have dinner at about 7.30. _____

9 They have a new car. _____

10 They're having a game of chess. _____

★ (ii) We can use *got* with *have* and *has* in three of these sentences. Write out the three sentences with *got*.

_1 Tony has got a good job._____

31 Review of talking about the present

Exercise 31A (▷ Units 23–25, 28)

Add *am, are, is, have* or *has*.

1 Sophia _is_ 26 years old.

2 She _____ two sisters.

3 You _____ tired.

4 You _____ got nice hands.

5 We _____ waiting for the bus.

6 The children _____ hungry.

7 George _____ leaving now.

8 I _____ listening to you.

9 There _____ a phone in my room.

10 There _____ two banks near here.

11 It _____ raining again.

Exercise 31B (▷ Units 29–30)

Choose the correct answer.

1 *I listen/I'm listening* to the radio every morning.

2 Be quiet! *I listen/I'm listening* to the radio.

3 Jill is in the kitchen. *She has/She's having* breakfast.

4 *She often has/She's often having* yoghurt for breakfast.

5 *She has/She's having* a brother and two sisters.

6 How many languages *do you speak/are you speaking*?

7 *Do you like/Are you liking* this music?

Exercise 31C (▷ Units 23–25, 27–28)

Make the sentences into negatives and questions.

1 It's cold.
   It isn't cold.
   Is it cold?

2 I'm late.
   _____
   _____

3 You're working.
   _____
   _____

4 She's leaving.
   _____
   _____

5 There's a film on TV.
   _____
   _____

6 He's got a camera.
   _____
   _____

7 We've got time.
   _____
   _____

8 They live in Rome.
   _____
   _____

9 She likes tennis.
   _____
   _____

32 Past tense of the verb *be*

I **was** at home yesterday. I **wasn't** at work.
'**Were** you and Julie at the cinema last night?'   'Yes, we **were**.'

Use

Last week

Now

Alex and Anna Stewart are at home in England now. They ***were*** *on holiday in Spain last week. The weather is terrible today. It* ***was*** *beautiful in Spain last week. Alex and Anna* ***were*** *happy last week. They aren't very happy now!*

■ We use the past tense of the verb *be* to talk about a definite time in the past eg *last week, yesterday, last night, in 1988.*

Form

AFFIRMATIVE (+)

I **was**
you **were**
he **was**
she **was**
it **was**
we **were**
you **were**
they **were**

NEGATIVE (−)

FULL FORMS	SHORT FORMS
I **was not**	I **wasn't**
you **were not**	you **weren't**
he **was not**	he **wasn't**
she **was not**	she **wasn't**
it **was not**	it **wasn't**
we **were not**	we **weren't**
you **were not**	you **weren't**
they **were not**	they **weren't**

QUESTION (?)

was I?
were you?
was he?
was she?
was it?
were we?
were you?
were they?

SHORT ANSWERS

Yes, I/he/she/it **was**.
Yes, you/we/they **were**.

No, I/he/she/it **wasn't**.
No, you/we/they **weren't**.

Practice

Exercise 32A

Sylvester Stallone

Sting

Madonna

Clint Eastwood

Rod Stewart

Julio Iglesias

Mark Knopfler

What were the first jobs of these famous people? Complete the sentences. Use *is*, *was*, *are* or *were*.

Sylvester Stallone _is_ (1) an actor and a film maker now. His first job _was_ (2) in an Italian restaurant. He _____ (3) a pizza chef.

Sting _____ (4) a singer and an actor now. His first job _____ (5) in a primary school. He _____ (6) a teacher.

Madonna _____ (7) a singer and an actress now. Her first job _____ (8) in a Burger King restaurant. She _____ (9) a waitress.

Clint Eastwood _____ (10) an actor and a film maker now. His first job _____ (11) in the army. He _____ (12) a swimming instructor.

Rod Stewart and Julio Iglesias _____ (13) singers now. Before they _____ (14) singers, they _____ (15) both footballers.

Mark Knopfler _____ (16) a singer and a guitarist now. His first job _____ (17) with the *Yorkshire Evening Post* newspaper. He _____ (18) a journalist.

Exercise 32B

Where were you yesterday? Make true sentences.

1 at home at 7 o'clock yesterday morning
2 at the cinema at 2 o'clock yesterday afternoon
3 in bed at 6 o'clock yesterday evening
4 at home at 9 o'clock last night
5 at a disco at midnight last night

Example:

1 *I was at home at 7 o'clock yesterday morning.*
or *I wasn't at home at 7 o'clock yesterday morning.*

1 _____

_____

2 _____

_____

3 _____

_____

4 _____

_____

5 _____

_____

Exercise 32C

(i) Complete the questions with *was* or *were*.

1 _Were_ you ill last week?
2 _____ the weather fine yesterday?
3 _____ your parents in Paris in 1980?
4 _____ you and your family in England last year?

(ii) Give true short answers to the questions in (i).

Example:

1 Were you ill last week?

– _Yes, I was._   or _No, I wasn't._

1 – _____   3 – _____

2 – _____   4 – _____

(iii) Now make sentences about these things.

Example:

1 I _was_ ill last week.

or I _wasn't_ ill last week.

1 I _____ ill last week.

2 The weather _____ fine yesterday.

3 My parents _____ in Paris in 1980.

4 My family and I _____ in England last year.

Exercise 32D

1

Maria Callas

2

Yuri Gagarin

3

James Dean

4

Laurel and Hardy

5

Agatha Christie

6

Marilyn Monroe

7

Marie and Pierre Curie

8

Indira Gandhi

These famous people are not alive now. Who were they? Complete the questions and answers with *was* or *were*.

QUESTIONS

1 Who __was__ Maria Callas?

2 Who _____ Yuri Gagarin?

3 Who _____ James Dean?

4 Who _____ Laurel and Hardy?

5 Who _____ Agatha Christie?

6 Who _____ Marilyn Monroe?

7 Who _____ Marie and Pierre Curie?

8 Who _____ Indira Gandhi?

ANSWERS

– She __was__ a Greek opera singer.

– He _____ the first man in space.

– He _____ an American actor.

– They _____ comedians.

– She _____ an English writer.

– She _____ an American actress.

– They _____ scientists.

– She _____ India's first woman prime minister.

33 Past simple

> We **played** tennis yesterday.
> Tony **stayed** at home last night. He **didn't go** out.
> 'I **went** to Canada in 1990.'   '**Did** you **go** to Ottawa?'

Use

Last year

Now

*Joe lives in New York now. He **lived** in a small town in Ohio last year. He works for a computer company now. Last year he **worked** for an export company. Joe **liked** his old job, but he likes his new job better.*

- We use the past simple to talk about a definite time in the past eg *last year, yesterday, last night, in 1990.*

Form

AFFIRMATIVE (+)

☐ Many verbs are 'regular'. The past simple of regular verbs ends in *-ed* eg *work → work**ed**.*

☐ Some verbs have 'irregular' past simple forms eg *go → **went**.* ▷ See pages 219–220.

I you he she it we you they	**worked** **went**

NEGATIVE (−)

FULL FORMS

I you he she it we you they	**did not**	**work** **go**

SHORT FORMS

I you he she it we you they	**didn't**	**work** **go**

QUESTION (?)

did	I you he she it we you they	**work**? **go**?

SHORT ANSWERS

Yes, I/you/he/she/it/we/ they **did**.
No, I/you/he/she/it/we/ they **didn't**.

Practice

Exercise 33A

(i) Write the *-ed* forms of these words.

1

start *started*

play _____

watch _____

need _____

finish _____

cook _____

sail _____

2

use *used*

live _____

dance _____

like _____

hate _____

3

stop *stopped*

plan _____

slip _____

4

hurry *hurried*

carry _____

tidy _____

▷ What are the *-ed* spelling rules? See page 218.

(ii) How do we say the *-ed* endings? Practise saying these words.

/ɪd/	/d/	/t/
visited	stayed	reached
ended	called	brushed
	closed	worked
	arrived	kissed
	cleaned	helped
	married	
	studied	

(iii) Now put the *-ed* forms from (i) into three groups.

/ɪd/	/d/	/t/
started	*played*	*watched*
___	___	___
___	___	___
	___	___
	___	___
	___	___
	___	

▷ What are the *-ed* pronunciation rules? See page 217.

Exercise 33B

(i) What do you usually do at weekends? Do you do any of these things?

> visit friends   play tennis   study   clean the car
> cook meals   clean your room   work in the garden
> stay at home and watch TV   tidy your flat or house

Tick (✓) the things that you do.

(ii) Look at the pictures. They show what Liz and George did **last** weekend. What did they do?

Saturday

1 They *tidied their flat.*

2 They _____

3 They _____

Sunday

1 Liz _____

2 George _____

3 They _____

_____

★ (iii) What about you, and your family and friends? What did you do last weekend? Did you do any of the things in (i)?

Examples:

> *I cleaned my room.*
> *I visited a friend.*
> *My friend and I played tennis.*

Saturday

1

2

3

Sunday

1

2

3

Exercise 33C

```
R E A D C D I E B S W A M B O
A R T A U G H T W O R E N D I   B
N M E T T C A M E U R N O R S U   U
S A W O M A D E G G G T O O P I   I
B U S O L D G O T H R G A V E L   L
S P O K E R L O S T E A R E N   T
S A T D R A N K E L W L E F T Y
K N E W T F L E W M O W R O T E
```

Find the past simple of these irregular verbs.

build	*built*	lose	*lost*
buy	_____	make	_____
come	_____	meet	_____
cut	_____	read	_____
do	_____	run	_____
drink	_____	see	_____
drive	_____	sell	_____
eat	_____	sit	_____
fly	_____	speak	_____
get	_____	spend	_____
give	_____	swim	_____
go	_____	take	_____
grow	_____	teach	_____
have	_____	wear	_____
know	_____	write	_____
leave	_____		

Exercise 33D

Mr Bird

(i) Mr Bird always does the same things every day. Read what he does.

> *He gets up at 6.45 every morning and has a shower. Then he has breakfast. He always has tea and cornflakes for breakfast. He leaves home at 7.55 and goes to work by bus. He always takes the 8.05 bus and gets to work at 8.30. He has lunch from 1.00 till 2.00 and leaves work at 6.00 in the evening. When he gets home, he reads the newspaper. Then he has dinner. He always has dinner at 7.15. After dinner he takes his dog for a walk. He always goes to bed at 10.30 exactly!*

★ (ii) What did Mr Bird do **yesterday**? Yesterday was a normal day for Mr Bird. What did he do?

Examples:

> *He got up at 6.45 and had a shower. Then he had breakfast. He had tea and cornflakes for breakfast.*

Exercise 33E

Complete the sentences. Use *did, have* or *had*.

1 Emily _had_ a big breakfast yesterday, so she
  did n't _have_ any lunch.

2 _____ you _____ a lot of homework last week?
  – No, I _____ n't.

3 What _____ you _____ for dinner last night?
  – We _____ chicken.

4 It was Tony's birthday last week. He _____ a party
  on Friday.
  – Where _____ he _____ the party?
  – He _____ it at his flat.

5 _____ Nick and Sarah _____ a good time at the
  concert last weekend?
  – Yes, they _____. They _____ a great time.

Exercise 33F

(i) Complete the questions. Give true short answers.

1 you | go | out last night?
2 you | play | tennis yesterday?
3 you | study | last weekend?
4 you | have | a haircut last week?
5 you | have | a birthday party last year?
6 you | have | a holiday last summer?

Example:

1 _Did you go out last night?_
  – _Yes, I did._ or _No, I didn't._

1 _____
  – _____

2 _____
  – _____

3 _____
  – _____

4 _____
  – _____

5 _____
  – _____

6 _____
  – _____

(ii) Now make true sentences about the things in (i).

Example:

1 _I went out last night._
  or _I didn't go out last night._

1 _____
2 _____
3 _____
4 _____
5 _____
6 _____

Exercise 33G

Henry Ford
(1863–1947)   **The Ford Model T**

(i) Read about Henry Ford. Some of the information is missing.

American engineer Henry Ford started the Ford Motor
Company in __1__. Ford produced __2__. He called the
car __3__. He started making the Model T in __4__ in
1908. Millions of people bought __5__ and Ford became
__6__.

(ii) Ask about the missing information.

1 When *did* Henry Ford *start* the Ford Motor

  Company?

2 What _____ he _____ ?

3 What _____ he _____ the car?

4 Where _____ he _____ making the Model T?

5 What _____ millions of people _____ ?

6 What _____ Ford _____ ?

(iii) Now find answers to the questions.

American engineer Henry Ford started the Ford Motor
Company <u>in 1903</u>. Ford produced the first cheap motor
car. He called the car the Ford Model T. He started
making the Model T in Detroit in 1908. Millions of
people bought the car and Ford became a very rich
man.

Exercise 33H

Look at the answers. What are the questions?

QUESTIONS	ANSWERS
1 you | out last Saturday?	– Yes, I went to the cinema.
2 you | on your own?	– No, I went with a friend.
3 Which film | you?	– We saw a film called *Zero*.
4 you | the film?	– Yes, we enjoyed it very much.
5 What time | the film?	– It started at 3.30.
6 When | it?	– It finished at 5.00.
7 Where | you | after the film?	– We went for a coffee in the Tropical Cafe.
8 What | you | after that?	– I went home.

1 *Did you go out last Saturday?* _____

2 _____

3 _____

4 _____

5 _____

6 _____

7 _____

8 _____

34 Past continuous

> 'What **were** you **doing** at 3 o'clock yesterday?'
> 'I **was cleaning** my flat.'

Use

At 8.30 yesterday morning I **was driving** to work. It was a beautiful morning. The sun **was shining** and the birds **were singing** in the trees.

- We use the past continuous for something that was in the middle of happening at a past time.

Past continuous

I **was driving** to work.

Past ————————————————————— **Present** ———

    8.15   8.30   8.45

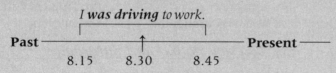

- Compare:

  I **was driving** along East Street **when** I saw a fire.
  (Past continuous)   (when = at the time that)
  I **telephoned** the fire brigade **when** I saw the fire.
  (Past simple)   (when = after)

Form

AFFIRMATIVE (+)

I **was working**
you **were working**
he **was working**
she **was working**
it **was working**
we **were working**
you **were working**
they **were working**

NEGATIVE (−)

FULL FORMS	SHORT FORMS
I **was not working**	I **wasn't working**
you **were not working**	you **weren't working**
he **was not working**	he **wasn't working**
she **was not working**	she **wasn't working**
it **was not working**	it **wasn't working**
we **were not working**	we **weren't working**
you **were not working**	you **weren't working**
they **were not working**	they **weren't working**

QUESTION (?)

was I **working**?
were you **working**?
was he **working**?
was she **working**?
was it **working**?
were we **working**?
were you **working**?
were they **working**?

SHORT ANSWERS

Yes, I/he/she/it **was**.
Yes, you/we/they **were**.

No, I/he/she/it **wasn't**.
No, you/we/they **weren't**.

Practice

Exercise 34A

The Wilson family had a surprise visitor at 9.00 last Sunday morning. This is what was happening when Tina Wilson opened the door.

(i) Tina is telling a friend about last Sunday morning. Complete what Tina says. Use these verbs:

> play sit wear bark have listen sing
> stand watch wear

It was terrible! I opened the door and a policeman
was standing _____ (1) there. My parents
_____ (2) breakfast in the
kitchen. Mum _____ (3)
her old dressing gown. Dad _____
_____ (4) his pyjamas. My sister Zoe
was in the hall. She _____ (5)
to her Walkman and _____ (6)
at the top of her voice. My brother Mark _____
_____ (7) on the stairs. He _____
_____ (8) his guitar. The dog _____
_____ (9) at the front door. And our
neighbours _____ (10)
everything from their garden, as usual!

★ (ii) What were you doing at these times yesterday?
Make true sentences.

> at 8.00 in the morning   at 11.00 in the morning
> at 3.00 in the afternoon   at 10.00 last night

Examples:

> I was having breakfast at 8.00 in the
> morning. I was working at 11.00 in the morning.

Exercise 34B

Ask and answer two questions about the man in each pair of pictures. Use the past continuous, then the past simple.

QUESTIONS

1 he | do | when | it | start | to rain?
2 he | do | when | his car | break | down?
3 he | do | when | the dog | run | in front of him?
4 he | do | when | he | see | the shark?

ANSWERS

– hang | out his washing
– take | the washing inside
– drive | into town
– phone | a garage
– cycle | along the street
– fall | off his bicycle
– swim | in the sea
– get | out of the water

1 What was he doing when it started to rain?
– He was hanging out his washing.
* What did he do when it started to rain?*
– He took the washing inside.

35 Present perfect simple

> *I've lived here for four years.*
> *Have you ever been to Australia?*
> *Look! Andrew has grown a beard!*

Use

■ Mrs Fish is a teacher. She became a teacher in 1955.

1955   **Now**

Past ———————————————————— **Present**

Present perfect

*Mrs Fish **has been** a teacher since 1955.*

■ We use the present perfect to talk about something that started in the past and continues up to the present.

I've had my car since 1990. (I still have the car.)
How long have you lived here? (You still live here.)

We often use *for* and *since* with the present perfect to say how long something has continued. Compare:

We've been here for two hours.	*We've been here since 2 o'clock.*

▷ For *for* and *since*, see Unit 69.

> Have you ever flown in a balloon?

Past ———————————————————— **Present**

Present perfect

Have you ever flown in a balloon?
(= at any time in your life)

■ We also use the present perfect to talk about experiences in our lives, up to now.

Julia hasn't been to Australia. (= in her life)
I've seen that film. (= in my life)

We often use *ever* and *never* with the present perfect.

***Have** you **ever driven** a Rolls Royce?* (= at any time in your life)
*Some people **have never seen** snow.* (= at no time in their lives)

Last month   **Now**

■ We also use the present perfect to talk about a past action, when we can see the result of the action now.

Action	Result
Tim **has grown** *a moustache.* →	He has a moustache now.
He **has had** *a haircut.* ⟶	His hair is shorter now.

We often use *just, already* and *yet* with the present perfect.

Diana **has just gone** *out.* (= a short time before now)
I've **already seen** *that film.* (= before now)
It's 10.00, but Tim **hasn't woken** *up yet.* (= up to now)
Have *you* **finished** *your homework yet?* (= up to now)

Note that we use *yet* in negatives and questions.

■ Compare *gone* and *been*:

Tony isn't at home. He
has gone *out.* (He has
not returned.)

Tony is back home now. He
has been *out.* (He has
returned.)

Form

■ *have/has* + past participle

□ The past participle of regular verbs ends in *-ed* eg
work + *work**ed***.

□ Some verbs have irregular past participle forms eg
be → *been*. ▷ See pages 219–220.

AFFIRMATIVE (+)

FULL FORMS

I you we they	**have**	**worked** **been**
he she it	**has**	

SHORT FORMS

I you we they	**'ve**	**worked** **been**
he she it	**'s**	

NEGATIVE (−)

FULL FORMS

I you we they	**have not**	**worked** **been**
he she it	**has not**	

SHORT FORMS

I you we they	**haven't**	**worked** **been**
he she it	**hasn't**	

QUESTION (?)

have	I you we they	**worked?** **been?**
has	he she it	

SHORT ANSWERS

Yes, I/you/we/they **have.** Yes, he/she/it **has.**
No, I/you/we/they **haven't.** No, he/she/it **hasn't.**

Practice

Exercise 35A

Complete the crossword. Use the past participle of these irregular verbs.

A = Across   **D** = Down

1D ride	**7D** teach	**13D** break	**19A** drink
2A grow	**8A** write	**14A** put	**20D** read
3D fly	**9D** steal	**15A** become	**21A** see
4D be	**10D** eat	**16A** begin	**22A** win
5A lose	**11A** go	**17D** do	**23A** have
6A drive	**12D** speak	**18D** know	**24A** wear

Exercise 35B

(i) Complete what Sylvia says. Use the present perfect simple, and *for* or *since*.

1 I'm from Switzerland, but I live in London now.

I **'ve lived** *(live)* here **since** 1988.

2 I'm a photographer. I work for a sports magazine in London. I _____ *(work)* there _____ two years.

3 I'm married. My husband's name is Theo.

We _____ *(be)* married _____ 1989.

4 Theo works in a bank. He _____ *(work)* there _____ three years.

5 We have a flat in north London. We _____ _____ *(have)* the flat _____ last January.

★ (ii) Look at Sylvia's answers. What are the questions? Use *How long . . .?*.

Example:

1 *How long have you worked for the sports magazine?*

1 For two years. 3 Since 1988.   5 For three years.
2 Since 1989.   4 Since last January.

Exercise 35C

1

eat | Chinese food

2

ride | a camel

3

be | sailing

4

climb | a mountain

5

fly | in a helicopter

6

see | a UFO

(i) What have you done in your life? Look at the pictures. Have you ever done these things?

Example:

1 _I've eaten Chinese food._
or _I haven't eaten Chinese food._

1 _____
2 _____
3 _____
4 _____
5 _____
6 _____

(ii) Now ask someone if he or she has ever done the things in (i).

1 _Have you ever eaten Chinese food ?_
2 _____
3 _____
4 _____
5 _____
6 _____

Exercise 35D

Last month

Now

★ Look at the picture of these people last month. Then look at the picture of them now. What have they done?

Example:

Jane has had a haircut.

break	grow		his beard	a moustache
have	shave off		an argument	a haircut
get	have		engaged	his leg

Exercise 35E

Look at the picture of the hotel kitchen. What have the different people **just** done?

1 *He's just done the washing up.*

2 _____

3 _____

4 _____

5 _____

6 _____

111

Exercise 35F

Alex and Anna are getting ready to go on holiday.

(i) Here is their list of things to do before they leave for the holiday. Ask and answer if they have done each thing **yet**.

Collect the plane tickets ✓ ☺
Pack the suitcases
Buy a film for the camera ✓
Collect the traveller's cheques ✓
Order a taxi to the airport ✓
Find the passports
Take the cat to the cattery

Have they collected the plane tickets yet?
– Yes, they have.
Have they packed the suitcases yet?
– No, they haven't.

–

–

–

–

(ii) What have Alex and Anna **already** done? What haven't they done **yet**? Make sentences.

They've already collected the plane tickets.
They haven't packed the suitcases yet.

36 Present perfect simple and past simple

*I'**ve had** my present job for two years.* ***Have** you **ever been** to Los Angeles?*	*I **had** my old job for five years.* ***Did** you **go** to Los Angeles last summer?*

■ We use the present perfect simple for something that started in the past and continues up to the present.

> ROME
>
> *I'**ve lived** in Rome for three years.*
>
> (I live in Rome now.)

Past ——————————————— **Present**

■ We use the past simple for something that started and finished in the past.

> PARIS
>
> *I **lived** in Paris for three years.*
>
> (I do **not** live in Paris now.)

Past ——————————————— **Present**

■ We use the present perfect simple to talk about an indefinite time up to the present eg *ever, never*.

***Have** you **ever been** to Rome?* (= at any time in your life)
*I'**ve never played** golf.* (= at no time in my life)

■ We use the past simple, not the present perfect, to talk about a definite past time eg *last week, yesterday, two years ago*.

***Did** you **go** to Rome **last week**?* (Not: ~~Have you been to Rome last week?~~)
*I **played** tennis **yesterday**.* (Not: ~~I've played tennis yesterday.~~)

We normally use the past simple, not the present perfect, to ask **when** something happened.

***When did** you **buy** your car?* (Not: ~~When have you bought your car?~~)

■ We use the present perfect when we can see the result of a past action at the present time. Compare:

Present perfect simple
*Bob **has broken** his leg.*
(His leg is broken now.)

Past simple
*Tim **broke** his leg last year.*
(His leg is better now.)

113

Practice

Exercise 36A

(i) Complete the text. Use the present perfect simple or the past simple.

Film maker David Morris *has been* _____ (1) (*be*) interested in the cinema since he _____ (2) (*be*) a small child. He _____ (3) (*make*) his first film when he _____ (4) (*be*) just twelve years old. He is now almost 40 and he _____ (5) (*make*) 30 films. David loves travelling. His work _____ _____ (6) (*take*) him all over the world. He _____ (7) (*be*) to Africa, India, Australia, China, the USA and South America. Last year he _____ (8) (*visit*) Russia for the first time. David is married to the singer, Leena Lennox.

They _____ (9) (*be*) married for ten years. They live with their two children on the Greek island of Crete. They _____ (10) (*buy*) a house on the island in 1987 and they _____ _____ (11) (*live*) there since then.

(ii) Ask and answer questions about the text.

1 How long *has David been* _____ interested in the cinema?
   – Since he was a small child.
2 When _____ his first film?
   – When he was 16.
3 How many films _____?
   – 30.
4 _____ to Russia?
   – Yes, he has.
5 When _____ there?
   – He went there last year.
6 When _____ David and Leena _____ married?
   – Ten years ago.
7 How long _____ on Crete?
   – Since 1987.

Exercise 36B

★ Which countries and cities have you been to in your life? When did you go to each place?
Examples:

> *I've been to New York.*
> *I went there in 1990.*

37 Review of talking about the past

Exercise 37A (▷ Units 32–33)

(i) Complete the sentences. Use the past tense of the verbs.

1 She *played* _____ tennis last Saturday. (*play*)

2 He _____ to the cinema last week. (*go*)

3 The train _____ late yesterday. (*be*)

4 They _____ at home last night. (*be*)

5 She _____ the letter yesterday. (*post*)

6 You _____ TV last night. (*watch*)

(ii) Now make the sentences from (i) into negatives and questions.

1 *She didn't play tennis last Saturday.*
   Did she play tennis last Saturday?

2 _____

   _____

3 _____

   _____

4 _____

   _____

5 _____

   _____

6 _____

   _____

Exercise 37B (▷ Unit 34)

Make sentences. Put the verbs into the past simple or the past continuous.

1 It | rain | when | I | get | up this morning.
2 When | I | get | up, I | have | a shower.
3 We | go | home | when | we | see | the accident.
4 When | we | see | the accident, we | phone | the police.
5 John | ride | on his bike | when | he | fall | off.
6 He | break | his leg | when | he | fall | off.
7 1 | get | undressed | when | I | hear | a strange noise outside my bedroom window.
8 When | I | hear | the noise, I | go | over to the window and | look | outside.

1 *It was raining when I got up this morning.*

_____

_____

_____

_____

_____

_____

_____

_____

_____

_____

_____

_____

_____

Exercise 37C (▷ Unit 35)

Make the sentences into negatives and questions.

1 She's arrived.

She hasn't arrived.

Has she arrived?

2 They've gone out.

_____

_____

3 The train has left.

_____

_____

4 We've finished.

_____

_____

Exercise 37D (▷ Unit 36)

(i) Complete the table.

INFINITIVE	PAST TENSE	PAST PARTICIPLE
_be_	_____	_____
_____	_____	_broken_
_____	_did_	_____
eat	_____	_____
_go_	_____	_____
_____	_had_	_____
_____	_____	_known_
live	_____	_____

(ii) Complete the sentences. Use verbs from (i) in the present perfect simple or the past simple.

1 _Did_ _____ you _go_ _____ to the cinema last night?

2 _____ you ever _____ to Australia?

3 We _____ to Canada last summer.

4 I _____n't _____ to work last Monday.

5 Tony isn't here. He _____ home.

6 We aren't hungry. We _____ lunch.

7 We _____ lunch at McDonald's last Saturday.

8 _____ you _____ breakfast yesterday?

9 How long _____ you _____ in your present flat?

10 How long _____ you _____ in your old flat?

Exercise 37E (▷ Units 35–36)

Choose the correct answer.

1 I had/~~I've had~~ my old job for three years.

2 I had/I've had my present job for a year.

3 We were/We've been at home last night.

4 The bus left/has left five minutes ago.

5 When did you get/have you got married?

6 I'm/I've been a teacher since 1980.

7 Curtis has lived in New York for/since ten years.

38 Present continuous for the future

> *I'm meeting a friend this evening.*
> *Diana is flying to Milan next Monday.*
> *What are you doing on Saturday?*

■ We can use the present continuous to talk about the future:

Look at David's diary for next week.

'What **is** David **doing** next week?' 'He'**s playing** basketball on Monday evening. He'**s going** to the doctor's on Wednesday afternoon. Then on Friday evening he'**s having** dinner with Monica.'

■ We use the present continuous for something that we have already arranged to do in the future.

I'm meeting a friend this evening. (= I have arranged to meet a friend.)
David is going to the doctor's next Wednesday. (= He has got an appointment with the doctor.)
What are you doing next weekend? (= What have you arranged to do?)

117

Practice

Exercise 38A

Diana Snow is going away on a business trip next week.

(i) Ask about Diana's trip next week. Look at the answers. What are the questions?

QUESTIONS	ANSWERS
1 Where | Diana | go?	– To Milan.
2 Where | she | fly | from?	– From Heathrow Airport.
3 When | she | leave?	– On Monday morning.
4 How long | she | stay | in Milan?	– She's staying there for three days.
5 Which hotel | she | stay | at?	– At the Hotel Mediterraneo.
6 When | she | come | back to England?	– She's coming back on Wednesday.
7 What time | she | arrive | in London?	– At 8 o'clock in the evening.

1 *Where is Diana going?*

(ii) Now write what Diana is doing next week.

1 *She's going to Milan.*

2 *She's flying from Heathrow Airport.*

Exercise 38B

Have you made any arrangements for the future? What are you doing? Make true sentences.

1 go | out this evening
2 have | an English lesson tomorrow
3 meet | a friend tomorrow evening
4 go | to the doctor's this week
5 play | tennis next weekend
6 go | away on holiday next month

Example:

1 *I'm going out this evening.*

or *I'm not going out this evening.*

Exercise 38C

(i) What are you doing next weekend? Complete the questions.

1 you | go | out on Friday evening?
2 What | you | do | on Saturday afternoon?
3 you | go | out on Saturday evening?
4 you | do | anything on Sunday morning?
5 you | stay | at home on Sunday evening?

1 Are you going out on Friday evening?

★ (ii) Now answer the questions in (i).

Example:

1 Are you going out on Friday evening?

– *Yes, I am. I'm going to the cinema.*
or *No, I'm not.*

119

39 Going to

> I'**m going to write** some letters this evening.
> Look at those black clouds. It'**s going to rain**.

Use

Julia: We'**re going to play** tennis this afternoon. Would you like to come?
Annie: Thanks, but I'**m going to stay** at home this afternoon. I'**m going to do** my washing.

■ We use *going to* to talk about something that we have already decided to do in the future.

Look. That man **is going to fall** into the river!

■ We also use *going to* when we can see a future action coming because of the present situation.

Form

AFFIRMATIVE (+)

FULL FORMS	SHORT FORMS
I **am going to work**	I'**m going to work**
you **are going to work**	you'**re going to work**
he **is going to work**	he'**s going to work**
she **is going to work**	she'**s going to work**
it **is going to work**	it'**s going to work**
we **are going to work**	we'**re going to work**
you **are going to work**	you'**re going to work**
they **are going to work**	they'**re going to work**

NEGATIVE (−)

FULL FORMS	SHORT FORMS
I **am not going to work**	I '**m not going to work**
you **are not going to work**	you **aren't going to work**
he **is not going to work**	he **isn't going to work**
she **is not going to work**	she **isn't going to work**
it **is not going to work**	it **isn't going to work**
we **are not going to work**	we **aren't going to work**
you **are not going to work**	you **aren't going to work**
they **are not going to work**	they **aren't going to work**

QUESTION (?)

QUESTION (?)	SHORT ANSWERS
am I **going to work?**	Yes, I **am**.
are you **going to work?**	Yes, he/she/it **is**.
is he **going to work?**	Yes, you/we/they **are**.
is she **going to work?**	No, I'**m not**.
is it **going to work?**	No, he/she/it **isn't**.
are we **going to work?**	No, you/we/they **aren't**.
are you **going to work?**	
are they **going to work?**	

Practice

Exercise 39A

(i) Look at the picture. Can you find these people?

1 an old woman	4 an old man
2 some children	5 a motorcyclist
3 a young couple	6 two young women

What are the people going to do in the picture? Are these sentences correct?

1 The old woman is going to post some letters.
2 The children are going to play golf.
3 The old man is going to make a phone call.
4 The motorcyclist is going to turn right.
5 The young women are going to cross the road.
6 The young couple are going to see a play.

Correct the mistakes.

1 ✓

2 The children aren't going to play golf.
They're going to play tennis.

(ii) What are the people going to do in the picture? Can you remember? Cover page 121. Ask and answer.

1 the motorcyclist | turn | right?
2 How many children | play | tennis?
3 the young women | cross | the road?
4 the old man | make | a phone call?
5 Which film | the young couple | see?
6 How many letters | the old woman | post?

1 Is the motorcyclist going to turn right?
—No, he isn't. He's going to turn left.

Exercise 39B

(i) What have you decided to do this evening? Are you going to do these things?

1 watch TV	4 wash your hair
2 read a book	5 go to bed early
3 cook dinner	

Make true sentences.

Example:

1 *I'm going to watch TV.*
   or *I'm not going to watch TV.*

1 _____
2 _____
3 _____
4 _____
5 _____

(ii) Now ask someone if he or she is going to do these things this evening.

1 *Are you going to watch TV this evening?*
2 *Are you going to read a book?*
3 _____
4 _____
5 _____

40 Will

> *'I'm cold.'* *'Are you? I'll close the window, then.'*
> I think Brazil **will win** the football match tomorrow.

Use

Jason: *What can I buy your brother for his birthday? I know! I'll get him a calculator.*
Tina: *He's already got one. But he needs a new watch.*
Jason: *Really? Oh. I'll buy him a watch, then.*

- We use *will* when we decide to do something at the moment we speak.

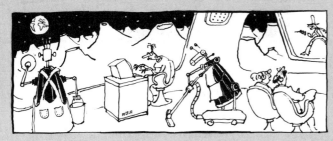

*In the future people **will live** on the moon. Robots **will do** all the housework.*

- We also use *will* to talk about what we think or know will happen in the future.

Form

AFFIRMATIVE (+)

FULL FORMS	SHORT FORMS
I **will work**	I**'ll work**
you **will work**	you**'ll work**
he **will work**	he**'ll work**
she **will work**	she**'ll work**
it **will work**	it**'ll work**
we **will work**	we**'ll work**
you **will work**	you**'ll work**
they **will work**	they**'ll work**

NEGATIVE (−)

FULL FORMS	SHORT FORMS
I **will not work**	I **won't work**
you **will not work**	you **won't work**
he **will not work**	he **won't work**
she **will not work**	she **won't work**
it **will not work**	it **won't work**
we **will not work**	we **won't work**
you **will not work**	you **won't work**
they **will not work**	they **won't work**

QUESTION (?)

QUESTION	SHORT ANSWERS
will I **work?**	Yes, I/you/he/she/it/ we/they **will.**
will you **work?**	
will he **work?**	No, I/you/he/she/it/ we/they **won't.**
will she **work?**	
will it **work?**	
will we **work?**	
will you **work?**	
will they **work?**	

▷ For *will* and *shall*, see also Units 50 and 51.

Practice

Exercise 40A

Read the sentences in A and decide what to do. Use *I think I'll . . .* and the words in B.

A
1 It's hot in this room.
2 I'm hungry.
3 My flat is in a mess.
4 I haven't got any stamps.
5 I want some new glasses.
6 I'm cold.
7 I've just missed my bus.
8 There's a good film on TV.
9 My watch is broken.

B
go to the optician's
buy a new one
open a window
turn on the heating
watch it
take a taxi home
get something to eat
go to the post office
tidy it

1 *I think I'll open a window*.

2 _____

3 _____

4 _____

5 _____

6 _____

7 _____

8 _____

9 _____

Exercise 40B

(i) What will life be like in 100 years from now?
Complete the questions with *will*.

1 children | go | to school in 100 years?
2 people | watch | more TV than they do now?
3 people | read | fewer books?
4 people | live | longer?
5 everyone | speak | the same language?
6 the world's climate | be | different?
7 life | be | better?

1 Will children go to school in 100 years?

(ii) What do you think about the ideas in (i)? Write sentences with *will* or *won't*.

Example:

1 Children will go to school in 100 years.
or Children won't go to school in 100 years.

Exercise 40C

Do you think that, in the future, you will:

1 learn a new language?
2 travel a lot?
3 move to a different country?
4 learn a musical instrument or a new musical instrument?
5 be richer?

Write sentences.

I think Perhaps I don't think	I'll _____.

Example:

1 I think I'll learn a new language.
or Perhaps I'll learn a new language.
or I don't think I'll learn a new language.

I'll clean my car. *He'll bite you.*	*I'm going to clean my car.* *He's going to bite you.*

■ We can use *will* and *going to* to talk about things we decide to do in the future. Note the difference:

■ We use *will* when we decide now – at the moment we speak.

What can I do this morning?

I know! I'll clean my car.
(She decides now.)

■ We use *going to* when we decide before now.

I'm going to clean my car. (She decided before now.)

■ We also use *will* to say what we think or know will happen in the future.

Don't touch that dog. He'll bite you.

■ We use *going to* when we can see a future action coming because of the present situation.

Look out! He's going to bite you!

Practice

Exercise 41A

(i) What do these people decide to do? Use *I'll . . . .*

1. Have you cleaned your room?

   Oh, no, I forgot. I'll clean it now.

2. I've got a letter for the post.

   Oh, _____ _____ for you.

3. What can we have for lunch? I know! _____ some spaghetti.

4. Oh, no! It's starting to rain! I think _____ a taxi.

(ii) What have these people decided to do? Use *I'm going to . . . .*

1. I'm going to make some spaghetti.

2.

3.

4.

Exercise 41B

What are these people saying? Use *going to* or *will('ll)*.

42 Review of talking about the future

Exercise 42A (▷ Units 38–40)

When can we use the present continuous to talk about the future? Can you find mistakes in some of these sentences?

1 Tony is meeting a friend tomorrow evening. ✓

2 I think ~~it's snowing~~ soon.

3 I'm visiting my parents at the weekend.

4 Perhaps I'm visiting New York one day.

5 What time are you leaving tomorrow?

6 Who is winning the next World Cup?

7 I'm sure you aren't failing the exam next week.

Exercise 42B (▷ Unit 41)

Choose the correct answer.

1 Don't touch that dog. *~~It's going to bite~~/It'll bite* you.

2 I'm going out for a walk now.

  – But it's raining.

  – Oh, is it? Well, *I'm going/I'll go* out later.

3 Why don't you change your hair style? *You're going to look/You'll look* much better.

4 Why do you want to sell your flat?

  – *I'll move/I'm going to move* to Madrid.

Exercise 42C (▷ Units 38–40)

Make the sentences into negatives and questions.

1 You'll be at home tonight.

  You won't be at home tonight.

  Will you be at home tonight?

2 I'm going to see you tomorrow.

3 He's working next Saturday.

4 It'll rain tomorrow.

5 They're coming next week.

6 She's going to be late tonight.

7 We'll be here tomorrow.

> *Tony **can swim**, but he **can't windsurf**.*
> ***Can** you **speak** Chinese?*

Use

Man: *I **can drive** a racing car. I **can ski**. I **can windsurf**. I **can speak** Chinese. I **can play** the violin . . .*
Woman: *But you **can't dance**!*

- We use *can* to talk about ability.

- We also use *can* to talk about possibility.

*The doctor **can see** you at 3.00*. (= It is possible for the doctor to see you at 3.00.)

Form

AFFIRMATIVE (+)

I **can swim**
you **can swim**
he **can swim**
she **can swim**
it **can swim**
we **can swim**
you **can swim**
they **can swim**

NEGATIVE (—)

FULL FORMS	SHORT FORMS
I **cannot swim**	I **can't swim**
you **cannot swim**	you **can't swim**
he **cannot swim**	he **can't swim**
she **cannot swim**	she **can't swim**
it **cannot swim**	it **can't swim**
we **cannot swim**	we **can't swim**
you **cannot swim**	you **can't swim**
they **cannot swim**	they **can't swim**

QUESTION (?)

QUESTION	SHORT ANSWERS
can I **swim**?	Yes, I/you/he/she/it/we/they **can**.
can you **swim**?	
can he **swim**?	No, I/you/he/she/it/we/they **can't**.
can she **swim**?	
can it **swim**?	
can we **swim**?	
can you **swim**?	
can they **swim**?	

▷ For *can* in requests eg ***Can** you help me?*, see Unit 49.

Practice

Exercise 43A

What can Tony do?

He can ... (✓)   **He can't ...** (×)

1

2

3

(i) What can Tony do? What can't he do? Make sentences.

| play golf |
| ski |
| windsurf |
| play tennis |
| swim |
| ice-skate |

1 *He can swim.*
   He can't windsurf.

2 _____

   _____

3 _____

   _____

(ii) Can you do these things?

Examples:

1 *I can swim.*   *or* *I can't swim.*
   I can windsurf.   *or* *I can't windsurf.*

1 _____

   _____

2 _____

   _____

3 _____

   _____

Exercise 43B

(i) Ask someone if he or she can do the things in the pictures.

1 *Can you play the piano?*

2 _____

3 _____

4 _____

5 _____

6 _____

stand on your head	type
dance the tango	play the piano
whistle	touch your toes

(ii) Give true short answers to the questions in (i).

Example:

1 Can you play the piano?

– *Yes, I can.* _____ *or* *No, I can't.*

1 – _____

2 – _____

3 – _____

4 – _____

5 – _____

6 – _____

Exercise 43C

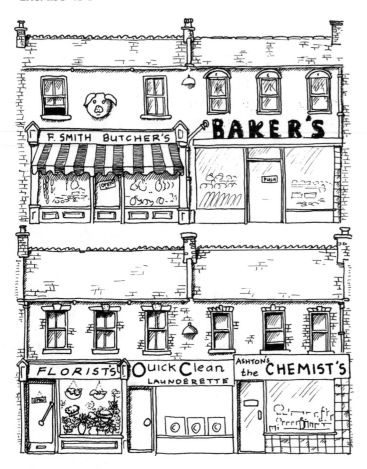

What can you do in these places? Make sentences.
Use *You can ... in a ....*

buy flowers	baker's
buy medicine	butcher's
buy bread and cakes	launderette
wash your clothes	florist's
buy meat	chemist's

You can buy flowers in a florist's.

_____

_____

_____

_____

_____

_____

_____

_____

_____

Exercise 43D

What can you do in your town in your free time? Write
four (or more) sentences.

Examples:

You can play tennis.

You can go to the cinema.

_____

_____

_____

_____

_____

_____

_____

> *Tony **could swim** when he was six years old.*
> ***Could** you **speak** Japanese before you went to Japan?*

Use

*I **could swim** when I was four years old. I **could dive** when I was six. I **could sail** a boat when I was ten. But I couldn't **windsurf** until I was 60!*

Form

AFFIRMATIVE (+)

I **could swim**
you **could swim**
he **could swim**
she **could swim**
it **could swim**
we **could swim**
you **could swim**
they **could swim**

NEGATIVE (−)

FULL FORMS

I **could not swim**
you **could not swim**
he **could not swim**
she **could not swim**
it **could not swim**
we **could not swim**
you **could not swim**
they **could not swim**

SHORT FORMS

I **couldn't swim**
you **couldn't swim**
he **couldn't swim**
she **couldn't swim**
it **couldn't swim**
we **couldn't swim**
you **couldn't swim**
they **couldn't swim**

QUESTION (?)

could I **swim**?
could you **swim**?
could he **swim**?
could she **swim**?
could it **swim**?
could we **swim**?
could you **swim**?
could they **swim**?

SHORT ANSWERS

Yes, I/you/he/she/it/ we/they **could**.

No, I/you/he/she/it/ we/they **couldn't**.

---

134 ■ We use *could* as the past form of *can*.

▷ For *could* in requests eg ***Could** you **help** me?*, see Unit 49.

Practice

Exercise 44A

This is Peter now.

Look at the pictures of Peter when he was a child. They show how old Peter was when he could do these things.

four years old

six years old

seven years old

eight years old

(i) Make sentences about Peter.

> He could _____ when he was _____.

1 *He could swim when he was four.*

2 _____

3 _____

4 _____

(ii) Could you do these things?

Example:

1 *I could swim when I was four.*
  or *I couldn't swim when I was four.*

1 _____

2 _____

3 _____

4 _____

Exercise 44B

1

2

3

4

5

Hello. What's your name?

ENGLISH

(i) What could you do when you were six years old? Ask someone if he or she could do the things in the pictures.

1 *Could you read when you were six?*

2 *Could you write?*

3 _____

4 _____

5 _____

cook   speak English   read   use a calculator   write

(ii) Give true short answers to the questions in (i).

Example:

1 Could you read when you were six?

– *Yes, I could.* or *No, I couldn't.*

1 – _____

2 – _____

3 – _____

4 – _____

5 – _____

45 Must

> I'm really tired. I **must go** home now.
> You **mustn't be** late for work tomorrow.

Use

Father: *You **must put** away your things. You **must keep** your room tidy.*

■ We use *must* when we think that something is necessary.

■ We use *must* to talk about the present eg *I **must do** my homework now*, or the future eg *I **must do** my homework tomorrow*.

To talk about the past, we use *had to* eg *I **had to do** my homework last night.* ▷ See Unit 46.

Father: *You **musn't pull** the cat's tail.*

■ We use *mustn't* to tell someone not to do something.

Form

AFFIRMATIVE (+)

I **must go**
you **must go**
he **must go**
she **must go**
it **must go**
we **must go**
you **must go**
they **must go**

NEGATIVE (−)

FULL FORMS

I **must not go**
you **must not go**
he **must not go**
she **must not go**
it **must not go**
we **must not go**
you **must not go**
they **must not go**

SHORT FORMS

I **mustn't go**
you **mustn't go**
he **mustn't go**
she **mustn't go**
it **mustn't go**
we **mustn't go**
you **mustn't go**
they **mustn't go**

QUESTION (?)

must I **go**?
must you **go**?
must he **go**?
must she **go**?
must it **go**?
must we **go**?
must you **go**?
must they **go**?

SHORT ANSWERS

Yes, I/you/he/she/it/ we/they **must**.
No, I/you/he/she/it/ we/they **mustn't**.

Practice

Exercise 45A

What is Alice's mother saying to Alice in the pictures?

You	must mustn't	touch do eat wake play go	with matches. your vegetables. your homework. to sleep. my camera. the baby.

You must do your homework.

Exercise 45B

Make sentences from B to go with the sentences in A.
Use *must* or *musn't*.

A

1 You're ill.
2 I'm very thirsty.
3 That dog is dangerous.
4 My glasses are broken.
5 It's Joe's birthday soon.
6 My room is in a mess.
7 I'm late for work.
8 Be quiet.
9 I'm very tired.
10 We're having a party on Saturday.

B

You | go | near it.
I | go | to the optician's.
You | come.
I | hurry.
I | go | to bed.
We | make | any noise.
You | see | the doctor.
I | have | a drink.
I | tidy | it.
We | forget | to send him a card.

1 *You must see the doctor.*
2 _____
3 _____
4 _____
5 _____
6 _____
7 _____
8 _____
9 _____
10 _____
   _____

Exercise 45C

(i)

This man is very unhappy with some things in his life.
He has decided to make some changes. Complete what
he says. Use these words:

| must buy   must lose   must have   mustn't eat |

1 *I must lose* _____ some weight.
2 _____ so much junk food.
3 _____ some new clothes.
4 _____ a haircut.

★ (ii) Are you unhappy with any things in your life?
Decide what changes to make!

Examples:

I must stop smoking.
I must study harder.
I mustn't spend so much money on clothes.

46 Have to

> You **have to be** eighteen to vote in Britain.
> We **don't have to hurry**. We aren't late.
> I **had to wear** a uniform when I was at school.

Use

You **have to drive** on the left in Britain. You **have to wear** a seat belt when you drive a car. You **have to wear** a crash helmet when you ride a motorbike.

■ We use *have to* when something is necessary.

■ The difference between *must* and *have to* is small:

□ Use *must* when **you** think that something is necessary.

You **must drive** more slowly. (**I** think it is necessary.)

□ Use *have to*, for example, when a law or another person says that something is necessary.

You **have to drive** on the right in the USA. (That is the law.)

■ We use *don't have to* or *doesn't have to* when something is not necessary.

I **don't have to wear** a uniform at my school. I can wear what I like.

■ There is a big difference in meaning between *mustn't* and *don't have to/doesn't have to*:

You **mustn't wash** this sweater. (= Do not wash it.)

You **don't have to wash** this sweater. It isn't dirty. (= It is not necessary to wash it.)

Form

AFFIRMATIVE (+)

I **have to go**
you **have to go**
he **has to go**
she **has to go**
it **has to go**
we **have to go**
you **have to go**
they **have to go**

NEGATIVE (−)

FULL FORMS

I **do not have to go**
you **do not have to go**
he **does not have to go**
she **does not have to go**
it **does not have to go**
we **do not have to go**
you **do not have to go**
they **do not have to go**

SHORT FORMS

I **don't have to go**
you **don't have to go**
he **doesn't have to go**
she **doesn't have to go**
it **doesn't have to go**
we **don't have to go**
you **don't have to go**
they **don't have to go**

QUESTION (?)

do I **have to go**?
do you **have to go**?
does he **have to go**?
does she **have to go**?
does it **have to go**?
do we **have to go**?
do you **have to go**?
do they **have to go**?

SHORT ANSWERS

Yes, I/you/we/they **do**.
Yes, he/she/it **does**.

No, I/you/we/they **don't**.
No, he/she/it **doesn't**.

Had to

I **had to wear** *a uniform when I was at school.*

■ To talk about the past, we use *had to*, with *did* and *didn't* in questions, negatives and short answers.

*My grandmother **had to go** into hospital last month.*
*'**Did** you **have to work** late yesterday?'   'Yes, I **did**.'*
*We **didn't have to pay** for the meal last night. Our friends paid for us.*

Practice

Exercise 46A

(i) Annie is a shop assistant in London. She has to do these things every day.

What does Annie have to do every day?

1 *She has to get up at 6.30.*

2 _____

3 _____

4 _____

stand	the Underground to work
be	at 6.30
get up	all day
take	polite to all the customers

(ii) Annie is on holiday this week.

Make sentences about Annie now.
Use *She doesn't have to . . . .*

1 *She doesn't have to get up at 6.30.*

2 _____

3 _____

4 _____

Exercise 46B

★ What do you have to do every day? Make sentences.

I have to ____. *or* I usually have to ____.
I don't have to ____. *or* I don't usually have to ____.

1 get up early
2 start work/school before 9.00
3 work/study hard
4 work/study in the evenings

Example:

1 *I have to get up early.*
or *I don't usually have to get up early.*

Exercise 46C

(i) Complete the sentences about the law in Britain. Add *have to* or *has to*.

In Britain

1 Children _have to_____ start school when they are five.

2 Everyone _has to_____ stay at school until the age of sixteen.

3 Nobody _____ do military service.

4 You _____ be sixteen to get married.

5 You _____ have your parents' permission to get married before you are eighteen.

6 You _____ be eighteen to vote.

7 Not everyone with a job _____ pay taxes.

8 You _____ have a licence for a TV.

★ (ii) Are these things the same in your country?

Examples:

In my country

> Children have to start school when they are six. Everyone has to stay at school until the age of sixteen.

Exercise 46D

(i) Ask someone about his or her country. Complete the questions. Add *do, does* or *have to*.

1 How old _do___ you _have to_____ be to drive in your country?

2 _____ you _____ have a licence to drive?

3 _____ everyone _____ wear a seat belt in a car?

4 How old _____ you _____ be to ride a motorbike?

5 _____ you _____ wear a crash helmet on a motorbike?

6 _____ you _____ have a licence to ride a bicycle?

7 How old _____ you _____ be to get a job?

8 _____ everyone _____ have an identity card?

★ (ii) Now answer the questions about your country. Use:

> You have to be eighteen/sixteen etc.
> Yes, you do.
> Yes, everyone has to.
> No, you don't.
> No, nobody has to.
> No, not everyone has to.

Exercise 46E

1

smoke

2

FREE CAR PARK

pay to park

3

light fires

4

CREDIT CARDS WELCOME

pay cash

5

turn right

6

drink the water

What do these signs mean? Make sentences. Use *You mustn't . . .* or *You don't have to . . . .*

1 *You mustn't smoke.*

2 _____

3 _____

4 _____

5 _____

6 _____

Exercise 46F

★ (i) Ask someone if he or she had to do these things. Use *Did you have to . . .?*

1 get up early yesterday
2 do a lot of housework last weekend
3 take an exam last week
4 go to the dentist's last month
5 go into hospital last year

Example:

Did you have to get up early yesterday?

(ii) Now say if you had to do these things. Use *I had to . . .* or *I didn't have to . . . .*

Example:

1 *I had to get up early yesterday.*

or *I didn't have to get up early yesterday.*

_____

_____

_____

_____

_____

_____

_____

_____

47 May, might

> I **may go** to the beach tomorrow.
> You **might be** rich one day.

Use

■ What am I going to do this evening? I'm not sure.

I **may stay** at home.   Or I **may go** to a disco!
(= Perhaps I will stay   (= Or perhaps I will go to
at home.)   a disco!)

■ We use *may* to say that perhaps something will happen
in the future.

■ We also use *might* to say that perhaps something will
happen in the future.

Be careful. You **might burn** yourself. (= Perhaps you
will burn yourself.)

■ The difference between *may* and *might* is very small –
might is a little less sure than *may*.

Form

May	Might

AFFIRMATIVE (+)

I **may stay**	I **might stay**
you **may stay**	you **might stay**
he **may stay**	he **might stay**
she **may stay**	she **might stay**
it **may stay**	it **might stay**
we **may stay**	we **might stay**
you **may stay**	you **might stay**
they **may stay**	they **might stay**

NEGATIVE (−)

I **may not stay**	I **might not stay**
you **may not stay**	you **might not stay**
he **may not stay**	he **might not stay**
she **may not stay**	she **might not stay**
it **may not stay**	it **might not stay**
we **may not stay**	we **might not stay**
you **may not stay**	you **might not stay**
they **may not stay**	they **might not stay**

QUESTION (?)

We do not normally use *may* or *might* in questions
with this meaning. For example, we do not say ~~May
you stay at home this evening?~~.

▷ For requests with *may* eg **May** *I use your pen?*, see
Unit 49.

Practice

Exercise 47A

★ Say what *may* or *might* happen in the pictures.

Example:

> 1 *The girl may cut herself.*
> or *The girl might cut herself.*

Exercise 47B

(i) Make a sentence with the same meaning. Use the word in brackets.

1 Perhaps it will rain tomorrow. *(might)*

> *It might rain tomorrow.*

2 Perhaps a friend will visit me next weekend. *(may)*

3 Perhaps I will buy a new computer next month. *(may)*

4 Perhaps I will change my job next year. *(might)*

5 Perhaps I won't go to work tomorrow. *(might)*

6 Perhaps we won't have a holiday next summer. *(may)*

★ (ii) Now make some true sentences. Say what *may* or *might* happen:

tomorrow	next month
next weekend	next summer
next week	next year

Examples:

> *It might be sunny tomorrow.*
> *My brother and I may play golf next weekend.*
> *I may go swimming next week.*

48 Should

> You've got a bad cold. You **should go** to bed.
> Parents **shouldn't hit** their children.

Use

Man: *I feel tired all the time.*
Woman: *You **should have** a holiday. You **shouldn't work** so hard.*

- We use *should* to give advice and, generally, to say what we think is good or right.

- We use *should* to talk about the present eg *I **should go** now*, or the future eg *I **should go** soon*.

- We often say *I think/I don't think . . . should . . . .*
  I think *you **should have** a holiday.*
  I don't think *you **should work** so hard.*

We often use *do you think* with *should* in questions.

Do you think *I **should have** a holiday?*
*What **do you think** I **should do**?*

Form

AFFIRMATIVE (+)

I **should work**
you **should work**
he **should work**
she **should work**
it **should work**
we **should work**
you **should work**
they **should work**

NEGATIVE (−)

FULL FORMS	SHORT FORMS
I **should not work**	I **shouldn't work**
you **should not work**	you **shouldn't work**
he **should not work**	he **shouldn't work**
she **should not work**	she **shouldn't work**
it **should not work**	it **shouldn't work**
we **should not work**	we **shouldn't work**
you **should not work**	you **shouldn't work**
they **should not work**	they **shouldn't work**

QUESTION (?)

should I **work**?
should you **work**?
should he **work**?
should she **work**?
should it **work**?
should we **work**?
should you **work**?
should they **work**?

SHORT ANSWERS

Yes, I/you/he/she/it/ we/they **should**.

No, I/you/he/she/it/ we/they **shouldn't**.

Practice

Exercise 48A

1

2

3

4

5

Give advice to a friend in the pictures.
Use *You should . . .* or *You shouldn't . . . .*

1 **You should try it on first.**

2 _____

3 _____

4 _____

5 _____

| get up today   wear walking boots   go out more |
| try it on first   swim straight after a meal |

Exercise 48B

What do you think? Make sentences. Use *I think . . .
should . . .* or *I don't think . . . should . . . .*

1 people|watch|less TV
2 boys and girls|go|to the same schools
3 men and women|get|the same pay for the same job
4 people|be|free to smoke in public places
5 we|stop|testing medicine on animals
6 we|destroy|nuclear weapons

Example:

1 I think people should watch less TV.
or *I don't think people should watch less TV.*

Exercise 48C

You want to visit a foreign country for a holiday. You
ask someone from that country for advice. Complete
the questions. Use *do you think I should*

1 When|visit|your country?
2 go|in the summer?
3 How|travel|when I'm there?
4 hire|a car?
5 Which places|visit?
6 stay|in hotels?
7 take|traveller's cheques?

1 When do you think I should visit your country?

49 Requests

> **Can** I **have** a coffee, please?
> **Could** you **tell** me the way to East Street?
> **May** I **ask** you a question?

Asking for something

■ We use *can*, *could* and *may* to ask for something.

Could I **have** a menu, please?
Could I **have** spaghetti bolognese?
May I **have** some mineral water, please?

■ *Could* is more polite than *can*. *May* is more formal than *can* or *could*.

Asking for permission

■ We use *can*, *could* and *may* to ask for permission to do something.

Can I **sit** here?
Could I **look** at your newspaper?
May I **use** your dictionary?

Asking someone to do something

■ We use *can* and *could* (but not *may*) to ask someone to do something for us.

Can you **lend** me some money?
Could you **help** me?

Practice

Exercise 49A

★ Ask for these things in a restaurant. Use:

Can Could May	I have _____, please?

a burger with French fries   some coffee   the bill a glass of water   a menu

Example:

1 Can I have a menu, please?
or Could I have a menu, please?
or May I have a menu, please?

Exercise 49B

What are these people saying?

Can I try on	my bag there?
May I borrow	your driving licence, sir?
Could I see	£10?
Can I put	these trousers?

Exercise 49C

What are these people saying?

Could you open	the phone?
Can you help	this form, please?
Can you answer	your suitcase, please?
Could you fill in	me move this table?

1

2

_____

3

4

_____

Exercise 49D

(i) What requests can you make in these places?

1	a bank	4	a hairdresser's
2	a garage	5	a florist's
3	a post office	6	a hotel

Find one request for each place.

| Can Could May | I | have a room with a shower? cut my hair very short? change some money for me? repair my car today? |
| Can Could | you | have ten roses, please? have a stamp, please |

1 *Can you change some money for me?*

2 _____

3 _____

4 _____

5 _____

6 _____

★ (ii) What requests can you make to a teacher in class?

Examples:

May I ask a question, please?
Could you spell that word, please?

Make four more requests.

50 Offers and invitations: *would like, will, shall*

> **Would** you **like** a drink?
> **I'll lend** you some money.
> **Shall** I **help** you?

Offering something

- **Would you like** (noun)?

Would you like a newspaper?
Would you like some coffee?

Inviting someone

- **Would you like to** (infinitive)?

Would you like to go to a concert on Saturday?
Would you like to come to a party tomorrow?

Offering to do something

- **I'll** (infinitive). (*I'll* = I will)

I'll help you.
I'll open the door for you.

- **Shall I** (infinitive)? (= Do you want me to . . .?)

Shall I get you some aspirins?
Shall I phone for the doctor?

- **Would you like me to** (infinitive)?

Would you like me to phone for a taxi?
Would you like me to lend you an umbrella?

Practice

Exercise 50A

B is at A's home. A offers B things in the pictures.
Complete what A says. Use *Would you like a/an/ some. . .?*

Example:

1 *Would you like a cup of tea?*

1 **A:** _____

  B: Oh, yes, please. I'm really thirsty.

2 **A:** _____

  B: Oh, yes, please. I love ice cream!

3 **A:** Are you hungry? _____

  B: No, it's all right. I'm fine, thanks.

4 **B:** I've got a headache.

  A: _____

  B: Oh, yes, please. Thank you.

Exercise 50B

A invites B to do these things. Complete what A says.
Use *Would you like to . . .?*

1 **A:** *Would you like to go to a disco this evening?*

  B: Yes, I would.

2 **A:** _____

  B: I'm sorry, but I can't on Saturday.

3 **A:** _____

  B: Yes, I'd love to.

4 **A:** _____

  B: No, thanks. I hate football!

Exercise 50C

Complete B's offers in the conversations. Use *I'll . . .* and these words:

> show you on the map
> look it up in my dictionary
> get you a ticket, then
> lend you mine
> close the window
> help you clean it

1 **A:** I need to borrow a camera.

  B: *I'll lend you mine.*

  A: That's very kind of you. Thanks.

2 **A:** I'd like to go to the concert on Saturday.

  B: _____

  A: That's very nice of you. Thank you.

3 **A:** Where's Northwood Street?

  B: _____

  A: Thank you.

4 **A:** My flat is in a mess.

  B: _____

  A: No, it's all right, thanks. I can do it.

5 **A:** It's cold in this room.

  B: _____

  A: Oh, thanks.

6 **A:** What does this word mean?

  B: _____

  A: All right. Thanks.

Exercise 50D

You visit a friend. He has a lot of jobs to do. Look at the picture. How many jobs can you find?

You want to help your friend. Offer to do the jobs you can see in the picture. Use *Shall I . . . ?*

1 *Shall I do the washing up?*

2 _____

3 _____

4 _____

5 _____

155

Exercise 50E

(i)

What do petrol station attendants offer to do for customers? Use *Would you like me to . . . ?* and these words:

| check   clean   fill up   check |

1 *Would you like me to fill up* _____

the tank?

2 _____

the oil?

3 _____

the windscreen?

4 _____

the tyres?

(ii)

What do secretaries offer to do for their bosses? Use *Would you like me to . . . ?* and suitable verbs.

Example:

1 *Would you like me to type* _____ this letter?

or *Would you like me to send* _____ this letter?

1 _____

this letter?

2 _____

that report?

3 _____

a fax message?

4 _____

this memo?

'What **shall** we **do** this evening?'   '**Let's stay** at home.'
'**Why don't we go** out?'   '**How about going** to the cinema?'

What shall we do?   Let's go parasailing.

How about having lunch first?

Asking for a suggestion

■ (What/Where etc) **shall we** (infinitive)?

What **shall we do** this morning?
Where **shall we go**?

Making a suggestion

We can make suggestions in these ways:

■ **Shall we** (infinitive)?

Shall we go to a restaurant?
Shall we have a swim?

■ **Let's** (infinitive).

Let's play golf.
Let's have a swim later.   (Let's = Let us)

■ **Why don't we** (infinitive)?

Why don't we have a drink?
Why don't we go to a disco tonight?

■ **How about** (-*ing* or noun)?

How about going for a swim?
How about having some coffee?
How about a swim?
How about some coffee?

157

Practice

Exercise 51A

A and B are friends. Complete B's suggestions when he/she sees the places in the picture.

> Shall we _____?   Let's _____.
> Why don't we _____?   How about _____?

1 **A:** What shall we do now?

   B: L *et's have* _____ a coffee in that cafe.

   A: Yes, all right.

2 **A:** What shall we do later on?

   B: H_____ tennis?

   A: I don't really want to play tennis today.

3 **A:** Where shall we have lunch?

   B: Sh_____ to that Italian restaurant?

   A: Yes, okay.

4 **A:** What shall we do this afternoon?

   B: Wh_____ that film at the cinema?

   A: I've already seen it.

5 **A:** Where shall we go this evening?

   B: L_____ to that disco.

   A: Yes. Why not?

6 **A:** What shall we do tomorrow morning?

   B: Wh_____ for a swim?

   A: Yes, all right. Let's do that!

Exercise 51B

You are spending this evening with a friend. What are you going to do? Complete the conversation.

You: (we | this evening | shall | do | what?)
Friend: (somewhere | go out | let's.)
You: All right. (go | where | we | shall?)
Friend: (for a meal | we | go out | why don't?)
You: Okay. (shall we | to Pizza Hut | go?)
Friend: We went there last Saturday. (go | this evening | let's | somewhere different.)
You: All right. (trying | how | that new Chinese restaurant in East Street | about?)
Friend: Okay. Good idea. (that | do | let's.)

You: *What shall we do this evening?*

Friend: _____

You: _____

Friend: _____

You: _____

Friend: _____

_____

You: _____

_____

Friend: _____

_____

Exercise 51C

Carla and Kim are planning a holiday together. Complete the conversation. Use:

| Let's   Why don't we   How about   shall we |
| Shall we |

Carla: So where _____*shall we*_____ (1) go?

Kim: _____ (2) go somewhere warm and sunny.

Carla: All right. _____ (3) go to Spain?

Kim: We went to Spain last summer. _____ (4) go somewhere different this year.

Carla: All right. But where?

Kim: _____ (5) going to Turkey?

Carla: Turkey? Mmm. Okay. _____ (6) do that.

Kim: So when _____ (7) go there?

Carla: _____ (8) going in April?

Kim: April is fine with me. All right.

Carla: How long _____ (9) go for?

Kim: _____ (10) go for two weeks?

Carla: Yes, all right.

52 Review of modal verbs

Exercise 52A (▷ Units 43–48)

Make the sentences into negatives.

1 I can cook.
 I can't cook.

2 My grandmother could ski.

3 We must stop now.

4 The letter may arrive tomorrow.

5 He might be here next week.

6 You should buy that car.

7 They can speak French.

8 She might remember you.

9 You must go out today.

10 I have to work late tomorrow.

11 She has to get up early.

12 They had to walk home yesterday.

Exercise 52B (▷ Units 43–44, 46, 48)

Make the sentences into questions.

1 We should ask for help.
 Should we ask for help?

2 You can come to the concert.

3 He could ride a horse.

4 I should go to the police.

5 She can dance the tango.

6 He should see the doctor.

7 I have to pay for the ticket.

8 She has to work on Saturdays.

9 They had to sell their car.

Exercise 52C (▷ Units 45–46)

★ (i) There is a mistake in one of these sentences. Find the mistake and correct it.

(a) *I must clean my room now.*
(b) *I must clean my room yesterday.*
(c) *I must clean my room tomorrow.*

(ii) Read these four sentences.

(a) *You must go.*

(b) *You mustn't go.*

(c) *You have to go.*

(d) *You don't have to go.*

★ 1 Which two sentences have only a small difference in meaning?

2 Which sentence means 'Don't go'?

3 Which sentence means 'It isn't necessary for you to go'?

Exercise 52D (▷ Unit 47)

Read these three sentences.

(a) *I may be here tomorrow.*

(b) *I'll be here tomorrow.*

(c) *I might be here tomorrow.*

★ 1 Which sentence means 'I'm sure I'll be here tomorrow'?

2 Which two sentences mean 'Perhaps I'll be here tomorrow'?

Exercise 52E (▷ Units 45, 48)

Read these two sentences.

(a) *You must stop.*

(b) *You should stop.*

★ 1 Which sentence means 'It's a good idea for you to stop'?

2 Which sentence means 'It's necessary for you to stop'?

Exercise 52F (▷ Units 49–51)

Give examples.

1 **Asking for something**

Can I have *a cup of coffee, please?*

Could I have *some bananas, please?*

May I have _____

2 **Asking for permission**

Can I _____

Could I _____

May I _____

3 **Asking someone to do something**

Can you _____

Could you _____

4 **Offering something**

Would you like _____

5 **Inviting someone**

Would you like to _____

6 **Offering to do something**

I'll _____

Shall I _____

Would you like me to _____

7 **Asking for a suggestion**

_____ shall we _____

8 **Making a suggestion**

Shall we _____

Let's _____

Why don't we _____

How about _____ 161

53 Question words

> **What ...?** **Who ...?** **Which ...?** **Whose ...?**
> **Where ...?** **When ...?** **Why ...?** **How ...?**

■ *What* normally asks about things.

'**What**'s your favourite drink?' 'Orange juice.'
'**What** kind of music do you like?' 'Jazz.'

■ *Who* asks about people.

'**Who**'s your favourite singer?' 'Madonna.'

■ *Which* asks about things or people when there is a small choice.

'**Which** do you prefer – jazz or pop music?' 'Jazz.'
'**Which** singer do you like best – Diana Ross, Natalie Cole or Whitney Houston?' 'Whitney Houston.'

■ *Whose* asks about possession.

'**Whose** coat is this?' 'It's mine.'
'**Whose** are these books?' 'They're John's.'

■ Compare *whose* and *who's*:

who's = *who is* or *who has*

Who's that man? (= Who is that man?)
Who's got my bag? (= Who has got my bag?)
'**Whose** bag is this?' 'It's Diana's.'

■ *Where* asks about place.

'**Where**'s Santa Monica?' 'It's in California.'

■ *When* asks about time.

'**When**'s your birthday?' 'It's on 3rd July.'

■ *Why* asks about reason.

'**Why** are you in a hurry?' 'Because I'm late for work.'
'**Why** are you going out?' 'To do some shopping.'

■ *How* asks 'in what way?'.

'**How** do you spell your name?' 'D-A-V-I-S.'

■ Note also:

□ *How old ...? How tall ...?*

'**How old** are you?' 'I'm 23.'
'**How tall** are you?' '1 metre 70.'

□ *How much ...? How many ...?*

'**How much** money have you got?' '£5.'
'**How many** tickets do you want?' 'Two.'

□ *How often ...?*

'**How often** do you go swimming?' 'About twice a week.'

□ *How long ...?*

'**How long** have you lived in this town?' 'For two years.'

Practice

Exercise 53A

Look at these answers.

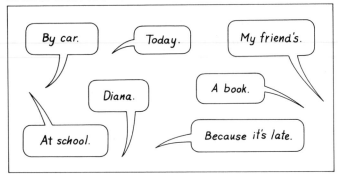

Find one answer for each question word.

What?

A book.

Who?

_____

Whose?

_____

How?

_____

Where?

_____

When?

_____

Why?

_____

Exercise 53B

Ask questions with *Who, What, How, Where, When* or *Why*.

1 *What* _____ is your name?

2 _____ do you spell your name?

3 _____ are you from?

4 _____ do you live?

5 _____ old are you?

6 _____ is your birthday?

7 _____ tall are you?

8 _____ kind of films do you like?

9 _____ is your favourite singer?

10 _____ is your favourite TV programme?

11 _____ do you like it?

Exercise 53C

Ask questions with *What, Who* or *Which*.

1 _____ kind of books do you like?

2 _____ hand do you write with?

3 _____ is your favourite actor?

4 _____ actor do you prefer – Al Pacino or Jack Nicholson?

Exercise 53D

What do you usually do every day? Look at the answers. Ask questions with *Who, What, How, When* (or *What time*), *How many, How much* or *How often*.

QUESTIONS	ANSWERS
1 _____ do you usually get up?	– At 6.30.
2 _____ do you have for breakfast?	– Coffee and toast.
3 _____ do you have breakfast with?	– My family.
4 _____ do you go to work/school?	– By train.
5 _____ do you start work/school?	– At 8.30.
6 _____ coffee do you drink every day?	– Not very much.
7 _____ do you usually have lunch?	– In a cafe.
8 _____ do you go out in the evenings?	– Once or twice a week.
9 _____ hours' sleep do you have a night?	– I usually have eight.
10 _____ do you usually go to bed?	– At about 11.00.

Exercise 53E

Look at the answers. Ask questions with *What, Who, How, When, Where* or *How long*.

QUESTIONS	ANSWERS
1 _____ did you go on your last holiday?	– To Greece.
2 _____ did you go there?	– Last June.
3 _____ in Greece did you go?	– To Crete.
4 _____ did you go with?	– I went with some friends.
5 _____ did you go there?	– We went by plane.
6 _____ did you stay in Crete?	– At a hotel.
7 _____ was the hotel like?	– It was very good.
8 _____ did you stay there?	– For two weeks.
9 _____ was the weather like?	– It was hot and sunny.

54 Subject and object questions

| Who **loves** Tina? | Who **does** Tina **love**? |

Tomiko is painting Frank.

Joe wants to see Mr Reed.

Karen wrote to Gary.

■ Note:

SUBJECT		OBJECT
Tomiko	is painting	**Frank.**
Joe	wants to see	**Mr Reed.**
Karen	wrote to	**Gary.**

■ *Who* can ask about the subject or the object:

□ Asking about the subject

| 'Who **is painting** Frank?' 'Tomiko.' |
| 'Who **wants** to see Mr Reed?' 'Joe.' |
| 'Who **wrote** to Gary?' 'Karen.' |

□ Asking about the object

| 'Who **is** Tomiko **painting**?' 'Frank.' |
| 'Who **does** Joe **want** to see?' 'Mr Reed.' |
| 'Who **did** Karen **write** to?' 'Gary.' |

■ When we ask about the subject:

□ the verb has the same form as in a statement

STATEMENT	QUESTION
Tomiko **is painting** Frank. →	Who **is painting** Frank?
Joe **wants** to see Mr Reed. →	Who **wants** to see Mr Reed?
Karen **wrote** to Gary. →	Who **wrote** to Gary?

□ we do not use *do* or *does* in the present simple or *did* in the past simple.

Who **wants** to see Mr Reed? (Not: ~~Who does want to see Mr Reed?~~)

Who **wrote** to Gary? (Not: ~~Who did write to Gary?~~)

■ *What* can also ask about the subject or the object:

Asking about the subject	Asking about the object
What **made** you late for work?	What **did** you **make** for dinner?

165

Practice

Exercise 54A

(i) What is happening in the picture? Read about the people. Some of the names are missing.

> __1__ is sitting next to Oscar. Oscar is talking to __2__. __3__ is standing next to Ella. Ella is talking to __4__. __5__ is playing table tennis with Carmen. Rob is waving to __6__. __7__ is looking at Marty. Marty is looking at __8__ in the mirror!

(ii) Ask about the missing names. Use *Who . . . ?*

1 *Who is sitting next to Oscar?*

2 *Who is Oscar talking to?*

3 _____

4 _____

5 _____

6 _____

7 _____

8 _____

(iii) Now find the answers to the questions. Write the names of the people in the picture.

> *Gina is sitting next to Oscar. Oscar is talking to Nancy. Bernie is standing next to Ella. Ella is talking to James. Franco is playing table tennis with Carmen. Rob is waving to Yoshiko. Judy is looking at Marty. Marty is looking at himself in the mirror!*

Exercise 54B

(i) These singers all like each other. But who likes who the best?

> *Sammy likes Cindy the best. Cindy likes Dizzy the best. Dizzy likes Lisa the best. And Lisa likes Sammy the best.*

★ (ii) Cover (i). Ask and answer *Who likes . . . the best?* and *Who does . . . like the best?*

Example:

> Who likes Sammy the best? - Lisa.
> Who does Sammy like the best? - Cindy.

Exercise 54C

(i) Read these facts.

1 Mary Shelley wrote *Frankenstein* in 1818.
2 Guglielmo Marconi invented the radio in 1894.
3 Hubert Booth invented the vacuum cleaner in 1901.
4 King Camp Gillette invented the razor in 1901.
5 Henry Ford produced the first cheap car in 1908.
6 Peter Chilvers built the first windsurfer in 1958.

★ (ii) Ask and answer questions about the facts in (i). Use *Who . . .?, When . . .?, What . . .?*

Examples:

> 1 Who wrote Frankenstein?
>   When did she write it?
> 2 What did Marconi invent?

55 Question tags

> You aren't married, **are you?**
> It's a nice day, **isn't it?**

You're angry, aren't you?

■ We can use question tags to check if something is true or to ask someone to agree with us.

You're angry, **aren't you?** (= Am I right?)
The weather isn't very nice today, **is it?** (= Do you agree?)

■ When we think that the statement is true, we use a falling intonation (the voice goes down).

You're angry, **aren't you?**
The weather isn't very nice today, **is it?**

■ We normally put:

□ affirmative question tags with negative sentences

	−		+
You	**aren't**	English,	**are you?**
Tina	**can't**	ski,	**can she?**

□ negative question tags with affirmative sentences

	+		−
You	**are**	English,	**aren't you?**
Tina	**can**	ski,	**can't she?**

■ The verbs are normally the same:

They	**are**	sleeping,	**aren't they?**
I	**am** not	late,	**am I?**
You	**have**	got a car,	**haven't you?**
Tony	**wasn't**	at work,	**was he?**

But note that we say I **am** ..., **aren't I?**

■ We use do, don't, does or doesn't in present simple question tags.

You	don't live here,	**do you?**
Annie	works in a shop,	**doesn't she?**

We use did or didn't in past simple question tags.

You	didn't go to work,	**did you?**
Frank	went to cinema,	**didn't he?**

Practice

Exercise 55A

(i) Read about Martha Miller.

◀ACTRESS MARTHA MILLER

Martha Miller has always wanted to be an actress. She appeared on stage for the first time when she was only four years old. Martha was born in Toronto. When she left school, she moved to New York, where she studied at acting school for two years. Then she started her acting career. Martha, 24, now lives in London with her English husband and their two young children.

(ii) You are interviewing Martha. Check what you read about her in (i). Complete the conversation.

You: Martha. You've always wanted to be an actress, *haven't you?* _____ (1)

Martha: Yes, I have.

You: You started acting when you were a small child, _____ (2)

Martha: Yes. I appeared on stage for the first time when I was only four.

You: You're Canadian, _____ (3)

Martha: Yes, I am.

You: You were born in Toronto, _____ (4)

Martha: That's right.

You: But you didn't go to acting school in Canada, _____ (5)

Martha: No, I studied acting in New York.

You: You were there for two years, _____ (6)

Martha: That's right.

You: You live in London now, _____ (7)

Martha: Yes, I do.

You: And you're married, _____ (8)

Martha: Yes, I am.

You: Your husband isn't Canadian, _____ (9)

Martha: No, he isn't. He's English.

You: And you've got two children, _____ (10)

Martha: Yes, we have. A boy and a girl.

169

56 Review of questions

Exercise 56A (▷ Unit 53)

Complete the questions. Use question words from Unit 53 eg *What, Where, How, How old*, etc.

1 _What_ kind of car have you got?

2 _____ is your favourite sport?

3 _____ ocean is bigger – the Atlantic or the Pacific?

4 _____ book is this? Is it yours?

5 _____ are you from? Are you English?

6 _____ do you usually have your summer holiday? Do you have it in August?

7 _____ are you in bed? Are you ill?

8 _____ do you go to work? Do you go by car?

9 _____ is your friend? Is he over 21?

10 _____ are you? Are you over I metre 80?

11 _____ children have you got?

12 _____ were your shoes? Were they expensive?

13 _____ do you go to the cinema? Do you go more than once a week?

14 _____ have you lived in this town? Have you been here for very long?

Exercise 56B (▷ Unit 54)

Ask questions with *Who . . . ?* or *What . . . ?*

1 Jack is waiting for someone.
Who is Jack waiting for?

2 Someone is waiting for Jack.
_____

3 Something is happening.
_____

4 Someone has got the money.
_____

5 Carmen wants to see someone.
_____

6 Someone wants to see Carmen.
_____

7 Carmen wants to see something.
_____

8 Steven smiled at someone.
_____

9 Someone smiled at Steven.
_____

10 Steven smiled at something.
_____

11 Something happened.
_____

Exercise 56C (▷ Unit 55)

You are talking to a friend. Ask him/her to agree with these statements. Use question tags.

1 Smoking is bad for you.
2 Money isn't everything.
3 Computers are very useful.
4 Some people watch too much TV.
5 People didn't have TV 100 years ago.
6 Life was better 100 years ago.
7 We can all make mistakes.
8 Parents shouldn't hit their children.

1 Smoking is bad for you, isn't it?

Exercise 56D (▷ Units 53–55)

Correct the mistakes.

1 What Tony is writing?

What is Tony writing ?

2 What Julia want to do?

3 Who does wants a cup of tea?

4 Who President John F. Kennedy killed?

5 Who did invented the telephone?

6 Whose your favourite actor?

7 Who's is this coat?

8 What hand do you write with?

9 Arthur is 21, hasn't he?

10 You're a student, isn't it?

11 They live in Milan, doesn't it?

12 Does Diana like golf, doesn't she?

57 Word +infinitive or *-ing* form

> I can **play** tennis.
> I want **to play** tennis.
> I enjoy **playing** tennis.

■ Note the three forms:

INFINITIVE WITHOUT *to*	*to* INFINITIVE	*-ing* FORM
play	*to play*	*playing*
go	*to go*	*going*
be	*to be*	*being*

When do we use each form?

Infinitive without *to* (eg *play, go, be*)

■ We use the infinitive without *to* after 'modal verbs' such as:

can   could   may   might   must   shall   should   will

> modal verb + infinitive without *to*

I **can play** basketball.
We **may go** to the cinema tomorrow.
I **mustn't be** late for work.
Shall we **watch** a video?

■ We also use the infinitive without *to* after *let's* and *why don't we*.

Let's go for a walk.
Why don't we eat now?

To infinitive (eg *to play, to go, to be*)

■ After some verbs, we use the *to* infinitive. For example:

(can) afford   decide   expect   hope   learn promise   want   would like

> verb + *to* infinitive

I can't **afford to go** on holiday.
I **hope to see** you soon.
When did you **learn to drive**?
I **promise to be** very careful with your car.
I don't **want to eat** now. I'm not hungry.
Would you **like to play** chess?

After the verb *help*, we can use the *to* infinitive or the infinitive without *to*.

I'll **help to clean** (or **help clean**) the flat.

■ After some verbs, we often use an object (eg *Peter, me, us*) and the *to* infinitive. For example:

ask   expect   invite   teach   tell   want   would like

> verb + object + *to* infinitive

I **asked Peter to play** tennis with me.
My boss **expects me to work** late tomorrow.
Alex and Anna **invited us to have** dinner with them.
The teacher **told the children to be** quiet.
Do you **want me to lend** you some money?

After the verbs *want* and *would like,* we cannot use
that . . . .

I *want* you *to go* now. (Not: ~~I want that you go now~~.)
Would you **like me to help** you? (Not: ~~Would you like that~~
~~I help you?~~)

After the verb *help,* we can use an object + the *to*
infinitive or the infinitive without *to.*

Can you **help me to push** (or **help me push**) the car?

■ We use the *to* infinitive after some adjectives eg *easy,*
difficult, important, possible, expensive, stupid.

adjective + *to* infinitive

It's **easy to drive** an automatic car.
It isn't **expensive to play** tennis in Britain.
It's **stupid to smoke** cigarettes.

▷ We can also use the *to* infinitive after *too* and *enough*
(see Unit 64) and after *someone, anything,* etc (see
Unit 20).

-ing form (eg *playing, going, being*)

■ After some verbs, we use the *-ing* form. For example:

enjoy finish mind

verb + *-ing* form

I **enjoy playing** computer games.
They **finished painting** the house last week.
I don't **mind working** at weekends.

■ We often use the *-ing* form after *go* to talk about sports
eg *go swimming, go windsurfing, go sailing, go jogging, go*
skiing.

go + *-ing* form

I **go swimming** every weekend.
Julia **went jogging** yesterday.
We're **going skiing** tomorrow.

■ We use the *-ing* form after all prepositions eg *about, at,*
in, for, before.

preposition + *-ing* form

How **about playing** tennis tomorrow?
I'm not very good **at cooking**.
Are you interested **in gardening**?
Thank you **for helping** me.
I washed my hair **before going** out.

-ing form or *to* infinitive

■ After some verbs, we can use the *-ing* form or the *to*
infinitive with very little difference in meaning. For
example:

begin hate like love start

verb + *-ing* form or *to* infinitive

Mike **hates going** to the dentist's. or Mike **hates to go** to
the dentist's.
I **like walking** to work. or I **like to walk** to work.
Diana **started learning** Italian last year. or Diana
started to learn Italian last year.

Practice

Exercise 57A

Ask questions. Put the verbs into the correct form.
(Sometimes two forms are possible.)

1 Do you enjoy _listening_ (listen) to classical music?

2 Do you like _cooking or to cook_ (cook)?

3 How many languages can you _speak_ (speak)?

4 When did you start _____ (learn) English?

5 Do you think it's easy _____ (learn) a foreign language?

6 Are you interested in _____ (garden)?

7 Do you ever go _____ (jog)?

8 Who taught you _____ (swim)?

9 Did you hate _____ (go) to bed early when you were a small child?

10 Are you good at _____ (draw)?

11 Could you _____ (play) chess when you were ten?

12 Do you like _____ (get) up early in the morning?

13 Do you hope _____ (travel) a lot in the future?

14 Do you expect _____ (move) to a new flat or house in the near future?

15 Do you think you'll _____ (move) to a different country one day?

16 Do you think it's important _____ (have) a lot of money?

17 Do you think it's possible _____ (be) happy if you haven't got much money?

18 Do you ever worry about _____ (get) older?

19 Would you like _____ (learn) _____ (fly) a plane?

20 Have you ever wanted _____ (be) taller or shorter?

21 Have you ever wanted _____ (be) someone else?

22 Do you mind _____ (answer) all these questions?

Exercise 57B

Complete the sentences. Use suitable verbs in the correct form. (Sometimes two forms are possible.)

1 I can *play*_____ tennis.

2 I'm good at _____ chess.

3 I taught myself _____ the guitar.

4 I enjoy _____ computer games.

5 I love _____ to the theatre.

6 Next summer I may _____ to Australia.

7 Next year I hope _____ to university.

8 I hate _____ to the dentist's.

9 I started _____ Spanish two years ago.

10 It isn't easy _____ a new language.

11 One day I might _____ Chinese.

12 I'm interested in _____ languages.

13 I could _____ a boat when I was ten.

14 One day I'd like _____ around the world.

15 I like _____ jeans.

16 I learnt _____ when I was seven.

17 I often go _____ in the sea.

18 I don't mind _____ up early in the morning.

Exercise 57C

Jason is visiting his friend Andy. Complete the conversation. Use the verbs in the correct form.

Jason: I'm going into town this afternoon. Would you like *to come*_____ (1) (*come*)?

Andy: I can't. I haven't finished _____ (2) (*clean*) my room. And I promised _____ (3) (*do*) it this afternoon.

Jason: I don't mind _____ (4) (*help*) you _____ (5) (*clean*) the room.

Andy: No, it's all right, really. Thanks for _____ (6) (*offer*), but I'll _____ (7) (*do*) it myself. Why don't we _____ (8) (*go*) out somewhere this evening?

Jason: Okay. Where shall we _____ (9) (*go*)?

Andy: How about _____ (10) (*go*) to the cinema?

Jason: I can't _____ (11) (*afford*) _____ (12) (*go*) to the cinema at the moment.

Andy: All right, then. How about _____ (13) (*go*) to The Zap Bar for a coffee?

Jason: Okay. Good idea. Let's _____ (14) (*do*) that.

Exercise 57D

Complete sentences about the people. Use *to . . .* or
him/her/them to . . . and these words:

> open his mouth   go to a concert   play chess
> drive   close the door   open the bottle

She'd like *to open the bottle*.

She'd like _____

He wants _____

He wants _____

He's teaching _____

She's telling _____

She's asking _____

He's inviting _____

176

58 Purpose: *to* . . . and *for* . . .

> *We went to a cafe **to have** lunch.*
> *We went to a cafe **for** lunch.*
> *A lawn mower is a machine **for cutting** grass.*

■ Tony went to Luigi's Hair Salon yesterday.

*Tony went to Luigi's **to have** a haircut.* (That is why he went to Luigi's.)

■ We use *to* + the infinitive to say why someone does something.

*We went to the Sports Centre **to play** basketball.*
*I must leave now **to catch** my bus.*

■ We can use *for* + a noun to say why someone does something.

I must go to the post office for some stamps.

■ Compare:

to + INFINITIVE	*for* + NOUN
Tony went to Luigi's **to have** *a haircut.* *I must go to the post office* **to get** *some stamps.*	*Tony went to Luigi's* **for** *a haircut.* *I must go to the post office* **for** *some stamps.*

We do not use *for* before a verb to say why someone does something. For example, we do not say *Tony went to Luigi's* ~~for have a haircut~~ or ~~for to have a haircut~~.

What's that?

It's a thing for making holes in paper.

■ We use *for* before the *-ing* form to talk about the purpose of a thing.

'What's that?' 'It's a thing **for making** holes in paper.'
*A lawn mower is a machine **for cutting** grass.*

Practice

Exercise 58A

(i) Look at the pictures. They show what Alex and Anna did last Saturday.

Where did Alex and Anna go last Saturday? Why did they go to each place? Use:

| They went to _____ to _____. |

see	lunch
do	tennis
borrow	a film
have	some books
play	some shopping

1 They went to the supermarket to do some shopping.

★ (ii) Think of some places you went to last week. Why did you go to each place?

Examples:

I went to the cinema to see a film.
I went to a restaurant to have a meal.

Exercise 58B

Why do you go to these places?

1 a baker's   2 a hairdresser's
3 a restaurant   4 a petrol station
5 a disco   6 a launderette

Make sentences.

| You go to a ____ | to (+ infinitive) |
| | for (+ noun) |

Use these words:

a haircut	petrol
dance	buy bread and cakes
wash your clothes	a meal

1 You go to a baker's to buy bread and cakes.

2 You go to a restaurant for a meal.

_____

_____

_____

_____

_____

_____

_____

_____

_____

_____

Exercise 58C

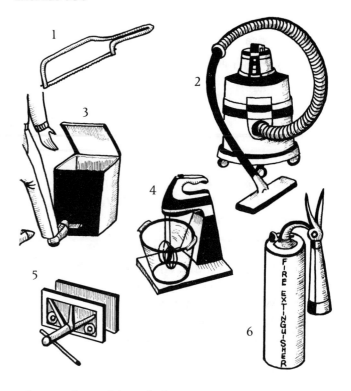

What are these things for?

1 It's a tool *for cutting metal.* _____

2 It's a machine _____

3 It's a thing _____

4 It's a machine _____

5 It's a tool _____

6 It's a thing _____

| put rubbish in   clean carpets   cut metal |
| mix food   put out fires   hold things |

179

59 Review of infinitive and -ing form

Exercise 59A (▷ Unit 57)

(i) Remember the three forms:

INFINITIVE WITHOUT *to*	*to* INFINITIVE	*-ing* FORM
dance	*to dance*	*dancing*
go	*to go*	*going*

★ Which form do we use after these words?

1 *I would like* _____.   4 *I love* _____.
2 *You can* _____.   5 *Teach me* _____.
3 *You're good at* _____.

(ii) Note the five groups of words:

1 Word + infinitive without *to*
   eg **can** (*You can dance.*)
2 Word + *to* infinitive
   eg **would like** (*I would like to dance.*)
3 Word + object + *to* infinitive
   eg **teach** (*Teach me to dance.*)
4 Word + *-ing* form
   eg **at** (*You're good at dancing.*)
5 Word + *-ing* form or *to* infinitive
   eg **love** (*I love dancing.* or *I love to dance.*)

★ Look back at Unit 57 and add more words to each group.

1 Word + infinitive without to
eg can, could, may, might, must, shall,

Exercise 59B (▷ Units 57–58)

There are mistakes in some of these sentences. Find the mistakes and correct them.

1 We must ~~to~~ go now.
2 Shall we stay at home this evening?
3 Do you enjoy to play chess?
4 They want get married next year.
5 We hope to see you tomorrow.
6 Do you mind to work at the weekends?
7 How about to go to the cinema?
8 Do you often go sailing?
9 I finished to write the report yesterday.
10 Tony phoned Julia before to leave work.
11 They went to the park for playing tennis.
12 A hacksaw is a tool for cutting metal.
13 Did you go out for to do some shopping?
14 Let's go to that cafe for a coffee.
15 I must go to the bank for get some money.
16 I'd like that you come to the party.
17 We don't want that you worry.

60 Adjectives

That's a **good** film.
I'm **happy**.
You look **tired**.

*an **old** man*

*a **white** shirt*

***big** feet*

■ *Old*, *white* and *big* are adjectives. We use adjectives to describe people and things.

■ An adjective always has the same form to talk about singular, plural, masculine, feminine, etc.

an **old** man   two **old** men
an **old** woman   two **old** women
an **old** house   two **old** houses

■ An adjective can normally go in two places in a sentence:

□ before a noun eg *man, shoes, hair, room*

ADJECTIVE + NOUN		
He's a	**tall**	**man**.
I've got some	**new**	**shoes**.
Maria has got	**lovely**	**hair**.
This is a	**cold**	**room**.

□ or after the verb *be* (eg *is, are*) and after verbs such as *look, feel* and *seem*.

VERB + ADJECTIVE		
That man	**is**	**tall**.
These shoes	**are**	**new**.
Maria's hair	**looks**	**lovely**.
This room	**feels**	**cold**.

You look hot.

Practice

Exercise 60A

(i) What's in the pictures? Use these words:

young   dirty   tall   old   short   clean

1

a *tall woman*

2

a _____

3

a _____

4

two _____

5

some _____

6

a _____

(ii) Now make sentences about the pictures: Use:

| He's/She's/It's ____.
They're |
|---|

1 *She's tall.*   2 _____

3 _____   4 _____

5 _____   6 _____

Exercise 60B

How do they *look*? Use these words:

sad   poor   hot   happy   rich   cold

1 *She looks rich.*

2 _____

3 _____

4 _____

5 _____

6 _____

61 Word order with adverbs and adverbial phrases

> *I play basketball **in the Sports Centre on Tuesdays**.*
> *Frank **always** sings in the bath. He's **always** happy.*

Place and time

- Adverbs and adverbial phrases of **place** answer the question **where**? eg *here, in an office, to work*.

  Adverbs and adverbial phrases of **time** answer the question **when**? eg *now, at 7 o'clock, on Saturdays*.

- Note the usual word order:

	VERB	+	PLACE OR TIME
We	*live*		*here*.
Diana	*works*		*in an office*.
Tony	*is going*		*now*.
I	*get up*		*at 7 o'clock*.

	VERB	+	OBJECT	+	PLACE OR TIME
Kurt	*takes*		*the bus*		*to work*.
We	*play*		*tennis*		*in the park*.
Mike	*starts*		*school*		*at 9 o'clock*.
I	*clean*		*my flat*		*on Saturdays*.

- We normally put **time** after **place**:

	PLACE	+	TIME
Kurt takes the bus	*to work*		*in the mornings*.
We play tennis	*in the park*		*on Saturdays*.
They watch TV	*at home*		*in the evenings*.

- We do not normally put **place** or **time** between the verb and the object.

  *They watch TV **at home**.* (Not: *They watch at home TV*.)
  *We play tennis **on Saturdays**.* (Not: *We play on Saturdays tennis*.)

Frequency

- Adverbs of **frequency** answer the question **how often**? eg *always, usually, often, sometimes, rarely, never*.

- We normally put these adverbs:

  - before a full verb eg *drive, stay, feel*

	ADVERB	+	VERB	
Diana	*always*		*drives*	*to work*.
We	*sometimes*		*stay*	*up late*.
I	*never*		*feel*	*bored*.

  - after the verb *be* (eg *is, are, am*)

	be	+	ADVERB	
Diana	*is*		*always*	*at work at 8.30*.
We	*are*		*sometimes*	*tired in the mornings*.
I	*am*		*never*	*bored*.

- We normally put phrases of frequency such as *every day* or *once a week* at the end of a sentence.

Jack walks to work	*every day*.
We go swimming	*once a week*.
I listen to the radio	*every evening*.

Practice

Exercise 61A

Put the words in the correct order.

1 teaches | in Paris | Edith | French.
   Edith teaches French in Paris.

2 on Saturdays | in town | go | I | shopping.

_____

3 play | We | at weekends | volleyball | at the beach.

_____

_____

4 lunch | They | in the school canteen | have | at 1 o'clock.

_____

_____

5 in the evenings | watches | Mr Wilson | TV | in his room.

_____

_____

Exercise 61B

★ What kind of person are you? Make true sentences.
   Add *always, usually, often, sometimes, rarely, never.*

   1 I work hard.   3 I get angry.   5 I feel bored.
   2 I'm polite.   4 I'm nervous.   6 I'm happy.

Example:

1 I always work hard!

Exercise 61C

★ How often do you do these things?

		once		
	clean my bedroom	once	a	day.
	brush my teeth	twice		week.
I	eat in a restaurant	three		month.
	have a haircut	four	times a	year.
	go on holiday	five, etc		

Make true sentences from the table.

Example:

I clean my bedroom once a week.

Exercise 61D

Put the words in the correct order.

1 Do you | every day | English | usually | speak?
2 Are you | tired | sometimes | in the mornings?
3 Do you | usually | every evening | watch TV?
4 Are you | before 12.00 | in bed | always?
5 Do you | go | often | at weekends | to the cinema?

1 Do you usually speak English every day?

_____

_____

_____

_____

_____

62 Comparison of adjectives

> Today is **hotter** than yesterday.
> Which is the **hottest** country in the world?
> Greece isn't **as hot as** Saudi Arabia.

■ Compare these cars:

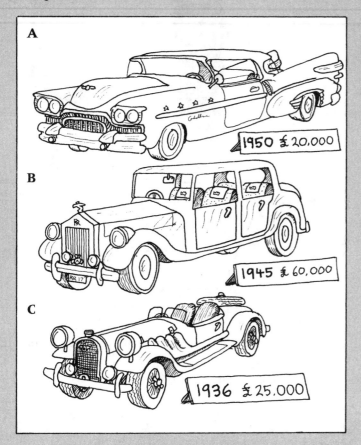

B is **older** than A. C is the **oldest** of the three cars. C is **more expensive** than A. B is the **most expensive** of the three.

■ Adjectives have comparative and superlative forms.

ADJECTIVE	COMPARATIVE	SUPERLATIVE
old	**older**	**oldest**
small	**smaller**	**smallest**
expensive	**more expensive**	**most expensive**
intelligent	**more intelligent**	**most intelligent**

■ We use the comparative when we compare two things or people.

> England is **smaller** than Spain.
> You're **more intelligent** than I am.

■ We use the superlative when we compare three or more things or people.

> Which is the **smallest** country in Europe?
> You're the **most intelligent** person I know.

■ We often use *than* after the comparative and *the* before the superlative.

> smaller **than**   **the** smallest

■ Form of comparative and superlative adjectives:

□ Short adjectives (adjectives of one syllable), add -er/-est.

	COMPARATIVE	SUPERLATIVE
old	older	oldest
small	smaller	smallest

□ Longer adjectives (adjectives of three or more syllables), take *more/most* . . . .

	COMPARATIVE	SUPERLATIVE
expensive (ex-pen-sive)	**more** *expensive*	**most** *expensive*
intelligent (in-tel-li-gent)	**more** *intelligent*	**most** *intelligent*

□ Adjectives of two syllables ending in a consonant + -*y* (eg -*py*), take away the -*y* and add -*ier/-iest*.

	COMPARATIVE	SUPERLATIVE
*hap**py*** (hap-py)	*hap**pier***	*hap**piest***

□ Most other adjectives of two syllables take *more/most*.

	COMPARATIVE	SUPERLATIVE
boring (bor-ing)	**more** *boring*	**most** *boring*
nervous (ner-vous)	**more** *nervous*	**most** *nervous*

□ Some words have irregular comparative and superlative forms. For example:

	COMPARATIVE	SUPERLATIVE
good	**better**	**best**
bad	**worse**	**worst**
far	**further/ farther**	**furthest/ farthest**

I'm as strong as you are.

■ We use *as . . . as* to say that two things or people are the same.

■ We use *not as . . . as* to say that two things or people are not the same.

   *England isn't **as big as** Spain.*
   *I'm **not as intelligent as** you are.*

■ After *than* and *as*, we often use an object pronoun.

   *My sister is taller than **me**.*
   *I'm not as slim as **her**.*

■ In a more formal style, we use a subject pronoun + a verb.

   *My sister is taller than **I am**.*
   *I'm not as slim as **she is**.*

Practice

Exercise 62A

Write the *-er* and *-est* forms of these words.

1

strong *stronger* – *strongest*

fast _____ – _____

small _____ – _____

loud _____ – _____

quick _____ – _____

cold _____ – _____

2

large *larger* – *largest*

nice _____ – _____

white _____ – _____

3

sad *sadder* – *saddest*

hot _____ – _____

slim _____ – _____

4

heavy *heavier* – *heaviest*

friendly _____ – _____

sunny _____ – _____

▷ What are the *-er/-est* spelling rules? See page **218**.

Exercise 62B

FRANK   GEORGE

★   Compare Frank and his brother George.

| Frank | is | ____-er | than | George. |
| George | looks | more ____ | | Frank. |

Use these words:

1 tall   2 friendly   3 old   4 slim
5 serious   6 fit   7 relaxed   8 good-looking

Examples:

> 1 George is taller than Frank.
> 2 Frank looks friendlier than George.

Exercise 62C

(i) Complete these questions about the students in a class. Use superlatives.

1 Who is *the youngest?*_____ (*young*)

2 Who is _____ (*old*)

3 Who is _____ (*tall*)

4 Who is _____ (*short*)

5 Who is _____ (*funny*)

6 Who is _____ (*serious*)

7 Who is _____ (*nice*)

8 Who is _____
    (*good-looking*)

9 Who is _____
    (*intelligent*)

★ (ii) Look at the questions in (i) again. Answer the same questions about the people in your family. Make true sentences.

Example:

> In my family....
> 1 my sister is the youngest.

Exercise 62D

★ Compare these animals. Use . . . *isn't as . . . as.*

Example:

> 1 A cheetah isn't as big as a lion.

1 a lion and a cheetah (*big/fast*)
2 an elephant and a giraffe (*tall/heavy*)
3 a swan and a duck (*strong/beautiful*)
4 a shark and a whale (*dangerous/big*)

63 Adjectives and adverbs

She's **nervous**.	She's waiting **nervously**.
I'm a **bad** dancer.	I dance **badly**.

■ Compare:

*He's a very **slow** driver.*
*He's driving very **slowly**.*

■ An adjective (eg *slow, clear, happy*) describes a person or thing.

*He's a very **slow** driver.*
*Your handwriting is very **clear**.*
*She was **happy**.*

We use adjectives with nouns (eg *driver, handwriting*) or pronouns (eg *she*).

■ An adverb of manner (eg *slowly, clearly, happily*) describes how something happens.

*He's driving very **slowly**.*
*You write very **clearly**.*
*She laughed **happily**.*

We use adverbs of manner with verbs (eg *drive, write, laugh*).

■ We form most adverbs of manner by adding -*ly* to the adjective.

ADJECTIVE	ADVERB
slow	*slow**ly***
clear	*clear**ly***

■ Words ending in a consonant + -*y* (eg -*py*), drop the -*y* and add -*ily*.

happy	*happ**ily***

■ Words ending in -*le*, change the -*le* to -*ly*.

terrible	*terrib**ly***

■ But note that the adverb of *good* is *well*.

*He's a **good** footballer.   He plays **well**.*

■ And we use some words as both adjectives and adverbs eg *fast* and *hard*.

*You're a **fast** walker.   You walk **fast**.*
*He's a **hard** worker.   He works **hard**.*

■ Note the usual word order:

VERB	+	ADVERB
They	*are talking*	**quietly**.
Julia	*can run*	**fast**.

VERB	+	OBJECT	+	ADVERB
I	*speak*	*German*		**badly**.
You	*passed*	*the exam*		**easily**.

Practice

Exercise 63A

What are these people doing? Use:

work	wave	run
laugh	walk	shout

happy	hard	slow
sad	fast	angry

1

He's walking slowly.

2

_____

3

_____

4

_____

5

_____

6

_____

Exercise 63B

Choose the correct answer.

1 Do you dance very ___*well*_____ ? (*good/well*)

2 Are you a _____ singer? (*good/well*)

3 How _____ do you ski? (*good/well*)

4 Do you walk very _____ ? (*quick/quickly*)

5 Are you a _____ swimmer? (*strong/strongly*)

6 Do you work _____ ? (*hard/hardly*)

7 How _____ can you type? (*fast/fastly*)

8 Do you drive _____ ? (*careful/carefully*)

Exercise 63C

Put the words in the usual order.

1 play | very well | the guitar | you |.
   You play the guitar very well.

2 speaks | my sister | fluently | Spanish |.

_____

3 very badly | chess | I | play |.

_____

4 his father's car | very carefully | drives | Mark |.

_____

_____

64 *Too* and *enough* with adjectives and adverbs

> *I can't go out tonight. I'm **too** tired.*
> *That bed isn't big **enough** for two people.*

The prince can't reach the princess.

- Compare:

  *The ladder is **too short**.*
  *The ladder is**n't long enough**.*

- *Too* goes before an adjective or adverb.

too + adjective or adverb

  *I can't play football. I'm **too old**.*
  *Ann is always tired. She works **too hard**.*

- *Enough* goes after an adjective or adverb.

adjective or adverb + *enough*

  *You can't drive a car. You aren't **old enough**.*
  *Mike is lazy. He doesn't work **hard enough**.*

- After *too* and *enough* we can use:

for + object

  *I don't like this weather. It's **too hot for me**.*
  *That suitcase isn't **big enough for all my things**.*

to + infinitive

  *That suitcase is **too small to carry** all my things.*
  *You aren't **old enough to drive** a car.*

- Compare *too* and *very*:

  Too means 'more than is good' or 'more than necessary'.

  *Sue is a good worker. She works **very hard**.*
  *Ann is always tired. She works **too hard**. (= harder than is good)*

The window is **very small**, but he can get through.

He can't get through. The window is **too small**. (= smaller than necessary)

Practice

Exercise 64A

Tessa stayed at a holiday camp last summer. She had a terrible time there.

(i) Why did Tessa have such a bad time at the camp? Complete the sentences. Use *too* and *enough* with these words:

sunny   dirty   bumpy   big   dangerous   windy

1 She couldn't lie on the beach.

   It **was too dirty**.

2 She couldn't windsurf.

   It **wasn't windy enough**.

3 She couldn't swim in the swimming pool.

   It _____

4 She couldn't sunbathe.

   It _____

5 She couldn't swim in the river.

   It _____

6 She couldn't play on the tennis courts.

   They _____

★ (ii) Make sentences about the things in (i). Use
. . . *too/enough . . . to . . . .*

Examples:

1 The beach was too dirty to lie on.
2 It wasn't windy enough to windsurf.

to sunbathe   to windsurf   to swim in to swim in   to play on   to lie on

65 Review of adjectives and adverbs

Exercise 65A (▷ Units 60–61, 63–64)

★ Put the words into the correct order.

Example:

> *1 New York is a very interesting city.*

1 New York is a city very interesting.
2 That's a film very good.
3 Julia is wearing a jacket green.
4 I meet every Saturday in town my friends.
5 We go once a week usually to the cinema.
6 Mr Bird arrives always at 8.30 at work.
7 Mr Bird never is late for work.
8 I like very much windsurfing.
9 You speak very well English.
10 Sue isn't enough old to get married.

Exercise 65B (▷ Unit 62)

★ Compare yourself and a friend. Use . . . -er than, more
. . . than, not as . . . as with some of these words:

> tall   serious   friendly   old   slim   quiet
> nervous   good-looking   intelligent

Examples:

> *I'm taller than my friend.*
> *She's more serious than I am.*
> *She isn't as friendly as I am.*

Exercise 65C (▷ Units 60, 62–63)

There are mistakes in some of these sentences. Find
the mistakes and correct them.

1 There are two youngs girls outside.
2 Your hair looks lovely today.
3 Which is the most large city in the world?
4 Mike is the younger student in his class.
5 Your English is very good.
6 Diana can sing very good.
7 I'm more old that Maria, but she's taller from me.
8 Boxing is much more dangerous as judo.
9 Loretta is a very hardly worker.
10 My father always drives very careful.

Exercise 65D (▷ Unit 64)

Complete the sentences with *too* or *enough* and the
words in brackets.

1 We couldn't move the piano because it was _____
_____ . *(heavy)*

2 We can't sail today. It isn't _____
_____ . *(windy)*

3 Mike is only 13. He isn't _____
to drive a car. *(old)*

4 We arrived at the station _____ , so
we missed our train. *(late)*

66 Place: *in, on, at*

> *The dictionary is **on** the desk **in** my room.*
> *Meet me **at** the airport.*

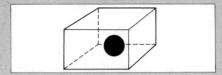

- ***in*** (a place with three dimensions)

  *There's a shower **in** the bathroom.*
  *My passport is **in** my suitcase.*
  *Annie is **in** the garden.*

- ***on*** (a surface)

  *The newspaper is **on** the table.*
  *Look, there's something **on** the floor.*

- ***on*** (a line)

  *Washington is **on** the Potomac River.*
  *Sydney is **on** the south-east coast of Australia.*

- ***at*** (a point)

  *There's a phone box **at** the end of West Street.*
  *Meet me **at** the airport.* (= a meeting point)

- We say *(be) at work* and *(be) at home.*

  *Nick isn't **at** work today. He's **at** home.*

- We often use *at* with places where people study.

  *Is Mike **at** school today?*
  *Tina is a student **at** university.*

- With buildings, we can often use *at* or *in.*

  *Diana sometimes stays **at** the Grand Hotel.*
  *or Diana sometimes stays **in** the Grand Hotel.*

- But we use *in* when we think of the building itself.

  *There are 200 rooms **in** the Grand Hotel.*

- When we say where we live, we use *in*, *at* and *on* in these ways:

  *I live **in** Brighton.* (in + city or town)
  *I live **in** Portland Street.* (in + street)
  *I live **at** 42 Portland Street.* (at + house number)
  *My flat is **on** the first floor.* (on + floor)

Practice

Exercise 66A

Add *in, on* or *at*.

on the car

_____ the car

_____ the park

_____ the bus stop

_____ work

_____ the cafe

_____ home

_____ the wall

_____ the river

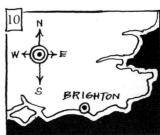

_____ the south coast

Exercise 66B

(i)

Gary Clench
2nd Floor Flat
33 Clifton Street
Brighton
BN1 3RS

Complete the sentences. Use *in, on* or *at*.

1 Gary Clench lives *in* _____ Brighton.

2 He lives _____ Clifton Street.

3 He lives _____ 33 Clifton Street.

4 His flat is _____ the second floor.

★ (ii) What about you? Where do you live? Make true sentences. Use *I live in/on/at* . . . .

195

67 Time: *in, on, at*

> **at** 8 o'clock   **on** Monday   **in** the morning   **at** night
> **at** the weekend   **in** October   **on** 5th October
> **in** 1954   **in** the winter

■ We use *at, on* and *in* in these ways:

☐ *at* + a time of the day
I usually get up **at 7 o'clock**.
We start work **at 9.30**.

☐ *on* + a day
You don't work **on Sundays**.
I play basketball **on Tuesdays**.

☐ *in* + a part of the day
The swimming pool is open **in the afternoon**.
We usually watch TV **in the evening**.

But we say *at night*:
I don't work **at night**.

☐ *on* + a day + a part of the day
I go shopping **on Saturday mornings**.

☐ *at* + weekends
We can meet **at the weekend**.
I usually play tennis **at weekends**.

☐ *at* + public holiday periods
I always visit my parents **at Christmas**.

But remember we say *on* + a day.
They always go to church **on Christmas Day**.

☐ *in* + a month — My birthday is **in June**.

☐ *on* + a date — My birthday is **on 10th June**.

☐ *in* + a year — I was born **in 1970**.

☐ *in* + the seasons — We often go swimming **in the summer**.

in the spring   *in the summer*

in the autumn   *in the winter*

■ We do not use *at, in* or *on* in time expressions with *this, next, last, every, tomorrow* or *yesterday*.

I'm busy **this weekend**.
Do you work **every Saturday?**
Meet me **tomorrow evening**.

Practice

Exercise 67A

Complete the questions. Add *in*, *on* or *at*.

1 Do you sometimes watch TV *in*____ the mornings?

2 Are you usually at home _____ 7 o'clock _____ the evenings?

3 Do you sometimes work _____ night?

4 What do you usually do _____ weekends?

5 Do you usually go shopping _____ Saturdays?

6 Do you go skiing _____ the winter?

7 Do you have a holiday _____ December?

8 Do you usually have a party _____ your birthday?

9 Is there a holiday in your country _____ 6th January?

Exercise 67B

Look at these time expressions.

*2 o'clock   Friday   the morning   last Friday   night
Tuesday   March   1st March   the afternoon
next Tuesday   1980   Monday morning   this morning
the summer   every summer   my birthday   the weekend
8.15   tomorrow evening   July   Friday night   1804
4th July   the spring   weekends   Christmas
New Year's Day   yesterday afternoon*

Do we use these time expressions with *in, on, at* or without a preposition? Make four lists:

in

in the morning
_____
_____
_____
_____
_____

on

on Friday
_____
_____
_____
_____
_____

at

at 2 o'clock
_____
_____
_____

without a preposition

last Friday
_____
_____
_____

68 Place and movement

> on in in front of behind near opposite
> next to between into out of onto off up
> down along across through over under
> past round from to

■ **on, in, in front of, behind, near**

on the wardrobe

in the wardrobe

behind the wardrobe

near the wardrobe

in front of the wardrobe

■ **opposite, next to, between**

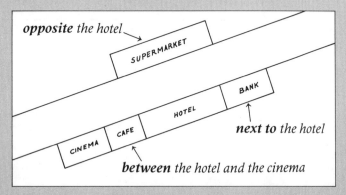

opposite the hotel

SUPERMARKET

BANK

HOTEL

CINEMA CAFE

next to the hotel

between the hotel and the cinema

■ **into, out of**

into the hairdresser's   **out of** the hairdresser's

■ **onto, off**

onto the roof   **off** the roof

■ **up, down**

up the mountain   **down** the mountain

■ **along, across, through**

along the road

across the road

through the pipe

■ **over, under**

over the fence

under the fence

■ **past, round**

past the bus stop

round the corner

■ **to, from**

to the beach

from the beach

Practice

Exercise 68A

Look at the picture. Complete the sentences. Use:

| across from on behind to round next to |
| opposite into off past under out of at |
| near along onto in front of |

There's a woman standing _under_ (1) a tree, _next to_ (2) the phone box. She's watching the house _____ (3) her. There's a man coming _____ (4) the house and another man going _____ (5) the house. A car is going _____ (6) the street, _____ (7) the house. There's a motorbike _____ (8) the car and a bicycle _____ (9) it. Can you see the man with the dog? He's waiting to go _____ (10) the street _____ (11) the post box _____ (12) the other side. A young couple are walking _____ (13) the bend away _____ (14) the post box. There's a bus waiting _____ (15) a bus stop _____ (16) the post box. There's a young man getting _____ (17) the bus and an old woman getting _____ (18) it.

(ii)

(iii)

Look at the picture. Complete the sentences. Use prepositions from this unit.

The woman is climbing ___*into*___ (1) the house _____ (2) a window now. There's a man outside the room. He's walking _____ (3) the stairs. What can you see _____ (4) the room? There's a briefcase _____ (5) the chair _____ (6) the desk. The desk drawer is open. Can you see a camera _____ (7) the drawer? There's a photograph _____ (8) the desk, _____ (9) a phone. _____ _____ (10) the phone, there's a key. A white cat is jumping _____ (11) the desk _____ (12) the floor. There's a large picture _____ (13) the wall _____ (14) two small pictures. _____ (15) the large picture there's a chair. _____ (16) the floor, _____ (17) the chair, there's a box.

★ Look at pictures (ii) and (iii). What is different in picture (iii)? Make sentences with prepositions from this unit.

Example:

In picture (iii) . . .

> *The woman is climbing out of the house.*

Exercise 68B

What are the opposites?

1 up _*down*_____

2 under _____

3 into _____

4 from _____

5 behind _____

6 onto _____

> *We arrived here* **three days ago***.*
> *We've been here* **for three days***.*
> *We've been here* **since Monday***.*

■ *Ago*

■ *Ago* means 'before now'.

It's 8.05 now. The Brighton train left five minutes **ago***.*
(= The Brighton train left at 8.00.)

■ We use *ago* with a past tense, not the present perfect.

I **visited** *Barcelona* **two years ago***.* (Not: ~~I've visited Barcelona two years ago~~.)

■ *Ago* comes after an expression of time eg *five minutes* **ago***, two years* **ago***, three days* **ago***.*

■ **For** *and* **since**

■ We can use *for* to talk about a length of time in the past, present or future.

We played tennis **for four hours** *yesterday.*
My grandfather usually sleeps **for an hour** *after lunch.*
Paul and Emma are going away **for a few days** *next week.*

■ We often use *for* and *since* with the present perfect to say how long something has continued. Compare:

PAST   PRESENT

I've been here **for an hour***.*

I've been here **since 1 o'clock**

■ We use:

for + a length of time		*since* + the starting point	
for	an hour two days three months ten years a long time	**since**	1 o'clock Saturday April 1982 I was a child

I've had my car **for two months***.*

I've had my car **since April***.*

Practice

Exercise 69A

(i) Make sentences with . . . *ago.*

1 It's Friday today. Diana went to Italy last Friday.
Diana went to Italy a week ago.

2 It's 2 o'clock now. The London train left at 1.50.

_____

3 It's 1st July now. Tim bought a new car on 1st May.

_____

★ (ii) Give true answers to the questions. Use . . . *ago.*

1 When did you start learning English?
2 When did you have your last holiday?
3 When did you first meet your best friend?

Example:

1 I started learning English two years ago.

Exercise 69B

(i) Add *since* or *for.*

1 *since* _____ Sunday   6 _____ four months
2 _____ five days   7 _____ last week
3 _____ two years   8 _____ six weeks
4 _____ 1990   9 _____ ten minutes
5 _____ March   10 _____ ten o'clock

★ (ii) Give true answers to the questions. Use the present perfect simple with *for* or *since.*

1 How long have you lived in your town or city?
2 Think of something you have (eg a car, a watch).
   How long have you had it?
3 Are you a student at a school? If you are, how long
   have you been at this school?
4 Think of someone you know. How long have you
   known him or her?

Example:

I've lived in Madrid for ten years.

Exercise 69C

What is Kate saying? Add *ago, for* or *since.*

I'm Australian. I was born in Canberra. I lived in
Canberra *for* ___ (1) sixteen years. Then my family
moved to Melbourne. I lived there _____ (2) two
years. Then I moved to Sydney. I've lived there
_____ (3) 1990. I work for a travel agency. I started
working there a year _____ (4). I'm married to Jack.
We got married three years _____ (5). We have a
house in Sydney. We've had the house _____ (6) last
year.

203

70 Review of prepositions

Exercise 70A (▷ Unit 66)

(i) *In* or *on*?

1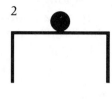

2

_____

_____

3

_____

(ii) Complete the sentences with *in*, *on* or *at*.

1 There are two bedrooms *in*____ the flat.

2 Santa Monica is _____ Southern California.

3 I've got a poster of Kevin Costner _____ my wall.

4 Heidelberg is _____ the River Neckar.

5 There's nobody waiting _____ the bus stop.

6 Meet me _____ the bus station.

7 I often have a coffee _____ the Calypso Cafe.

8 I'm a student _____ Brighton College.

9 My sister is _____ work at the moment.

10 Carlos lives _____ Barcelona.

11 I live _____ Main Street.

12 I live _____ 109 Main Street.

Exercise 70B (▷ Unit 67)

Do we use these time expressions with *in*, *on* or *at*?

ten o'clock, 2.15	(times of the day)
Monday, Tuesday	(days)
the morning, the afternoon,	(parts of the day –
the evening	except *night*)
night	(part of the day)
Monday morning,	(days + parts of the day)
Tuesday afternoon	
the weekend, weekends	(weekends)
Christmas, Easter	(public holidays)
January, February	(months)
1st May, 7th June	(dates)
1930, 1992, 2001	(years)
the summer, the winter	(the seasons)

Make three lists:

in

in the morning, in the afternoon, in the evening,
_____
_____
_____

on

_____
_____
_____

at

_____
_____
_____

Exercise 70C (▷ Unit 68)

Complete the crossword.

A = Across →   **D = Down ↓**

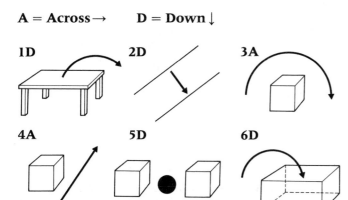

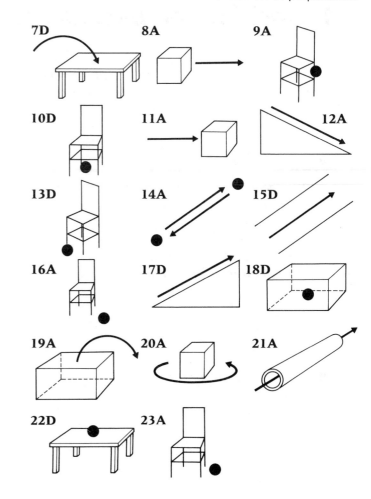

Exercise 70D (▷ Unit 69)

Choose the correct answer.

1 Peter changed his job *ago two years/two years ago*.
2 Julia *left/has left* home ten minutes ago.
3 I sold my car *for four weeks/four weeks ago*.
4 I've known Diana *since five years/for five years*.
5 We've been here *since two o'clock/for two o'clock*.

205

> I can surf **and** windsurf, **but** I can't water-ski.
> Do you prefer pop music **or** classical music?
> I can't buy a car **because** I haven't got enough money.
> I haven't got enough money, **so** I can't buy a car.

- ### And, but, or

We use *and*, *but* and *or* to join words or parts of a sentence:

- I like tea **and** coffee.
  I speak Spanish **and** Italian.
  I can sing **and** play the guitar.

- I like tea, **but** I don't like coffee.
  I speak Spanish, **but** I don't speak Italian.
  I can't sing, **but** I can play the guitar.

- Would you like tea **or** coffee?
  I don't speak Spanish **or** Italian.
  I can't sing **or** play the guitar.

Do you prefer pop music or classical music?

- ### Because, so

I can't play tennis because my racket is broken.

- ### *because* + the reason

I can't play tennis **because** my racket is broken.
We're going shopping **because** we haven't got any food.
Mark was late for school **because** he missed his bus.

- ### *so* + the result

My racket is broken, **so** I can't play tennis.
We haven't got any food, **so** we're going shopping.
Mark missed his bus, **so** he was late for school.

Practice

Exercise 71A

Join the sentences with *and, but* or *or*.

1 I can windsurf. I can't water-ski.
   I can windsurf, but I can't water-ski.

2 I play volleyball. I play basketball.
   I play volleyball and basketball.

3 I've got a cat. I haven't got a dog.
   _____

4 I go swimming. I do yoga.
   _____

5 Are you left-handed? Are you right-handed?
   _____

6 I can't speak Italian. I can speak Spanish.
   _____

7 I've got two brothers. I've got two sisters.
   _____

8 Are you married. Are you single?
   _____

9 I enjoy watching TV. I enjoy listening to music.
   _____

10 I like playing tennis. I don't enjoy watching it.
   _____
   _____

Exercise 71B

Complete the same sentence in different ways: *I was late for work* . . . . Use *because* or *so* and the words in the box.

1 my car broke down
2 I hurried
3 I took a taxi
4 my alarm clock didn't go off
5 I overslept
6 I didn't have time for breakfast
7 I apologised to my boss

1 I was late for work because my car broke down.

_____

_____

_____

_____

_____

_____

_____

72 When, if

I'll be at the station **when** your train arrives.
I'll take the driving test again **if** I fail it the first time.

■ Compare *when* and *if*:

I'll watch TV when I finish dinner.

I'll watch the news if I finish dinner before 9.00.

■ We use *when* for things we are sure will happen.
I'll watch TV **when** I finish dinner. (I'm sure I'll finish dinner.)

We use *if* for things we are not sure will happen.
I'll watch the news **if** I finish dinner before 9.00. (Perhaps I'll finish dinner before 9.00. I'm not sure.)

■ After *when* and *if*, we use the present simple to talk about the future.

I'll watch TV	**when**	I **finish** dinner.
Sue will lock the door	**when**	she **goes** to bed.
We'll take a taxi home	**if**	we **miss** the bus.
I'll stay at home	**if**	it **rains**.

We do not use *will* after *when* and *if*.

I'll post your letter **when** I **go** out. (Not: ... ~~when I will go out~~.)
We'll catch the bus **if** we **hurry**. (Not: ... ~~if we will hurry~~.)

■ We can begin a sentence with *when* or *if*.

| **When** | I go out, | I'll post your letter. |
| **If** | we hurry, | we'll catch the bus. |

We often use a comma when we begin with *when* or *if*.

▷ For *when* in sentences about the past, see Unit 34.

Practice

Exercise 72A

It is early in the morning and Tony is asleep. What will he do when he wakes up? Make sentences. Use *When he . . . he'll . . . .*

finish|the washing up	have|breakfast
be|dressed finish|breakfast	have|a shower
do|the washing up wake|up go|to work	

When he wakes up, he'll have a shower.

Exercise 72B

★ What will happen in the pictures? Make sentences.

sunbathe|for too long	get|wet
eat|all that ice cream	cut|herself
not|take|an umbrella	be|sick
touch|that broken glass	get|sunburnt

Example:

1 If she sunbathes for too long, she'll get sunburnt.

Exercise 72C

★ What will you do? Make true sentences.

1 When I finish this exercise, . . .
2 When I get up tomorrow, . . .
3 If I feel ill tomorrow, . . .
4 If it rains this weekend, . . .

Example:

1 When I finish this exercise, I'll go for a walk.

73 Review of linking words

Exercise 73A (▷ Unit 71)

Complete the sentences with *and*, *but* or *or*.

1 Mrs Williams is 55, _____ she looks younger.

2 Greg is 19 _____ comes from Sydney, Australia.

3 Would you like to stay at home _____ go out?

4 It's very sunny _____ the sky is blue.

5 I've got two brothers, _____ I haven't got any sisters.

Exercise 73B (▷ Unit 71)

Think of a way to complete each sentence.

1 I was late for work because _____

_____

2 I was late for work, so _____

_____

3 We can't play tennis because _____

_____

4 My watch is broken, so _____

_____

5 I stayed at home because _____

_____

6 It was a lovely day, so _____

_____

Exercise 73C (▷ Unit 72)

Complete the sentences with *if* or *when*.

1 I'll go shopping _when_ I finish lunch.

2 I won't go to the beach tomorrow _____ it rains.

3 I'll have a bath _____ I wake up tomorrow.

4 _____ you fail the exam, will you take it again?

5 _____ Mike is older, he wants to be a doctor.

Exercise 73D (▷ Unit 72)

Complete the sentences. Use *if* or *when* and the present simple or *will*.

1 I'm going out later. _When I go_ (*I go*) out, _I'll post_ (*I post*) your letter.

2 Perhaps I'll stay at home this evening. _____ _____ (*I stay*) at home, _____ (*I watch*) the film on TV.

3 Perhaps I'll sell my old car. _____ (*I sell*) it, _____ (*I buy*) a new one.

4 I'm going to finish this exercise soon. _____ _____ (*I finish*) it, _____ (*I go*) to bed.

5 Perhaps the weather will be fine tomorrow. _____ _____ (*it be*) fine, _____ (*I go*) swimming.

74 Days, months, numbers

> Monday, Tuesday . . .   January, February . . .
> one, two, three . . .   first, second, third . . .

Days

Monday
Tuesday
Wednesday
Thursday
Friday
Saturday
Sunday

- The first letter is always a capital eg *Monday* (not: ~~monday~~).

- Normally, we use *on*, without *the*, before a day.
  Meet me on Monday.

Months

January	July
February	August
March	September
April	October
May	November
June	December

- The first letter is always a capital eg *January* (not: ~~january~~).

- Normally, we use *in*, without *the*, before a month.
  My birthday is in March.

  But we use *on* before a date.
  My birthday is on 10th March.

Cardinal numbers

1	one	21	twenty-one
2	two	22	twenty-two
3	three	30	thirty
4	four	40	forty
5	five	50	fifty
6	six	60	sixty
7	seven	70	seventy
8	eight	80	eighty
9	nine	90	ninety
10	ten	100	a/one hundred
11	eleven	101	a/one hundred and one
12	twelve	102	a/one hundred and two
13	thirteen	150	a/one hundred and fifty
14	fourteen	200	two hundred
15	fifteen	320	three hundred and twenty
16	sixteen	1,000	a/one thousand
17	seventeen	5,010	five thousand and ten
18	eighteen	1,000,000	a/one million
19	nineteen	2,500,000	two million five hundred
20	twenty		thousand

- Notice the use of *and* before the units or tens:

  101 = *a/one hundred **and** one*
  312 = *three hundred **and** twelve*
  6,279 = *six thousand two hundred **and** seventy-nine*

■ After a number, *hundred* and *thousand* have no -s.

200 = **two hundred** (Not: ~~two hundreds~~)
5,000 = **five thousand** (Not: ~~five thousands~~)

■ Notice how we normally say years:

1740 = **seventeen forty**
1856 = **eighteen fifty-six**
1905 = **nineteen oh five** (*oh* = 0)

■ Notice how we say telephone numbers:

306291 = **three oh six two nine one**
584774 = **five eight four double seven four** (*double seven* = 77)

Ordinal numbers

1st	first	18th	eighteenth
2nd	second	19th	nineteenth
3rd	third	20th	twentieth
4th	fourth	21st	twenty-first
5th	fifth	22nd	twenty-second
6th	sixth	30th	thirtieth
7th	seventh	40th	fortieth
8th	eighth	50th	fiftieth
9th	ninth	60th	sixtieth
10th	tenth	70th	seventieth
11th	eleventh	80th	eightieth
12th	twelfth	90th	ninetieth
13th	thirteenth	100th	hundredth
14th	fourteenth	200th	two hundredth
15th	fifteenth	1,000th	thousandth
16th	sixteenth	1,000,000th	millionth
17th	seventeenth		

■ We often use *the* before ordinal numbers.
*Our flat is on **the first** floor.*

■ We can say the date in two ways:

26th January = **the twenty-sixth of** January
or January **the twenty-sixth**
3rd November = **the third of** November
or November **the third**

■ The most usual way of writing the date is:

26th January, 1993 or **26 January, 1993**

In British English, when we write the date in figures, we put the day before the month.

26.1.93 (= 26th January, 1993)
11.3.47 (= 3rd November, 1947)

■ We normally use *on* before dates.
*There's a holiday **on the twenty-sixth of January**.*

Practice

Exercise 74A

TUE   FRI   MON   SAT   WED   SUN   THU

★ Give the names of the days in the correct order.

Monday,

Exercise 74B

MAY   NOV   APR   JUL   JAN   SEPT
  MAR   DEC   OCT   JUNE   FEB   AUG

★ Give the names of the months in the correct order.

January,

Exercise 74C

How do we say these numbers?

1) 420 *four hundred and twenty*

2) 110 _____

3) 904 _____

4) 728 _____

5) 892 _____

6) 1,201 _____

7) 1,000,000 _____

Exercise 74D

How do we say these telephone numbers?

1) 269902 *two six double nine oh two*

2) 428095 _____

3) 737693 _____

4) 511481 _____

5) 006633 _____

Exercise 74E

★ Which is the first month? Which is the second, third, fourth? Make a list of all the months.

January is the first month.
February is the second month.

Exercise 74F

★ How do we say these dates?

Example:

1 the ninth of March nineteen eighty
or March the ninth nineteen eighty

1) 9/3/80   6) 21/9/92
2) 10/2/50   7) 3/6/11
3) 31/5/41   8) 2/11/25
4) 19/8/63   9) 13/1/30
5) 7/7/77   10) 30/10/08

75 The time

'What's the time?' 'It's **five o'clock**.'

Telling the time

- *o'clock*

We can only
use *o'clock*
on the hour.

two o'clock **ten o'clock**

- *half past*

half past two **half past ten**

- *(a) quarter to/past*

(a) quarter to two **(a) quarter past ten**

- *minutes to/past*

two minutes to seven **nine minutes past five**

- We normally say *five, ten, twenty, twenty-five* without *minutes*.

five to four **twenty past six**

- We can also tell the time by saying the hour + the minutes:

five fifteen **nine thirty-two** **six oh seven**

Asking the time

What's the time ?   It's twenty past three .

- When we want to know the time, we can ask *What's the time?* or *What time is it?*.

214

Practice

Exercise 75A

What is the time?

1

It's four o'clock.

2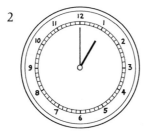

3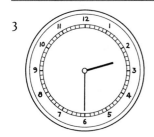

4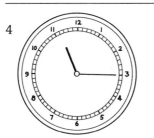

5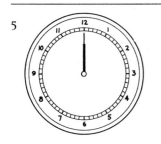

6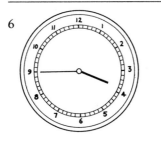

Exercise 75B

How do we say these times?

1)	6.05	half past six
2)	6.10	ten to seven
3)	6.15	ten past six
4)	6.20	a quarter to seven
5)	6.25	a quarter past six
6)	6.30	five past six
7)	6.35	five to seven
8)	6.40	twenty-five past six
9)	6.45	twenty-five to seven
10)	6.50	twenty past six
11)	6.55	twenty to seven

Exercise 75C

What is the time?

Example:

It's a quarter past three.
or *It's three fifteen.*

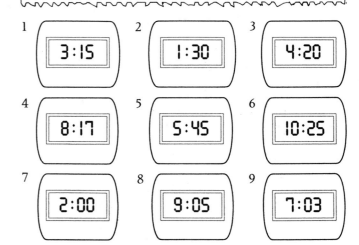

1 Short forms

FULL FORMS	SHORT FORMS	FULL FORMS	SHORT FORMS
I am	**I'm**	I will	**I'll**
you are	**you're**	you will	**you'll**
he is	**he's**	he will	**he'll**
she is	**she's**	she will	**she'll**
it is	**it's**	it will	**it'll**
we are	**we're**	we will	**we'll**
they are	**they're**	they will	**they'll**
are not	**aren't**	will not	**won't**
is not	**isn't**		
there is	**there's**	I would	**I'd**
that is	**that's**	you would	**you'd**
here is	**here's**	he would	**he'd**
		she would	**she'd**
I have	**I've**	it would	**it'd**
you have	**you've**	we would	**we'd**
he has	**he's**	they would	**they'd**
she has	**she's**	would not	**wouldn't**
it has	**it's**		
we have	**we've**	cannot	**can't**
they have	**they've**	could not	**couldn't**
have not	**haven't**	should not	**shouldn't**
has not	**hasn't**	must not	**mustn't**
do not	**don't**	let us	**let's**
does not	**doesn't**		
was not	**wasn't**		
were not	**weren't**		
did not	**didn't**		

■ We often use short forms when we speak or when we write to friends.

■ *'s = is* or *has*

He's Italian. (= He is Italian.)
He's got brown eyes. (= He has got brown eyes.)

■ Sometimes there are two negative short forms.

*He **isn't** French.* or *He's **not** French.* (= He is not French.)

■ We sometimes use a short form:

□ after a noun eg *Mario, brother*

***Mario's** Italian.* (= Mario is Italian.)
*My **brother's** got brown eyes.* (= My brother has got brown eyes.)

□ or after a question word eg *what, who*

***What's** your name?* (= What is your name?).
***Who's** got my newspaper?* (= Who has got my newspaper?)

■ We do not use an affirmative short form at the end of a sentence.

*I'm not Italian, but **Mario is**.* (Not: . . . *but Mario's*).
*'Has Jenny got a car?'   'Yes, **she has**.'* (Not: *Yes, she's*.)

But we can use a negative short form at the end of a sentence eg *Diana has got a car, but Sylvia **hasn't**.*

2 Pronunciation of endings: *-s/ -es, -ed*

■ The *-s/-es* ending has three pronunciations:

□ *-s/-es* is /ɪz/ after the sounds /tʃ/, /ʃ/, /s/, /z/, /dʒ/ and /ʒ/

watches	/tʃɪz/
finishes	/ʃɪz/
Alice's	/sɪz/
Liz's	/zɪz/
fridges	/dʒɪz/
garages	/ʒɪz/

□ *-s/-es* is /z/ after 'voiced' sounds (except /z/, /dʒ/, /ʒ/)

jobs	/bz/
opens	/nz/
Jim's	/mz/
shows	/əʊz/
lives	/vz/
stays	/eɪz/

With a voiced sound there is vibration.

□ *-s/-es* is /s/ after 'unvoiced' sounds (except /tʃ/, /ʃ/, /s/).

cups	/ps/
starts	/ts/
months	/əs/
Frank's	/ks/
laughs	/fs/

With an unvoiced sound there is *no* vibration.

■ The *-ed* ending has three pronunciations:

□ *-ed* is /ɪd/ after the sounds /t/ and /d/

started	/tɪd/
visited	/tɪd/
ended	/dɪd/
decided	/dɪd/

□ *-ed* is /d/ after voiced sounds (except /d/)

cleaned	/nd/
closed	/zd/
robbed	/bd/
showed	/əʊd/
lived	/vd/
enjoyed	/ɔɪd/

□ *-ed* is /t/ after unvoiced sounds (except /t/).

stopped	/pt/
finished	/ʃt/
watched	/tʃt/
worked	/kt/
danced	/st/
laughed	/ft/

3 Spelling of endings: *-s/-es, -ing, -ed, -er, -est, -ly*

■ Words ending in *-ch, -sh, -s, -x* or *-z*:

+ -es

teach	teach**es**	fox	fox**es**
brush	brush**es**	buzz	buzz**es**
bus	bus**es**		

The words *tomato, potato, do* and *go* also add *-es*.

tomato	tomato**es**	do	do**es**
potato	potato**es**	go	go**es**

■ Most nouns ending in *-f* or *-fe*:

~f/-fe + -ves

loaf	loa**ves**	wife	wi**ves**

■ Words ending in a consonant + *-y* (eg *-by, -ty, -ry*):

~y + -ies/-ied/-ier/-iest/-ily

baby	bab**ies**	happy	happ**ier**
city	cit**ies**	lovely	lovel**iest**
cry	cr**ied**	angry	angr**ily**

■ Words ending in one *-e*:

~e + -ing/-ed/-er/-est

write	writ**ing**	late	lat**est**
move	mov**ed**	nice	nic**est**

■ Words ending *-ie* and *-le*:

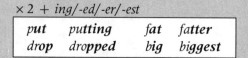

~ie + -ying   *~le + -ly*

die	d**ying**

simple	simp**ly**

■ Words of one syllable ending in one vowel + one consonant (eg *-ut, -op, -at, -ig*):

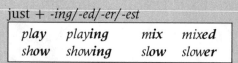

× 2 + ing/-ed/-er/-est

put	pu**tting**	fat	fa**tter**
drop	dro**pped**	big	bi**ggest**

But words ending in one vowel + *-y, -w* or *-x*:

just + -ing/-ed/-er/-est

play	play**ing**	mix	mix**ed**
show	show**ing**	slow	slow**er**

■ Words of two or more syllables ending in one vowel + one consonant:

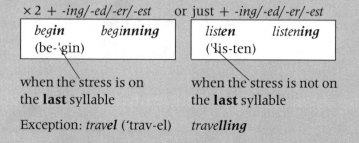

× 2 + -ing/-ed/-er/-est   or *just + -ing/-ed/-er/-est*

begin	begi**nning**
(be-'gin)	

listen	listen**ing**
('lis-ten)	

when the stress is on the **last** syllable

when the stress is not on the **last** syllable

Exception: *travel* ('trav-el)   *trave**lling***

218

4 Irregular verbs

■ Verbs can be 'regular' or 'irregular'.

■ Regular verbs add -ed in the past tense and the past participle.

INFINITIVE	PAST TENSE	PAST PARTICIPLE
watch	watched	watched
clean	cleaned	cleaned

■ Irregular verbs do not add -ed in the past tense or the past participle. Here are some of the most common irregular verbs:

INFINITIVE	PAST TENSE	PAST PARTICIPLE
be	was/were	been
beat	beaten	beaten
become	became	become
begin	began	begun
bite	bit	bitten
blow	blew	blown
break	broke	broken
bring	brought	brought
build	built	built
burn	burnt*	burnt*
buy	bought	bought
catch	caught	caught
choose	chose	chosen
come	came	come
cost	cost	cost
cut	cut	cut

INFINITIVE	PAST TENSE	PAST PARTICIPLE
do	did	done
draw	drew	drawn
dream	dreamt*	dreamt*
drink	drank	drunk
drive	drove	driven
eat	ate	eaten
fall	fell	fallen
feed	fed	fed
feel	felt	felt
fight	fought	fought
find	found	found
fly	flew	flown
forget	forgot	forgotten
freeze	froze	frozen
get	got	got
give	gave	given
go	went	gone
grow	grew	grown
have	had	had
hear	heard	heard
hide	hid	hidden
hit	hit	hit
hold	held	held
hurt	hurt	hurt
keep	kept	kept
know	knew	known

INFINITIVE	PAST TENSE	PAST PARTICIPLE
learn	learnt*	learnt*
leave	left	left
lend	lent	lent
light	lit	lit
lose	lost	lost
make	made	made
mean	meant	meant
meet	met	met
pay	paid	paid
put	put	put
read	read	read
/riːd/	/red/	/red/
ride	rode	ridden
ring	rang	rung
run	ran	run
say	said	said
see	saw	seen
sell	sold	sold
send	sent	sent
shine	shone	shone
shoot	shot	shot
show	showed	shown
shut	shut	shut
sing	sang	sung
sit	sat	sat
sleep	slept	slept
smell	smelt*	smelt*
speak	spoke	spoken
spell	spelt*	spelt*
spend	spent	spent

INFINITIVE	PAST TENSE	PAST PARTICIPLE
stand	stood	stood
steal	stole	stolen
swim	swam	swum
take	took	taken
teach	taught	taught
tear	tore	torn
tell	told	told
think	thought	thought
throw	threw	thrown
understand	understood	understood
wake	woke	woken
wear	wore	worn
win	won	won
write	wrote	written

*These can also be regular: *burned, dreamed, learned, smelled, spelled.*

5 American English

The differences between British and American English grammar are small. Here are the main differences:

- Americans often use the past simple where British people use the present perfect (especially with *just*, *already* and *yet*).

AMERICAN ENGLISH	BRITISH ENGLISH
Joe just **arrived**.	*Joe* **has** *just* **arrived**.
Did *you* **phone** *Carla yet?*	**Have** *you* **phoned** *Carla yet?*
I already **saw** *the film.*	*I've already* **seen** *the film.*

- Americans often use *have* (with *do* or *does* in negatives, questions and short answers) where British people use *have got*.

AMERICAN ENGLISH	BRITISH ENGLISH
I **have** *two brothers.*	*I've* **got** *two brothers.*
I **don't have** *a job.*	*I* **haven't got** *a job.*
'*Do you* **have** *any money?'*	'**Have** *you* **got** *any money?'*
'*Yes, I* **do**.'	'*Yes, I* **have**.'

- British people use *got* as the past participle of *get*. Americans often use *gotten*.

AMERICAN ENGLISH	BRITISH ENGLISH
I've **gotten** *fatter since I stopped smoking.*	*I've* **got** *fatter since I stopped smoking.*

- There are differences in the use of some prepositions. For example:

AMERICAN ENGLISH	BRITISH ENGLISH
on *the weekend*	**at** *the weekend*
Monday **through** *Friday*	*Monday* **to** *Friday*
stay home	*stay* **at** *home*
write someone	*write* **to** *someone*
a quarter **of** *four*	*a quarter* **to** *four*
a quarter **after** *four*	*a quarter* **past** *four*
I live **on** *Main Street*	*I live* **in** *Main Street.*

- There are some differences in spelling. For example:

AMERICAN ENGLISH	BRITISH ENGLISH
*trave**l**ed*	*trave**ll**ed*
color	*colour*
center	*cent**re***

- The past tense and past participle of the verbs *burn*, *dream*, *learn*, *smell* and *spell* normally ends in *-ed* in American English, but *-t* in British English.

AMERICAN ENGLISH	BRITISH ENGLISH
burned	*burnt*
dreamed	*dreamt*
learned	*learnt*
smelled	*smelt*
spelled	*spelt*

Progress tests

- These *Progress tests* will show how well you have learnt the main grammar points in the book.

- There are 62 tests. You can find a list of the tests in the *Progress tests contents* on pages 222–223.

- Each test covers the grammar in one or more of the units in the book.

  > **24** Present continuous (▷ Unit 28)

  In the title to each test there is a reference to the unit or units that teach the grammar in that test.

- Write your answers on a piece of paper.

- You can check your answers in the *Answers to the progress tests* on pages 255–256 of the *With answers* edition of the book.

- If any of your answers to the tests are wrong, look at the units again. Try to understand why your answers are wrong by studying the examples and explanations in the units again.

Progress tests contents

A Nouns and articles
1 Singular and plural nouns (▷ Unit 1)
2 *A, an* (▷ Unit 2)
3 Possessive *'s* (▷ Unit 3)
4 Countable and uncountable nouns (▷ Unit 4)
5 *A, an, the* (▷ Unit 5)
6 Talking in general (▷ Unit 6)
7 Proper nouns (▷ Unit 7)
8 Expressions with and without *the* (▷ Unit 8)

B Quantity
9 *Some, any, no* (▷ Unit 10)
10 *Much, many, a lot of, a little, a few, enough* (▷ Unit 11)

C Personal pronouns
11 Subject pronouns (▷ Unit 13)
12 Possessive adjectives (▷ Unit 14)
13 Subject and object pronouns (▷ Units 13, 15)
14 Possessive adjectives and pronouns (▷ Units 14, 16)

D Other pronouns
15 *This, that, these, those* (▷ Unit 18)
16 *One, ones* (▷ Unit 19)
17 *Something, anything, somebody, anybody,* etc (▷ Unit 20)
18 Reflexive pronouns (▷ Unit 21)

E Talking about the present
19 Present tense of the verb *be* (▷ Unit 23)
20 *There is, there are* (▷ Unit 24)
21 *Have got* (▷ Unit 25)

22 Imperative (▷ Unit 26)
23 Present simple (▷ Unit 27)
24 Present continuous (▷ Unit 28)
25 Present continuous and present simple
(▷ Unit 29)
26 Verbs not normally used in the continuous
(▷ Unit 30)

F Talking about the past
27 Past tense of the verb *be* (▷ Unit 32)
28 Past simple (▷ Unit 33)
29 Past continuous (▷ Unit 34)
30 Present perfect simple (▷ Unit 35)
31 Present perfect simple and past simple (▷ Unit 36)

G Talking about the future
32 Present continuous for the future (▷ Unit 38)
33 *Going to* (▷ Unit 39)
34 *Will* (▷ Unit 40)
35 *Will* and *going to* (▷ Unit 41)

H Modal verbs
36 *Can* (▷ Unit 43)
37 *Can, could* (▷ Units 43, 44)
38 *Must* (▷ Unit 45)
39 *Must, have to* (▷ Unit 46)
40 *May, might* (▷ Unit 47)
41 *Should* (▷ Unit 48)
42 Requests: *can, could, may* (▷ Unit 49)
43 Offers and invitations: *would like, will, shall*
(▷ Unit 50)
44 Suggestions: *shall, let's, why don't we, how about*
(▷ Unit 51)

I Questions
45 Question words (▷ Unit 53)
46 Subject and object questions (▷ Unit 54)
47 Question tags (▷ Unit 55)

J Infinitive and -*ing* form
48 Word + infinitive or -*ing* form (▷ Unit 57)
49 Purpose: *to . . .* and *for . . .* (▷ Unit 58)

K Adjectives and adverbs
50 Adjectives (▷ Unit 60)
51 Word order with adverbs and adverbial phrases
(▷ Unit 61)
52 Comparison of adjectives (▷ Unit 62)
53 Adjectives and adverbs (▷ Unit 63)
54 *Too* and *enough* with adjectives and adverbs
(▷ Unit 64)

L Prepositions
55 Place: *in, on, at* (▷ Unit 66)
56 Time: *in, on, at* (▷ Unit 67)
57 Place and movement (▷ Unit 68)
58 Time: *ago, for, since* (▷ Unit 69)

M Linking words
59 *And, but, or, because, so* (▷ Unit 71)
60 *When, if* (▷ Unit 72)

N Days, months, numbers, the time
61 Days, months, numbers (▷ Unit 74)
62 The time (▷ Unit 75)

Progress tests

1 Singular and plural nouns (▷ Unit 1)

★ Write the plurals.

Example: car
   cars

1 chair	4 student	7 life	10 house
2 pen	5 eye	8 child	11 fox
3 church	6 man	9 country	12 person

2 A, an (▷ Unit 2)

★ Put in *a, an* or *one* where necessary.

1 Suzanne is ___ teacher.
2 Jane is ___ actress.
3 Greg and Kylie are ___ students.
4 There is only ___ bathroom in the house.
5 Groningen is ___ city in Holland.
6 We've got two sons, but only ___ daughter.

3 Possessive 's (▷ Unit 3)

★ Join these nouns. Use *'s/s'* or *of . . . .*

Example: the husband | Anna
   Anna's husband

1 the office	Diana	4 the house	my parents
2 the wife	Bruce	5 the sister	Mike
3 the corner	the room	6 the end	Delaware Street

4 Countable and uncountable nouns (▷ Unit 4)

★ Complete the sentences with the correct words.

1 Anna has got lovely blonde ___ (*hair/hairs*).
2 You've got some new ___ (*furniture/furnitures*).
3 There ___ (*is/are*) some chairs in the kitchen.
4 There ___ (*is/are*) ___ (*a bread/bread*) on the table.
5 The ___ (*spaghetti/spaghettis*) ___ (*is/are*) cooked.
6 There ___ (*is/are*) ___ (*a/some*) bad ___ (*new/news*).

5 A, an, the (▷ Unit 5)

★ Correct the mistakes. Put in *a, an* or *the* where necessary.

1 My car has got radio.
2 Can you switch off radio, please?
3 There isn't telephone box near here.
4 Who is woman outside?
5 Astrid is secretary in office in Zurich.
6 My parents have got cat and dog. Cat's name is Ziggy and dog's name is Barry.

6 Talking in general (▷ Unit 6)

★ Put in *the* where necessary.

1 I never drink ___ coffee.
2 I like ___ clothes in that shop.
3 I don't like ___ pop music.
4 Look at ___ people in that car.
5 Do you think ___ money can buy ___ happiness?

7 Proper nouns (▷ Unit 7)

★ Correct the mistakes.

Example: The Chicago is in the United States.
   Chicago is in the United States.

1 Tahiti is in Pacific Ocean.
2 Rome is on River Tiber.
3 The Greece is in the Europe.
4 The British Museum is in the London.
5 Sicily is in Mediterranean.
6 The Peter's birthday is in the November.
7 The Sam is a student at the University of Bristol.
8 The Diana speaks the French and the German.
9 My sister is a student at the Oxford University.
10 Odeon Cinema is between Park Hotel and Playhouse Theatre in Shelley Street.

8 Expressions with and without *the* (▷ Unit 8)

★ Put in *the* where necessary.

1 Do you like listening to ___ radio?
2 Do you watch ___ TV every day?
3 What time do you usually have ___ lunch?
4 How often do you go to ___ cinema?
5 Do you go to ___ school on Saturdays?
6 I like swimming in ___ sea.
7 The children are in ___ bed asleep.
8 Can you play ___ guitar?
9 Peter isn't at ___ work. He's at ___ home.
10 Sylvia prefers ___ town to ___ country.

9 Some, any, no (▷ Unit 10)

★ Complete the conversation. Use *some, any* or *no*.

A: I'm making __ 1 __ coffee. Would you like __ 2 __?
B: No, thanks. I'm going shopping. What do we need?
A: Well. We haven't got __ 3 __ bread.
B: Have we got __ 4 __ cheese?
A: No, we haven't. And there aren't __ 5 __ eggs.
B: Is there __ 6 __ tea left?
A: No, there's __ 7 __ tea. And we haven't got __ 8 __ rice.
B: Right. Bread, cheese, eggs, tea and rice.
A: Have you got enough money?
B: I've got __ 9 __, but not much. Can you lend me __ 10 __?

10 Much, many, a lot of, a little, a few, enough (▷ Unit 11)

★ Choose the correct answer—A, B or C.

1 There are ___ books on the desk.
   A *much*   B *many*   C *a lot of*
2 There isn't ___ petrol in the car.
   A *much*   B *many*   C *a lot of*
3 How ___ cousins have you got?
   A *much*   B *many*   C *too many*
4 I can't go out. I've got ___ work to do.
   A *much*   B *many*   C *too much*
5 I've got ___ money, but not much.
   A *a lot of*   B *a little*   C *a few*
6 We can't all sit down. There aren't ___ chairs.
   A *too many*   B *too much*   C *enough*
7 I know ___ Americans, but not many.
   A *a lot of*   B *a little*   C *a few*

11 Subject pronouns (▷ Unit 13)

★ Complete the sentences with subject pronouns eg *I*, *you, he*.

1 Frank isn't English. ___'s American.
2 Diana isn't at home. ___'s at work.
3 My name is Mike. ___'m a student.
4 My friend and I are French. ___'re from Paris.
5 What's your name? Where are ___ from?
6 Sue and Bob are married. ___'ve got two children.
7 Where are my keys? – ___'re on the table.
8 Where is Saint Sofia? – ___'s in Istanbul.

12 Possessive adjectives (▷ Unit 14)

★ Complete the sentences with possessive adjectives eg *my, your, his*.

1 I've got two sisters. ___ names are Kate and Eva.
2 Tina and ___ brother are from Manchester.
3 Bruce and ___ wife have got two children.
4 I'm married. ___ husband's name is Walter.
5 The cat is washing ___ tail.
6 My friend and I are Spanish. ___ names are Pedro and Carmen. What about you? What's ___ name?

13 Subject and object pronouns (▷ Units 13, 15)

★ Choose the correct word.

1 Look! There is Diana. Can you see ___ (*she/her*)?
2 Tony isn't at home. ___ (*He/Him*) is at work.
3 Who is that man? Do you know ___ (*he/him*)?

4 Can you give ___ (*I/me*) your address?
5 Where are my keys? Have you got ___ (*they/them*)?
6 Our friends are late. ___ (*We/Us*) are waiting for ___ (*they/them*).

14 Possessive adjectives and pronouns (▷ Units 14, 16)

★ Choose the correct word.

1 This bag isn't ___ (*my/mine*).
2 Is Sue with ___ (*her/hers*) brother?
3 My name is Arthur. What's ___ (*your/yours*)?
4 That isn't ___ (*your/yours*) book.
5 Bob and Ann are having ___ (*their/theirs*) breakfast.
6 Your children are older than ___ (*our/ours*).

15 *This, that, these, those* (▷ Unit 18)

★ Complete the sentences with *this, that, these* or *those*.

1 Look at ___ picture here.
2 Look at ___ people over there.
3 Look at ___ shoes here.
4 Look at ___ man over there.

16 *One, ones* (▷ Unit 19)

★ Complete the sentences with *one* or *ones*. What does *one* or *ones* mean in each sentence?

1 I'm making a cup of coffee. Would you like ___?
2 I like the green trousers more than the blue ___.
3 I know that girl. – Which ___? – The ___ sitting next to Tony.

17 *Something, anything, somebody, anybody*, etc (▷ Unit 20)

★ Complete the sentences. Use *something, anything, nothing, everything, somebody/someone, anybody/anyone, nobody/no one, everyone, somewhere, anywhere, nowhere, everywhere*.

1 Would you like ____ to drink?
2 There isn't ____ good on at the cinema.
3 The factory is closed. ____ works there any more.
4 Can ____ help me carry these bags, please?
5 The office is empty now. ____ has gone home.
6 You look worried. Is ____ all right?
7 All my clothes are dirty. I've got ____ to wear.
8 There isn't ____ using the phone at the moment.
9 It's too late to go shopping now. ____ is closed.
10 I'm staying at home today. I'm not going ____.
11 We'd like to go away ____ for the weekend.
12 The waiting room is full. There's ____ to sit down.

18 Reflexive pronouns (▷ Unit 21)

★ Complete the sentences with reflexive pronouns eg *myself, yourself, himself*.

1 My grandfather often talks to ____.
2 Julia taught ____ to play the guitar.
3 Are you and your friend enjoying ____?
4 I'm making ____ a cheese sandwich.
5 Who painted your flat? – We painted it ____.
6 A lot of old people live by ____.

19 Present tense of the verb *be* (▷ Unit 23)

★ (i) Complete the sentences. Use *am, is* or *are*.

My name __1__ Mary Adams. I __2__ married. My husband's name __3__ Arthur. We __4__ from Bristol. That __5__ in the south-west of England. We've got one son and one daughter. Their names __6__ Nick and Emily. Nick __7__ 20. He __8__ a student. Emily __9__ 25. She __10__ a housewife.

(ii) Make the sentences negative.

1 I'm tired.   3 Mike is married.
2 You're late.   4 We're hungry.

(iii) Ask questions. Use *is* or *are*.

1 what your name?   3 your teacher English?
2 you a student?   4 what your parents' names?

20 *There is, there are* (▷ Unit 24)

★ Complete the conversation. Use *there is, there are, is there, are there, it is* and *they are*.

A: Where can you go in the Europa Holiday Camp?
B: __1__ a park and a zoo in the camp.
A: __2__ a swimming pool?
B: Yes, __3__, __4__ in the park.
A: __5__ any tennis courts?
B: Yes, __6__. __7__ in the park too.
A: How many restaurants __8__?
B: __9__ two. __10__ both near the swimming pool.

21   Have got (▷ **Unit 25**)

★   Complete the sentences. Use the correct form of *have got*.

1 I ___ a brother, but I ___ (*not*) any sisters.
2 My brother ___ (*not*) blue eyes. He ___ brown eyes.
3 ___ (*you*) a fax machine? – No, I ___ (*not*).
4 ___ (*your car*) a radio? – Yes, it ___.
5 ___ (*your parents*) a house or a flat? – They ___ a flat.

22   Imperative (▷ **Unit 26**)

★   Complete the sentences. Use these words:

close   not|forget   not|sit   switch   hurry

1 Are you cold? ___ the window.
2 ___ on that chair. It's broken.
3 ___ on the light, please. It's dark in here.
4 We're late. ___ up.
5 ___ your umbrella. It's raining outside.

23   Present simple (▷ **Unit 27**)

★   Complete the sentences. Use the present simple.

1 School ___ (*start*) at 9.00 and ___ (*finish*) at 4.00 every day.
2 Those people ___ (*not|come*) from England. They (*come*) from Scotland.
3 The post office ___ (*open*) at 9.00 every day. – What time ___ (*it|close*)?

4 Jill ___ (*get up*) early six days a week. She ___ (*not|get up*) early on Sundays.
5 I ___ (*speak*) French and Italian. I ___ (*not|speak*) Spanish. How many languages ___ (*you|speak*)?

24   Present continuous (▷ **Unit 28**)

★   Complete the sentences. Use these verbs in the present continuous:

wear   not|read   eat   play   talk   not|rain write   paint   shine

1 I ___ a letter to my sister at the moment.
2 Frank and Gina are at the beach. They ___ volleyball.
3 Look, George ___ a new Nike T-shirt.
4 Where's Julia? ___ she ___ on the phone?
5 We ___ our flat at the moment.
6 What ___ you ___? – A cheese sandwich.
7 You can look at my newspaper. I ___ it.
8 The weather is lovely now. It ___. The sun ___.

25   Present continuous and present simple (▷ **Unit 29**)

★   (i) Choose the correct answer—A, B or C.

1 Jenny ___ to Italy on holiday every summer.
   A *go*   B *goes*   C *is going*
2 Goodbye. ___ home now.
   A *I go*   B *I goes*   C *I'm going*
3 Charles ___ the bus to work in the mornings.
   A *usually take*   B *usually takes*   C *is usually taking*

4 Tony ___ at the moment. He's at the beach.
   A *don't work* B *doesn't work* C *isn't working*
5 Normally ___ to bed very late.
   A *I don't go* B *I doesn't go* C *I'm not going*

(ii) Complete the questions and the short answers. Use the present continuous or the present simple.

1 ___ (*you|work*) at the moment? – Yes, I ___.
2 ___ (*you|work*) every Saturday? – Yes, I ___.
3 ___ (*Pete|usually|walk*) to school? – No, he ___.

26 Verbs not normally used in the continuous (▷ Unit 30)

★ There are mistakes in some of these sentences. Find the mistakes and correct them.

1 Mmm! I'm liking this ice cream.
2 I'm not understanding this sentence.
3 Michael is having lunch at the moment.
4 Michael is having black hair and brown eyes.
5 You look sad. What are you thinking about?
6 Are you thinking Julia Roberts is a good actress?
7 Are you knowing those people?

27 Past tense of the verb *be* (▷ Unit 32)

★ Complete the sentences. Use *was* or *were*.

1 ___ Laurel and Hardy comedians? – Yes, they ___.
2 ___ Sylvia at work yesterday? – No, she ___n't.
3 ___ you ill last week? – Yes, I ___.
4 ___ your train late last night? – Yes, it ___.
5 ___ you and Sue here yesterday? – No, we ___n't.

28 Past simple (▷ Unit 33)

★ Complete the conversation. Use the past simple.

A: Where __ 1 __ you ___ (*go*) on holiday last summer?
B: I __ 2 __ (*go*) camping in the north of France.
A: __ 3 __ you ___ (*go*) on your own?
B: No, I __ 4 __. I __ 5 __ (*go*) with a friend. We __ 6 __ (*drive*) there in his car.
A: How long __ 7 __ you ___ (*stay*) there?
B: We __ 8 __ (*stay*) for two weeks.
A: What __ 9 __ (*be*) the weather like?
B: Well, we __ 10 __ (*not|have*) very good weather on the first day. It __ 11 __ (*rain*) all day. But it __ 12 __ (*be*) very hot and sunny after that.
A: __ 13 __ you ___ (*have*) a good time?
B: Yes, we __ 14 __. We really __ 15 __ (*enjoy*) ourselves!

29 Past continuous (▷ Unit 34)

★ You and a friend saw a bank robbery yesterday. What happened? Complete the sentences. Use the past simple or the past continuous.

It __ 1 __ (*be*) about 3 o'clock yesterday afternoon. We __ 2 __ (*sit*) in a cafe opposite the bank. A motorbike suddenly __ 3 __ (*stop*) outside the bank. There __ 4 __ (*be*) two men on the bike. One of the men __ 5 __ (*get*) off and __ 6 __ (*run*) into the bank. He __ 7 __ (*carry*) a gun. After a short time, he __ 8 __ (*come*) out of the bank. He __ 9 __ (*carry*) a large bag. He __ 10 __ (*get*) back on the bike. Then they __ 11 __ (*ride*) off down the street. A few minutes later the police __ 12 __ (*arrive*).

229

30 Present perfect simple (▷ Unit 35)

★ Complete the sentences. Use the present perfect simple.

1 Maria ___ (*live*) in Rome for two years.
2 I ___ (*visited*) New York three times.
3 How long ___ (*Diana | have*) her present job?
4 ___ (*you | ever | be*) camping?
5 Hurry up! The taxi ___ (*just | arrive*).
6 ___(*you | see*) Steven Spielberg's new film yet?

31 Present perfect simple and past simple (▷ Unit 36)

★ (i) Complete the sentences. Use the present perfect simple or the past simple.

My name is Ricky Dean. I live in London. I __ 1 __ (*live*) here for four years. I __ 2 __ (*be*) born in Liverpool. I __ 3 __ (*live*) there for eighteen years. I work for a travel company in London. I __ 4 __ (*work*) there since last summer. I __ 5 __ (*work*) for an export company before that. I __ 6 __ (*work*) there for three years.

(ii) Look at Ricky's answers. What are the questions? Use *How long have you . . . ?* or *How long did you . . . ?*

1 For four years.   3 Since last summer.
2 For eighteen years.   4 For three years.

(iii) Choose the correct form.

1 (*started* or *has started*?)
   a) It ___ snowing last night.
   b) Look! It ___ snowing!

2 (*Did you go* or *Have you been?*)
   a) ___ to work last Tuesday?
   b) ___ to many countries in your life?
3 (*did you have* or *have you had?*)
   a) How long ___ your present car?
   b) When ___ your first English lesson?

32 Present continuous for the future (▷ Unit 38)

★ (i) Ask Diana what she is doing this weekend. Complete the questions.

1 What ___ (*you | do*) on Friday evening?
2 ___ (*you | go*) out on Saturday evening?
3 ___ (*you | do*) anything on Sunday?

(ii) Now look at Diana's diary for this weekend. Give her answers to the questions in (i).

Example: 1 *I'm going to evening class.*

Friday	*Go to evening class*
Saturday	*Have dinner with Andrew*
Sunday	*Visit Jenny and Karen*

33 Going to (▷ Unit 39)

★ Complete the sentences. Use *going to* and these verbs:

be   live   do   buy   watch

1 I've decided to stay at home this evening. I ___ TV.
2 Why are you going out? – I ___ a newspaper.

3 There's a blue sky this morning. It ___ a fine day.
4 Sue is going to sell her flat. – Where ___ (*she*)?
5 I've missed the last bus home. – What ___ (*you*)?

34 *Will* (▷ Unit 40)

★ Complete the conversation. Use *will* or *won't* and suitable verbs.

A: I'm going out now, mum. See you later.
B: What time __ 1 __ (*you*) back home, Tina?
A: Well. I've got a lot to do, so I __ 2 __ (*not*) back before 7.00.
B: Have you cleaned your room yet?
A: Oh, no. I forgot. I __ 3 __ it when I get back.
B: And what about your homework? You haven't done that yet.
A: Oh, no. Well, I __ 4 __ it later. I promise.

35 *Will* and *going to* (▷ Unit 41)

★ Choose the correct form.

1 Hurry up! Look, the train ___ (*will leave/is going to leave*)!
2 Go and see the film. ___ (*You'll enjoy/You're going to enjoy*) it.
3 Peter has bought a bicycle because ___ (*he'll start/he's going to start*) cycling to work.
4 I've lost my pen. – Have you? ___ (*I'll lend/I'm going to lend*) you one.

36 *Can* (▷ Unit 43)

★ Choose the correct form.

1 You ___ (*can to/can*) buy stamps in a post office.
2 Caroline ___ (*can/cans*) speak Italian.
3 I ___ (*don't can/can't*) stand on my head.
4 ___ (*Do you can/Can you*) play the guitar?

37 *Can, could* (▷ Units 43, 44)

★ There are mistakes in some of these sentences. Find the mistakes and correct them.

1 I can play chess when I was eight.
2 Mike is a good runner. He could run very fast.
3 The room is very dark so I can't see very much.
4 When I was younger I can't swim.
5 Did you can ski when you were ten?

38 *Must* (▷ Unit 45)

★ Complete the sentences. Use *must* or *musn't* and these verbs:

tidy drive make forget

1 There's ice on the roads today. You ___ carefully.
2 The baby is asleep. We ___ a noise.
3 My room is in a mess. I ___ it.
4 It's Sue's birthday soon. We ___ to send her a card.

231

39 *Must, have to* (▷ Unit 46)

★ (i) Complete the sentences. Use *must, have to, has to* or *had to*. Sometimes two answers are possible.

1 You ___ be eighteen to vote in Britain.
2 Annie ___ get up early every day.
3 I ___ work late last night.
4 I ___ phone my friend tonight.
5 Does Tony ___ wear a uniform at his school?
6 Did you ___ get up early yesterday?

★ (ii) Complete the sentences with *mustn't* or *don't have to/doesn't have to*.

1 We aren't late. We ___ hurry.
2 You ___ swim here. It's dangerous.
3 Mike ___ wear a uniform at his school. He can wear what he likes.
4 You ___ smoke here. This is a no-smoking area.

40 *May, might* (▷ Unit 47)

★ Complete the conversations. Use *may* or *might* and these verbs:

play watch rain stay go

1 **A:** What are you doing this evening?
  B: I'm not sure. I ___ out or I ___ at home. There's a good film on TV. I think I ___ it.
2 **A:** What are you and Carla doing this afternoon?
  B: We don't know. We ___ tennis. But it depends on the weather. I think it ___ later on.

41 *Should* (▷ Unit 48)

★ Complete the sentences. Use *should* or *shouldn't* and these verbs:

help go wear do

1 I'm going out for a walk now. – You ___ a coat. It's cold outside.
2 I'm always tired. – You ___ to bed so late.
3 That girl looks lost. Do you think we ___ her?
4 I've just found somebody's driving licence in the street. What do you think I ___?

42 Requests: *can, could, may* (▷ Unit 49)

★ (i) Find the requests.

1 we|two coffees|, please|Could|have|?
2 a new cheque book|I|, please|have|May|?
3 I|try on|Can|these jeans|?
4 check|the oil|Could|, please|you|?

★ (ii) Which of the requests in (i) can you make in these places?

| a clothes shop |
| a bank |
| a petrol station |
| a cafe |

43 Offers and invitations: *would like, will, shall* (▷ Unit 50)

★ Find the offers and invitations.

1 Are you hungry? (*something to eat* | *you* | *like* | *Would* | ?)

2 I've got two tickets for the concert. (*you* | *to* | *go with me* | *Would* | *like* | ?)

3 Are you cold? (*I* | *the central heating* | *switch on* | *Shall* | ?)

4 Is your calculator broken? (*mine* | *you* | *lend* | *if you like* | *I'll*.)

5 Your shopping bags look heavy. (*to* | *like* | *you* | *Would* | *help you carry them* | *me* | ?)

44 Suggestions: *shall, let's, why don't we, how about* (▷ Unit 51)

★ Complete the conversation.

A: What sh__ 1 __ we d__ 2 __ this afternoon?

B: Sh__ 3 __ we s__ 4 __y at home?

A: I don't really want to stay at home.

B: All right. L__ 5 __ g__ 6 __ to the cinema, then.

A: There aren't any good films on at the moment.

B: Okay. H__ 7 __ ab__ 8 __ ha__ 9 __ a game of tennis?

A: It's too hot for tennis today.

B: Wh__ 10 __ __ 11 __n't we __ 12 __ swimming, then?

A: I don't want to go swimming today.

B: What *do* you want to do, then?

A: L__ 13 __ st__ 14 __ at home.

B: Stay at home! But you said . . .

45 Question words (▷ Unit 53)

★ Look at the answers. Ask questions with *What, Who, Which, Whose, Where, When, Why, How, How old* and *How often*.

Questions	Answers
1 ____ is that girl?	– She's Joe's sister.
2 ____ is the time?	– It's 2 o'clock.
3 ____ sport do you prefer— golf or tennis?	– Tennis.
4 ____ is your friend?	– She's 18.
5 ____ does your father work?	– In a bank.
6 ____ does that shop close?	– At 6 o'clock.
7 ____ do you go to work?	– By bus.
8 ____ is Sam going to bed now?	– Because he's tired.
9 ____ camera is this?	– It's my friend's.
10 ____ do you go jogging?	– About twice a week.

46 Subject and object questions (▷ Unit 54)

★ Ask questions with *who* or *what*.

Example: I'm writing to someone.
   Who are you writing to?

1 Someone is helping me.

2 I'm reading something.

3 Someone wants to see Jim.

4 Jim wants to say something.

5 Someone phoned me.

6 I phoned someone.

7 Diana gave me something.

47 Question tags (▷ Unit 55)

★ Add the correct question tag.

1 You've got a computer, ___
2 Gina is a student, ___
3 You aren't English, ___
4 You can type, ___
5 I'm coming with you, ___
6 Tony wasn't at home last night, ___
7 You live near here, ___
8 Julia doesn't speak French, ___
9 You posted that letter, ___

48 Word + infinitive or *-ing* form (▷ Unit 57)

★ Complete the sentences. Put the verbs into the correct form. (Sometimes two forms are possible.)

1 Can you ___ (*use*) a computer?
2 It's easy ___ (*ride*) a bicycle.
3 I'm thinking about ___ (*buy*) a new car.
4 Do you enjoy ___ (*go*) to the cinema?
5 It's a lovely day. Let's ___ (*go*) for a walk.
6 Mike hopes ___ (*pass*) all his exams this summer.
7 Annie locked all the doors before ___ (*go*) to bed.
8 It's late. We really must ___ (*go*) home now.
9 Do you want me ___ (*post*) that letter for you?
10 The old man often goes ___ (*sail*) in his boat.
11 Our friends invited us ___ (*have*) dinner with them.
12 Do you like ___ (*listen*) to the radio?
13 Would you like ___ (*listen*) to my new CD?
14 Can you help me ___ (*do*) the washing up?
15 I'm cold. Would you mind ___ (*close*) the window?

16 Is it expensive ___ (*play*) golf in Britain?
17 Have you finished ___ (*read*) that newspaper?
18 Emily started ___ (*learn*) French last year.

49 Purpose: *to* . . . and *for* . . . (▷ Unit 58)

★ Complete the sentences with *to* or *for*.

1 I went out ___ do some shopping on Saturday.
2 We must stop at a petrol station ___ some petrol.
3 A drill is a tool or a machine ___ making holes.
4 I'd like to go to the cinema ___ see Robert de Niro's new film.

50 Adjectives (▷ Unit 60)

★ There are mistakes in some of these sentences. Find the mistakes and correct them.

1 This room is very small.
2 I've got some pyjamas yellow.
3 Mrs Kent has got two youngs children.
4 Those people look angry.

51 Word order with adverbs and adverbial phrases (▷ Unit 61)

★ Put the words in the usual order.

1 We | in the garden | have | in the summer | breakfast.
2 once a week | I | to the disco | go | usually.
3 visits | Julia | often | at the weekends | her parents.
4 in the mornings | always | The roads | very busy | are.

52 Comparison of adjectives (▷ Unit 62)

★ Complete the sentences. Use the correct form of the adjectives. Add *than, the* or *as* where necessary.

1 (*tall*)
  a) How tall is ___ person in the world?
  b) You aren't as ___ me.
  c) A giraffe is ___ a horse.
2 (*good*)
  a) Mario's English isn't as ___ Carla's.
  b) I love my new flat. It's much ___ my old flat.
  c) Which is ___ hotel in Brighton?
3 (*interesting*)
  a) Which is ___ place you've ever visited?
  b) My old job wasn't as ___ my new job.
  c) I was surprised how good the film was. It was much ___ I expected.

53 Adjectives and adverbs (▷ Unit 63)

★ (i) Choose the correct word.

1 You're a ___ (*good/well*) swimmer.
2 You swim very ___ (*good/well*).
3 It's raining very ___ (*heavy/heavily*).
4 The rain is very ___ (*heavy/heavily*).
5 He's a ___ (*hard/hardly*) worker.
6 He works very ___ (*hard/hardly*).

★ (ii) Put the words in the usual order.

1 must read | You | carefully | the letter |.
2 I | very well | the guitar | don't play |.

54 *Too* and *enough* with adjectives and adverbs (▷ Unit 64)

★ Complete the sentences with the correct words.

1 Susie is only 14. She isn't ___ (*enough old/old enough*) to get married.
2 I don't want to go swimming. It's ___ (*too cold/cold enough*).
3 I love Tina's singing. Her voice is ___ (*too/very*) good.

55 Place: *in, on, at* (▷ Unit 66)

★ Complete the sentences with *in, on* or *at*.

1 Kevin is sleeping ___ the floor ___ the living room.
2 Alice isn't ___ school. She's ill ___ bed ___ home.
3 My father works ___ the post office ___ East Street.
4 Meet me ___ the bus stop ___ Brentwood Street.
5 We live ___ Acapulco, ___ the west coast of Mexico.
6 Charles lives ___ a flat ___ 109 Brentwood Street.

56 Time: *in, on, at* (▷ Unit 67)

★ Put in *in, on* or *at* where necessary.

1 School starts ___ 9 o'clock ___ the morning.
2 Can you meet me ___ 8.30 ___ tomorrow evening?
3 I often play tennis ___ the weekend ___ the summer.
4 I don't work ___ Saturday afternoons or ___ Sundays.
5 There's a meeting ___ 2 o'clock ___ next Tuesday.
6 We're on holiday ___ Easter and then again ___ July.
7 I was born ___ 2nd August ___ 1970.

235

57   Place and movement (▷ Unit 68)

★   (i) Complete the sentences. Put the words in the correct places.

1 I walked ____ the house, got ____ my car and drove away. (*into/out of*)
2 The dog was asleep ____ a tree when the cat jumped ____ the fence into the garden. (*over/under*)
3 The girl got ____ her motorbike and walked over to the post box. Then she got back ____ the bike and rode away. (*off/onto*)
4 We walked slowly ____ to the top of the hill. Then we ran all the way ____ to the bottom. (*up/down*)
5 I wrote a letter ____ the company last week and I had a reply ____ them today. (*from/to*)

★   (ii) Complete the sentences with the correct words.

1 Can you see someone hiding ____ (*in front of/behind*) that tree?
2 I can't see that woman's face because someone is standing ____ (*in front of/behind*) her.
3 There's a bank ____ (*between/opposite*) my flat. You can see it from my bedroom window.
4 Gatwick Airport is ____ (*between/opposite*) London and Brighton.
5 We drove ____ (*along/across*) the road for an hour.
6 The old man waited for a car to pass, then walked ____ (*along/across*) to the other side of the street.
7 The robbers climbed into the room ____ (*round/through*) a small window.
8 My flat is ____ (*round/through*) the next corner.
9 Who's that sitting ____ (*next to/past*) Peter?
10 We drove straight ____ (*next to/past*) the petrol station without stopping.

58   Time: *ago, for, since* (▷ Unit 69)

★   There are mistakes in some of these sentences. Find the mistakes and correct them.

1 We've been married since twenty years.
2 I've known Tony since 1990.
3 Diana bought her flat ago two years.
4 You've been at this school for five years.
5 I've started learning Italian five years ago.

59   *And, but, or, because, so* (▷ Unit 71)

★   Choose the correct word.

1 What would you like, tea ____ coffee? (*and/or*)
2 Jane has got one brother ____ one sister. (*and/but*)
3 Gina hasn't got a car ____ she's got a motorbike. (*and/but*)
4 I had a headache ____ I took an aspirin. (*because/so*)
5 I went to the shops ____ I wanted some bread. (*because/so*)

60   *When, if* (▷ Unit 72)

★   Complete the sentences with *when* or *if*.

1 I'll go to bed ____ this TV programme finishes.
2 ____ it doesn't rain this weekend, we'll go camping.
3 ____ I finish this cup of coffee, I'll start work.
4 John and Jane want to get married ____ they're 18.
5 ____ you lose your credit card, you should phone the credit card company immediately.

61   Days, months, numbers (▷ Unit 74)

★   (i) Complete the list of days.

> Monday
> ——————
> ——————
> ——————
> Friday
> ——————
> ——————

★   (ii) Find the correct number—A, B or C.

1 two hundred and twenty-two
A *220*   B *2222*   C *222*

2 eight hundred and thirteen
A *813*   B *830*   C *833*

3 one thousand two hundred and forty
A *1,214*   B *1,204*   C *1,240*

4 one million six hundred thousand
A *160,000*   B *1,600,000*   C *160,000,000*

★   (iii) How do we say these phone numbers?

Example: 581109
five eight double one oh nine

1) 631508
2) 417883
3) 220569
4) 103710
5) 001436
6) 774490

★   (iv) How do we say these dates?
Example: 10/6/90
the tenth of June nineteen ninety
or   **_June the tenth nineteen ninety_**

1) 8/2/91
2) 11/3/66
3) 4/10/59
4) 25/8/92
5) 16/5/78
6) 12/12/12

★   (v) Correct the mistakes.

1 Our holiday is on the april.
2 The next meeting is in monday.
3 Diana's birthday is on sixteen april.
4 I have ten thousands dollars.
5 You have hundred pounds.
6 There's a concert in first january.

62   The time (▷ Unit 75)

★   How do we say these times?
Example: 8.20
twenty past eight
or   **_eight twenty_**

1) 8.00   5) 7.55
2) 8.30   6) 8.25
3) 7.45   7) 8.03
4) 8.15   8) 7.40

Index

The reference numbers in this *Index* are **unit** numbers; not page numbers.

R = Review unit
Gen inf = General information
(pages **216–221**)

A

a, an 2, 4–5, 9R
a few 11, 12R
a little 11, 12R
a lot of 11, 12R
across 68, 70R
adjectives (position) 60, 65R
adjectives (comparison) 62, 65R
adjectives and adverbs (*bad, badly*, etc) 63, 65R
adjectives and adverbs (with *too* and *enough*) 64, 65R
adverbs (position) 61, 65R
ago 69, 70R
along 68, 70R
already 35
always 61, 65R
am 23, 31R
American English Gen inf 5
an, a 2, 4–5, 9R
and 71, 73R
any 10, 12R
anybody, anyone, anything, anywhere 20, 22R
are 23, 31R
articles 2, 4–8, 9R
as . . . as 62, 65R
at 66–67, 70R

B

be (*am, is, are*) 23, 31R

be (*was, were*) 32, 37R
because 71, 73R
been (and *gone*) 35
behind 68, 70R
between 68, 70R
but 71, 73R
by bus, by car, **etc** 8, 9R
by myself, by yourself, **etc** 21, 22R

C

can 43, 49, 52R
comparative adjectives 62, 65R
could 44, 49, 52R
countable and uncountable nouns 4, 9R

D

days 74
did 33
do, does 26–27
don't have to (and *mustn't*) 46, 52R
down 68, 70R

E

each other 21, 22R
enough 11, 12R, 64, 65R
ever 35
everybody, everyone, everything, everywhere 20, 22R

F

few (*a few*) 11, 12R
for (*went for a drink*, etc) 58, 59R
for (*too small for me*, etc) 64
for (and *since*) 69, 70R
from 68, 70R
front (*in front of*) 68, 70R
future (*going to*) 39, 41, 42R
future (present continuous) 38, 42R

future (*will*) 40–41, 42R
future (present simple) 72, 73R

G

go (+ *-ing* form) 57, 59R
going to (future) 39, 41, 42R
gone (and *been*) 35
got (*have got*) 25, 31R

H

had to 46, 52R
have got (and *have*) 25, 30, 31R
have to 46, 52R
he 13, 17R
her 14, 15, 17R
hers 16, 17R
herself 21, 22R
him 15, 17R
himself 21, 22R
his 14, 16, 17R
how 53, 56R
how about 51, 52R
how old, how much, how often, **etc** 53, 56R

I

I 13, 17R
if 72, 73R
imperative 26
in 66–67, 70R
in front of 68, 70R
infinitive 20, 57–58, 59R
infinitive of purpose 58, 59R
-ing **form** 57–58, 59R
into 68, 70R
irregular verbs Gen inf 4
is 23, 31R
it 13, 15, 17R
its 14, 17R
itself 21, 22R

J

just 35

L

let's 51, 52R
little (*a little*) 11, 12R
lot (*a lot of*) 11, 12R

M

many 11, 12R
may, might 47, 49, 52R
me 15, 17R
might, may 47, 49, 52R
mine 16, 17R
modal verbs 43–51, 52R
months 74
more, most 62, 65R
much 11, 12R
must 45, 52R
must (and *have to*) 46, 52R
mustn't (and *don't have to*) 46, 52R
my 14, 17R
myself 21, 22R

N

near 68, 70R
never 35, 61, 65R
next to 68, 70R
no (and *not any*) 10, 20, 12R
nobody, no one, nothing, nowhere 20, 22R
nouns 1–8, 9R
numbers 74

O

object pronouns 15, 17R
object questions (*who does Tina love?* etc) 54, 56R
of . . . (and possessive *'s*) 3, 9R

off 68, 70R
often 61, 65R
on 66–67, 70R
one (and *a, an*) 2
one, ones 19, 22R
onto 68, 70R
opposite 68, 70R
or 71, 73
our 14, 17R
ours 16, 17R
ourselves 21, 22R
out of 68, 70R
over 68, 70R

P

past 68, 70R
past continuous 34, 37R
past simple 33, 36, 37R
past tense of *be* 32, 37R
personal pronouns 13–16, 17R
plural and singular 7, 9R
possessive adjectives 14, 17R
possessive pronouns 16, 17R
possessive *'s* 3, 9R
prepositions 66–69, 70R
prepositions (+ *-ing* form) 57, 59R
present continuous 28–30, 31R
present continuous (future) 38, 42R
present perfect simple 35–36, 37R
present simple 27, 29–30, 31R
present simple (future) 72, 73R
present tense of *be* 23, 31R
pronunciation: *-s/-es, -ed* Gen inf 2

Q

questions 53–55, 56R
question words 53, 56R
question tags 55, 56R

R

rarely 61, 65R

reflexive pronouns 21, 22R
round 68, 70R

S

's/s' 3, 9R
shall 50, 51, 52R
she 13, 17R
short forms Gen inf 1
should 48, 52R
singular and plural 1, 9R
since (and *for*) 69, 70R
so 71, 73R
some 4, 9R, 10, 12R
somebody, someone, something, somewhere 20, 22R
sometimes 61, 65R
spelling: *-s/-es, -ing, -ed, -er,* etc Gen inf 3
subject pronouns 13, 17R
subject questions (*who loves Tina?* etc) 54, 56R
superlative adjectives 62, 65R

T

tags 55, 56R
that 18, 22R
than 62, 65R
the 5–8, 9R, 62
their 14, 17R
theirs 16, 17R
them 15, 17R
themselves 21, 22R
there is, there are 24, 31R
these 18, 22R
they 13, 17R
this 18, 22R
those 18, 22R
through 68, 70R
time (the time) 75

to (*something to drink*, etc) 20
to (*want to go*, etc) 57, 59R
to (*went out to see a friend*, etc) 58, 59R
to (*go to Africa*, etc) 68, 70R
too 64, 65R
too (and *very*) 64
too much, too many 11, 12R

U

uncountable and countable nouns 4, 9R
under 68, 70R
up 68, 70R
us 15, 17R
usually 61, 65R

V

verbs not used in the continuous 30, 31R
very (and *too*) 64

W

was, were 32, 37R
we 13, 17R
were, was 32, 37R
what 53, 56R
when 53, 56R
when (and *if*) 72, 73R
where 53, 56R
which 53, 56R

which one, which ones 19
who 53, 56R
whose 53, 56R
why 53, 56R
why don't we 51, 52R
will 40–41, 42R, 50, 52R
would like 50, 52R

Y

yet 35
you 13, 15, 17R
your 14, 17R
yours 16, 17R
yourself 21, 22R
yourselves 21, 22R

Answers to the exercises

Unit 1

Exercise 1A

(i)

1 chairs	7 pens	13 cities
2 cups	8 beds	14 offices
3 glasses	9 dogs	15 desks
4 books	10 rooms	16 boxes
5 watches	11 knives	
6 flats	12 dishes	

(ii)

Speaking practice

(iii)

/ɪz/	/z/	/s/
glasses	chairs	cups
watches	pens	books
dishes	beds	flats
offices	dogs	desks
boxes	rooms	
	knives	
	cities	

Exercise 1B

1 eyes 3 teeth 5 hands 7 feet
2 ears 4 arms 6 legs

Exercise 1C

(i)

1 zebras 3 tigers 5 mice
2 foxes 4 chickens 6 goldfish

(ii)

Some example answers:

in a zoo	on a farm	in a house
zebras	chickens	cats
elephants	cows	dogs
gorillas	sheep	goldfish
lions	lambs	parrots
penguins	pigs	canaries
giraffes	horses	mice
etc	*etc*	*etc*

Exercise 1D

1 trousers 3 pyjamas 5 jeans 7 scissors
2 shorts 4 tights 6 glasses

Unit 2

Exercise 2A

1 a burger   5 a milkshake
2 a sandwich   6 an apple
3 an ice cream   7 an egg
4 a bar of chocolate 8 a glass of water

Exercise 2B

(i)

1 a postman   4 an electrician
2 an actor   5 a taxi driver
3 a waiter   6 an optician

(ii)

a	an
a teacher	an architect
a mechanic	an artist
a nurse	an engineer
a housewife	
a singer	
a doctor	
a fireman	

Exercise 2C

1 a phone   4 robots
2 watches   5 a bicycle
3 an alarm clock 6 an umbrella

Exercise 2D

1 a car   4 a pen   7 one ticket
2 one sister   5 one bedroom
3 an architect 6 a key

Unit 3

Exercise 3A

(i)

1 my sister's car   6 Doris's TV
2 Nick's mother   7 Bruce's book
3 Liz's family   8 Tom's wife
4 Mike's school   9 the children's beds
5 Kurt's office   10 my parents' house

(ii)

/ɪz/	Liz's, Doris's, Bruce's
/z/	my sister's, Tom's, the children's
/s/	Nick's, Mike's, Kurt's, my parents'

Exercise 3B

1 Sherlock Holmes's pipe.
2 Charlie Chaplin's shoes.
3 Charlie Chaplin's cane.
4 Sherlock Holmes's hat.
5 Sherlock Holmes's violin.
6 Charlie Chaplin's trousers.

Exercise 3C

1 Gina's 3 Shizuo's 5 Rajah's
2 Frank's 4 Nicole's 6 Nancy's

Exercise 3D

1 What is your teacher's name?
2 What is the name of your school?
3 When is your teacher's birthday?
4 Who is your teacher's favourite actor?
5 When is the start of the next school
  holiday?
6 What is the name of your home town?
7 What is the number of your house?

Unit 4

Exercise 4A

COUNTABLE	UNCOUNTABLE
a shoe (2)	rain (1)
a glass (4)	sugar (3)
an engine (6)	oil (5)

Exercise 4B

1 is a 3 are 5 are 7 is
2 is 4 is an 6 is a 8 is an

Exercise 4C

Some tomatoes, some meat, a banana, some
spaghetti, an apple, a chicken, some
potatoes.

Exercise 4D

1 ✓
2 I've got some *information*.
3 We've got *some* bread. *or* We've got bread.
  or We've got *a loaf of* bread.
4 ✓
5 *Furniture is* expensive.
6 Your *hair is* lovely today.
7 ✓
8 *Is the spaghetti* cooked?

Exercise 4E

1 some coffee *or* a packet of coffee
2 some carrots
3 some apples
4 some (mineral) water *or* a bottle of
  (mineral) water
5 some lemonade *or* a can of lemonade
6 some soup *or* a tin of soup *or* a can of soup
7 some lemons
8 some milk *or* a carton of milk
9 some chocolates *or* a box of chocolates
10 some bread *or* a loaf of bread

Unit 5

Exercise 5A

1 a; the 6 a; the
2 the; a 7 the; the
3 a; the 8 an; the
4 the; a 9 the; the
5 the; a

Exercise 5B

1 a) The shower   3 a) the poster
  b) a shower   b) a poster
2 a) a garden   4 a) a woman
  b) the garden   b) the woman

Unit 6

Exercise 6A

(i)

1 She likes opera. She doesn't like pop
  music.
2 She likes golf. She doesn't like football.
3 She likes expensive restaurants. She
  doesn't like fast-food restaurants.

(ii)

1 I like opera. *or* I don't like opera.
  I like pop music. *or* I don't like pop music.
2 I like golf. *or* I don't like golf.
  I like football. *or* I don't like football.
3 I like expensive restaurants. *or* I don't like
  expensive restaurants.
  I like fast-food restaurants. *or* I don't like
  fast-food restaurants.

(iii)

1 Do you like computer games?
2 Do you like discos?
3 Do you like housework?
4 Do you like classical music?
5 Do you like basketball?
6 Do you like heavy metal music?

Exercise 6B

1 G 2 P 3 G 4 P 5 G 6 G 7 G 8 G

Exercise 6C

1 a) Sugar   3 a) bread
  b) The sugar   b) the bread
2 a) the elephants 4 a) the English people
  b) Elephants   b) English people

Unit 7

Exercise 7A

1 the	6 /	11 /	16 the
2 /	7 the	12 the	17 /
3 the	8 /	13 /	18 the
4 /	9 the	14 the	19 /
5 /	10 the	15 /	20 the

Exercise 7B

1 **Countries**
   Spain, Japan, the United States
2 **Continents**
   Asia, Europe, Africa
3 **Capital cities**
   Athens, Tokyo, Berne
4 **Oceans**
   the Pacific, the Atlantic, the Indian Ocean
5 **Seas**
   the Caribbean, the Aegean, the Mediterranean
6 **Rivers**
   the Rhine, the Danube, the Nile
7 **Museums**
   the Louvre, the Prado, the Uffizi
8 **Famous hotels**
   the Ritz, the Hilton, the Waldorf Astoria

Unit 8

Exercise 8A

1 TV	5 the cinema	9 church
2 the sea	6 the sun	10 university
3 breakfast	7 hospital	11 the piano
4 bed	8 the radio	12 foot

Exercise 8B

1 the	6 the; the	11 the; the
2 /	7 the	12 /
3 /;/	8 the	
4 /	9 /;/	
5 /	10 the	

Unit 9

Exercise 9A

(i)

SINGULAR	PLURAL	UNCOUNTABLE
car	tomatoes	bread
umbrella	houses	music
book	men	money

(ii)

1 a car	5 is
2 an umbrella	6 are
3 tomatoes *or* some tomatoes	7 is
4 bread *or* some bread	

Exercise 9B

1 a) a house	4 a) beds
b) The house	b) The bed
c) Houses	c) a bed
2 a) Money	5 a) Salt
b) the money	b) the salt
3 a) the teacher	6 a) a car
b) Teachers	b) The car
c) a teacher	c) cars

Exercise 9C

Example answers:

's	**of . . .**
Mike's camera	the name of my school
Diana's car	the end of the holiday
the cat's ears	the number of the house

We normally use *'s* for people and animals.
We normally use *of . . .* for things.

Exercise 9D

without *the*	*Example names:*
cities	– Tokyo, Dallas
countries	– Italy, China
days	– Monday, Tuesday
languages	– English, French
months	– January, February
people	– Diana, Tom
streets	– Madison Avenue
city + building	– London Airport

with *the*	*Example names:*
cinema	– the Odeon Cinema
hotels	– the Plaza, the Ritz
museums	– the Prado, the Louvre
oceans	– the Atlantic, the Pacific
rivers	– the Seine, the Danube
seas	– the Caribbean, the Black Sea
theatres	– the Shakespeare Theatre
of . . .	– the University of Rome

Exercise 9E

(i)

See Unit 8 for the two lists of expressions.

Unit 10

Exercise 10A

1 some	3 any; some	5 some	7 some; any
2 any	4 any	6 any

Exercise 10B

1 There's no hot water.
2 There's no soap.

3 There are no clean towels.
4 There's no toilet paper.
5 There are no hangers in the wardrobe.

Exercise 10C

1 There's no news.
2 We haven't got any pens.
3 He's got no time.
4 There aren't any chairs.
5 I haven't got any bread.

Exercise 10D

1 some 2 no 3 any 4 some 5 some 6 any

Unit 11

Exercise 11A

1 How many stamps do you want?
2 How many tickets do you want?
3 How many roses do you want?
4 How much money do you want?
5 How much petrol do you want?
6 How much bread do you want?

Exercise 11B

Example answers:
1 There is a little apple juice.
2 There isn't much coffee.
3 There is a lot of orange juice.
4 There isn't much spaghetti.
5 There is a little rice.
6 There aren't many bananas.
7 There are a few chicken sandwiches.
8 There are a lot of cheese sandwiches.

Exercise 11C

(i)

1 too much	3 enough; enough
2 too many; enough	4 too much; too many

(ii)

Example answers:
I don't take enough exercise. I have too many late nights. I eat too much junk food.

Unit 12

Exercise 12A

1 C or U	3 C or U	5 U	7 U	9 C or U
2 C or U	4 C	6 C or U	8 C	

Exercise 12B

1 /
2 Look! I've got *some* new shoes.
3 I can't make lunch. We haven't got *any* food.

4 I'm thirsty. Could I have *some* water, please?
5 /
6 We can't go to the concert. We've got *no* tickets. *or* We *haven't got* any tickets.
7 We can't sit down. There aren't *any* chairs. *or* There *are* no chairs.

Exercise 12C

3 ✓ 6 ✓
We normally say:
3 We've got *a lot of* food.
6 There are *a lot of* chairs in the room.

Exercise 12D

1 a little	3 a lot of	5 too much
2 a few	4 too many	6 enough

Unit 13

Exercise 13A

1 You	3 She	5 We	7 It
2 I	4 He	6 They	8 It

Exercise 13B

1 She 2 We 3 It 4 He 5 They 6 She

Unit 14

Exercise 14A

1 My	4 your	7 Our	10 Her
2 My	5 my	8 His	11 Her
3 your	6 His	9 Our	12 Their

Exercise 14B

1 Your	3 my	5 its	7 his; their
2 your	4 our	6 her	

Unit 15

Exercise 15A

1 them	3 him	5 me	7 them
2 her	4 it	6 you	8 us

Exercise 15B

1 I like it. *or* I don't like it.
2 I like her. *or* I don't like her.
3 I like them. *or* I don't like them.
4 I like it. *or* I don't like it.
5 I like him. *or* I don't like him.
6 I like them. *or* I don't like them.

Exercise 15C

1 me 3 him 5 it 7 you
2 her 4 us 6 them 8 me

Exercise 15D

1 He; her; she; him 3 We; them; they; us
2 I; you; you; me

Unit 16

Exercise 16A

1 mine 2 ours 3 his
4 theirs 5 hers 6 yours

Exercise 16B

1 your; yours 3 our; ours 5 my; mine
2 his; his 4 her; hers 6 their; theirs

Unit 17

Exercise 17A

(i)
Singular

I	me	my	mine
you	you	your	yours
he	him	his	his
she	her	her	hers
it	it	its	/

Plural

we	us	our	ours
you	you	your	yours
they	them	their	theirs

(ii)
You can use all these words:
1 my, your, his, her, its, our, your, their
2 mine, yours, his, hers, ours, yours, theirs
3 I, You, He, She, It, We, You, They
4 me, you, him, her, it, us, you, them

Exercise 17B

1 Her 4 his 7 He 10 its 13 ours
2 It 5 her 8 us 11 me 14 mine
3 him 6 Hers 9 yours 12 She 15 his

Unit 18

Exercise 18A

1 This 3 those 5 that 7 these
2 That 4 These 6 those 8 This

Unit 19

Exercise 19A

(i)
1 one; one; one; one 3 one; one; one
2 ones; ones; ones; ones 4 ones; ones; ones

(ii)
1 one = shirt 3 one = girl
2 ones = video tapes 4 ones = suitcases

Unit 20

Exercise 20A

(i)
1 somebody 3 Everybody 5 nobody
2 anybody 4 somebody 6 somebody

(ii)
1 something 3 nothing 5 Everything
2 anything 4 everything

(iii)
1 nowhere 3 everywhere
2 somewhere 4 anywhere

Exercise 20B

1 There's nothing in the fridge.
2 I haven't got anything to say.
3 There isn't anybody at home.
4 They've got nowhere to live.
5 There's no one outside.
6 We haven't got anywhere to sit down.
7 I've got nothing to do today.

Exercise 20C

1 anything to drink.
2 nothing to wear.
3 something to listen to.
4 anything to eat with.
5 anyone to play with.
6 nowhere to sleep.

Unit 21

Exercise 21A

1 yourself 5 myself
2 himself 6 yourselves
3 itself 7 themselves
4 herself 8 ourselves

Exercise 21B

1 seen each other. 3 know each other.
2 waving at each other. 4 talk to each other.

Exercise 21C

1 a) They're looking at themselves.
 b) They're looking at each other.
2 a) They're talking to each other.
 b) They're talking to themselves.

Unit 22

Exercise 22A

1 Look at these. 3 Who's that?
2 Look at this window. 4 Stop those men!

Exercise 22B

1 You've got a video, but I haven't got one.
2 Do you like the brown shoes or the black ones?
3 Who are those men—the ones in the car?
4 My house is the one next door.
5 We'd like to have a holiday in May and another one in September.
6 Our children are the ones near the tree.

Exercise 22C

(i)

	some	any
–thing	something	anything
–body	somebody	anybody
–one	someone	anyone
–where	somewhere	anywhere
	no	**every**
–thing	nothing	everything
–body	nobody	everybody
–one	no one	everyone
–where	nowhere	everywhere

(ii)
1 something 6 anybody *or* anyone
2 anything 7 nowhere
3 nothing 8 everything
4 Nobody *or* No one 9 anywhere; everywhere
5 somewhere

Exercise 22D

(i)
Singular

I	–	myself
you	–	yourself
he	–	himself
she	–	herself
it	–	itself

Plural

we	–	ourselves
you	–	yourselves
they	–	themselves

(ii)
1 My sister taught *herself* to swim.
2 ✓
3 ✓
4 I hurt *myself* when I fell down the stairs.
5 We're meeting *each other* at 8.00 this evening. (*or* We're meeting at 8.00 this evening.)
6 Do you live *by* yourself or with other people?
7 We're enjoying ourselves very much.
8 We're good friends. We like *each other* very much.

Unit 23

Exercise 23A

1 is 3 am 5 are 7 is 9 is
2 am 4 am 6 is 8 is

Exercise 23B

FULL FORMS	SHORT FORMS
I am	I'm
you are	you're
he is	he's
she is	she's
it is	it's
we are	we're
you are	you're
they are	they're

Exercise 23C

1 is *or* isn't 3 is *or* isn't 5 is *or* isn't
2 'm *or* 'm not 4 are *or* aren't

Exercise 23D

(i)
Reading about the people

(ii)
1 He isn't American. He's Australian.
2 He isn't an actor. He's a film maker.
3 She isn't Italian. She's Argentinian.
4 They aren't Australian. They're American.
5 He isn't Argentinian. He's Italian.
6 He isn't a singer. He's an actor.
7 They aren't actresses. They're tennis players.

Exercise 23E

1 Is the Sears Tower in New York? – No, it isn't. It's in Chicago.
2 Is the Parthenon in Rome? – No, it isn't. It's in Athens.
3 Is Brooklyn Bridge in Chicago? – No, it isn't. It's in New York.

4 Are the Spanish Steps in Athens? – No, they aren't. They're in Rome.
5 Is Saint Sofia in Istanbul? – Yes, it is.
6 Are the Pyramids in Egypt? – Yes, they are.

Exercise 23F

1 Are you a good singer? – Yes, I am. *or* No, I'm not.
2 Is your teacher married? – Yes, he/she is. *or* No, he/she isn't.
3 Is tennis your favourite sport? – Yes, it is. *or* No, it isn't.
4 Are your shoes new? – Yes, they are. *or* No, they aren't.
5 Is your best friend English? – Yes, he/she is. *or* No, he/she isn't.
6 Are you very intelligent? – Yes, I am. *or* No, I'm not.

Exercise 23G

Questions:
1 What is your name?
2 Where are you from?
3 How old are you?
4 When is your birthday?
5 What colour are your eyes?
6 Who is your best friend?

Example answers:
– Carlos Sanchez.
– Madrid.
– 25.
– 1st May.
– Brown.
– My sister.

Unit 24

Exercise 24A

(i)
West Street

(ii)
Middle Street
1 There is
2 There is
3 There isn't
4 There aren't
5 There are

East Street
1 There is
2 There is
3 There aren't
4 There are
5 There isn't

(iii)
Example answer:
There is a post office in the street. There are two restaurants. There isn't a hotel. There aren't any banks.

Exercise 24B

(i)
1 Is there; Yes, there is.
2 Is there; No, there isn't.
3 Are there; Yes, there are.
4 Is there; No, there isn't.
5 Are there; No, there aren't.
6 Are there; No, there aren't.
7 Is there; Yes, there is.

(ii)
1 Where's; It's
2 Where's; It's
3 Where are; They're
4 Where's; It's

(iii)
Example answer:
There's a TV in my room. There isn't a video. There are some posters on the wall. There's a bed and a desk. There are two chairs.

Unit 25

Exercise 25A

(i)
1 He's got a Walkman.
2 She's got a camera.
3 They've got a car.
4 They've got a bicycle.
5 She's got a computer.
6 He's got a dog.

(ii)
Example answers:
1 I've got a Walkman. *or* I haven't got a Walkman.
2 I've got a camera. *or* I haven't got a camera.
3 We've got a car. *or* We haven't got a car.
4 I've got a bicycle. *or* I haven't got a bicycle.
5 I've got a computer. *or* I haven't got a computer.
6 We've got a dog. *or* We haven't got a dog.

Exercise 25B

Full forms	Short forms
I have got	I've got
you have got	you've got
he has got	he's got
she has got	she's got
it has got	it's got
we have got	we've got
you have got	you've got
they have got	they've got

Exercise 25C

(i)
1 Have you got any brothers or sisters?
2 Have you got any children?
3 How many cousins have you got?
4 Have you got a cat or a dog?
5 Has your teacher got a car?
6 Has your house or flat got a garden?

(ii)
Example answers:
1 Yes, I have. I've got two sisters. *or* No, I haven't.
2 Yes, I have. I've got a son. *or* No, I haven't.
3 I've got four cousins.

4 Yes, I have. I've got a cat. *or* No, I haven't.
5 Yes, he/she has. *or* No, he/she hasn't.
6 Yes, it has. *or* No, it hasn't.

Unit 26

Exercise 26A

1 Put your hands up!
2 Close the door, please.
3 Sit down.
4 Open your mouth, please.
5 Don't touch that cake!
6 Don't forget your briefcase.
7 Be careful. Don't drop it.
8 Open your suitcase, please.

Unit 27

Exercise 27A

(i)

1	2	3
gets	teaches	carries
cooks	finishes	studies
leaves	kisses	flies
uses	goes	
sings		
stops		
tests		
reads		
starts		

(ii)
Speaking practice

(iii)

/ɪz/	/z/	/s/
uses	leaves	gets
teaches	sings	cooks
finishes	reads	stops
kisses	goes	tests
	carries	starts
	studies	
	flies	

Exercise 27B

(i)
get up; have; leave; start; finish; have; go

(ii)
1 Jill gets up at 5.00. I get up at . . . .
2 She has breakfast at 5.30. I have breakfast at . . . .
3 She leaves home at 6.00. I leave home at . . . .
4 She starts work at 6.30. I start work/school at . . . .

5 She finishes work at 2.00. I finish work/school at . . . .
6 She has dinner at 7.00. I have dinner at . . . .
7 She goes to bed at about 10.00. I go to bed at . . . .

(iii)
Example answer:
My father gets up at 6.30. He has breakfast at 7.00. He leaves home at 7.30. He starts work at 8.00. He finishes work at 6.00. He has dinner at 8.00. He goes to bed at about 11.30.

Exercise 27C

1 A fireman puts out
2 A porter carries
3 A chef cooks
4 A pilot flies
5 An optician tests
6 A swimming instructor teaches

Exercise 27D

Example answers:
I usually go shopping. I sometimes play tennis. My father often goes swimming. My friend and I sometimes go to the cinema. My friend often goes windsurfing. I never play football.

Exercise 27E

1 Do; live; do; live
2 do; live; live
3 do; live; live
4 Does; live; does
5 does; live; lives

Exercise 27F

(i)
1 Do you read a lot of books? – Yes, I do. *or* No, I don't.
2 Does your best friend drive a Ferrari? – Yes, he/she does. *or* No, he/she doesn't.
3 Does it rain a lot in your country? – Yes, it does. *or* No, it doesn't.
4 Do you do yoga? – Yes, I do. *or* No, I don't.
5 Does your teacher wear glasses? – Yes, he/she does. *or* No, he/she doesn't.

(iii)
1 read *or* don't read
2 drives *or* doesn't drive
3 rains *or* doesn't rain
4 do *or* don't do
5 wears *or* doesn't wear

Exercise 27G

(i)

Reading what Greg says

(ii)

1 do you come from?
2 do you get up?
3 do you go to college?
4 does college start?
5 does college finish?
6 do you usually have lunch?
7 do you go after college?
8 do you do there?

(iii)

1 f 2 h 3 a 4 e 5 b 6 g 7 d 8 c

Unit 28

Exercise 28A

1	2	3	4
raining	leaving	putting	dying
working	smoking	swimming	lying
eating	shining	sitting	
reading	writing	stopping	
cleaning	coming	running	
doing	dancing	jogging	
waiting	making		
looking			
walking			

Exercise 28B

(i)

Example answers:

A young man is waiting at a bus stop. He's reading a newspaper. An old woman is walking across the street. She's carrying a bag. Two old men are looking in a shop window. One of the men is smoking a pipe. Two young girls are sitting on a bench outside the park. They're eating sandwiches. A dog is running up some steps. A young woman is cleaning a car.

(ii)

Example answers:

1 The old woman isn't carrying a bag. She's carrying an umbrella.   2 The old man isn't smoking a pipe. He's smoking a cigarette.
3 The young girls aren't eating sandwiches. They're eating ice creams.   4 The dog isn't running up the steps. It's running down the steps. 5 The young woman isn't cleaning a car. She's cleaning a motorbike.

Exercise 28C

1 I'm writing a letter.
2 You're sitting in my seat.

3 I'm not feeling well.
4 You aren't listening to me.
5 We're going out.
6 We aren't watching the TV.

Exercise 28D

(i)

1 Ed	3 Bruce	5 Benny	7 Carla
2 Lillian	4 Loretta	6 Sam	

(ii)

1 Is Benny working on his computer? – No, he isn't. He's reading a report.
2 Are Bruce and Loretta talking on the phone? – No, they aren't. They're working on their computers.
3 Is Ed doing some photocopying? – Yes, he is.
4 Is Lillian reading a report? – No, she isn't. She's talking on the phone.
5 Are Sam and Carla looking at some posters? – Yes, they are.

(iii)

1 What are Bruce and Loretta doing? – They're working on their computers.
2 What are Sam and Carla looking at? – They're looking at some posters.
3 What is Ed doing? – He's doing some photocopying.
4 What is Lillian doing? – She's talking on the phone.
5 What is Benny reading? – He's reading a report.

Exercise 28E

(i)

1 Are you studying at home now? – Yes, I am. *or* No, I'm not.
2 Where are you sitting? – I'm sitting . . . .
3 What are you wearing? – I'm wearing . . . .
4 Is the sun shining? – Yes, it is. *or* No, it isn't.

(ii)

Example answers:

My brother and his wife are working now. My friend Astrid is playing tennis. My sister is studying. My friend Carlos is shopping.

Unit 29

Exercise 29A

1 's having	5 teaches	9 spends
2 has	6 's teaching	10 's teaching
3 leaves	7 come	
4 drives	8 don't speak	

Exercise 29B

Present continuous	Present simple
I am working	I work
you are working	you work
he is working	he works
she is working	she works
it is working	it works
we are working	we work
you are working	you work
they are working	they work

Exercise 29C

(i)

1 Do you often wear jeans? – Yes, I do. *or* No, I don't.
2 Are you wearing jeans now? – Yes, I am. *or* No, I'm not.
3 Is it raining now? – Yes, it is. *or* No, it isn't.
4 Does it often rain in your country? – Yes, it does. *or* No, it doesn't.
5 Do you study English every day? – Yes, I do. *or* No, I don't.
6 Are you studying English at the moment? – Yes, I am.

(ii)

1 I often wear jeans. *or* I don't often wear jeans.
2 I'm wearing jeans now. *or* I'm not wearing jeans now.
3 It's raining now. *or* It isn't raining now.
4 It often rains in my country. *or* It doesn't often rain in my country.
5 I study English every day. *or* I don't study English every day.
6 I'm studying English at the moment.

Unit 30

Exercise 30A

1 like
2 is watching
3 owns
4 love
5 Do you want
6 Are you going
7 Do you know
8 'm doing

Exercise 30B

1 *I hate* cold weather.
2 ✓
3 *Do you believe* me?
4 *This car doesn't belong* to me.
5 What *does* this word *mean*?
6 ✓
7 *I prefer* jazz to pop music.

8 ✓
9 *I can see* a dog in the garden.
10 *You seem* very happy.
11 ✓

Exercise 30C

(i)

1 NA	5 NA	9 NA
2 A	6 A	10 A
3 A	7 A	
4 NA	8 A	

(ii)

1 Tony has got a good job.
4 Tony has got a sister.
9 They have got a new car.

Unit 31

Exercise 31A

1 is	3 are	5 are	7 is	9 is	11 is
2 has	4 have	6 are	8 am	10 are	

Exercise 31B

1 I listen	5 She has
2 I'm listening	6 do you speak
3 She's having	7 Do you like
4 She often has	

Exercise 31C

1 It isn't cold. Is it cold?
2 I'm not late. Am I late?
3 You aren't working. Are you working?
4 She isn't leaving. Is she leaving?
5 There isn't a film on TV. Is there a film on TV?
6 He hasn't got a camera. Has he got a camera?
7 We haven't got time. Have we got time?
8 They don't live in Rome. Do they live in Rome?
9 She doesn't like tennis. Does she like tennis?

Unit 32

Exercise 32A

1 is	5 was	9 was	13 are	17 was
2 was	6 was	10 is	14 were	18 was
3 was	7 is	11 was	15 were	
4 is	8 was	12 was	16 is	

Exercise 32B

1 I was at home at 7 o'clock yesterday morning. *or* I wasn't at home at 7 o'clock yesterday morning.

245

2 I was at the cinema at 2 o'clock yesterday afternoon. *or* I wasn't at the cinema at 2 o'clock yesterday afternoon.

3 I was in bed at 6 o'clock yesterday evening. *or* I wasn't in bed at 6 o'clock yesterday evening.

4 I was at home at 9 o'clock last night. *or* I wasn't at home at 9 o'clock last night.

5 I was at a disco at midnight last night. *or* I wasn't at a disco at midnight last night.

Exercise 32C

(i)

1 Were   2 Was   3 Were   4 Were

(ii)

1 Yes, I was. *or* No, I wasn't.
2 Yes, it was. *or* No, it wasn't.
3 Yes, they were. *or* No, they weren't.
4 Yes, we were. *or* No, we weren't.

(iii)

1 was *or* wasn't   3 were *or* weren't
2 was *or* wasn't   4 were *or* weren't

Exercise 32D

1 was; was   4 were; were   7 were; were
2 was; was   5 was; was   8 was; was
3 was; was   6 was; was

Unit 33

Exercise 33A

(i)

1	2	3	4
started	used	stopped	hurried
played	lived	planned	carried
watched	danced	slipped	tidied
needed	liked		
finished	hated		
cooked			
sailed			

(ii)

Speaking practice

(iii)

/ɪd/	/d/	/t/
started	played	watched
needed	sailed	finished
hated	used	cooked
	lived	danced
	planned	liked
	hurried	stopped
	carried	slipped
	tidied	

Exercise 33B

(i)

Ticking the things that you usually do at weekends

(ii)

Saturday

1 tidied their flat.
2 played tennis.
3 visited some friends.

Sunday

1 worked in the garden.
2 cooked lunch.
3 stayed at home and watched TV.

(iii)

Example answers:
I cleaned my room. I visited a friend. My friend and I played tennis. I studied. I cooked a meal. I stayed at home and watched TV.

Exercise 33C

built	lost
bought	made
came	met
cut	read
did	ran
drank	saw
drove	sold
ate	sat
flew	spoke
got	spent
gave	swam
went	took
grew	taught
had	wore
knew	wrote
left	

Exercise 33D

(i)

Reading about Mr Bird

(ii)

He got up at 6.45 and had a shower. Then he had breakfast. He had tea and cornflakes for breakfast. He left home at 7.55 and went to work by bus. He took the 8.05 bus and got to work at 8.30. He had lunch from 1.00 till 2.00 and left work at 6.00 in the evening. When he got home, he read the newspaper. Then he had dinner. He had dinner at 7.15. After dinner he took his dog for a walk. He went to bed at 10.30 exactly!

Exercise 33E

1 had; did; have   4 had; did; have; had
2 Did; have; did   5 Did; have; did; had
3 did; have; had

Exercise 33F

(i)

1 Did you go out last night? – Yes, I did. *or* No, I didn't.
2 Did you play tennis yesterday? – Yes I did. *or* No, I didn't.
3 Did you study last weekend? – Yes, I did. *or* No, I didn't.
4 Did you have a haircut last week? – Yes, I did. *or* No, I didn't.
5 Did you have a birthday party last year? – Yes, I did. *or* No, I didn't.
6 Did you have a holiday last summer? – Yes, I did. *or* No, I didn't.

(ii)

1 I went out last night. *or* I didn't go out last night.
2 I played tennis yesterday. *or* I didn't play tennis yesterday.
3 I studied last weekend. *or* I didn't study last weekend.
4 I had a haircut last week. *or* I didn't have a haircut last week.
5 I had a birthday party last year. *or* I didn't have a birthday party last year.
6 I had a holiday last summer. *or* I didn't have a holiday last summer.

Exercise 33G

(i)

Reading about Henry Ford

(ii)

1 did; start   4 did; start
2 did; produce   5 did; do (*or* buy)
3 did; call   6 did; become

(iii)

American engineer Henry Ford started the Ford Motor Company in 1903. Ford produced the first cheap motor car. He called the car the Ford Model T. He started making the Model T in Detroit in 1908. Millions of people bought the car and Ford became a very rich man.

Exercise 33H

1 Did you go out last Saturday?
2 Did you go on your own?
3 Which film did you see?
4 Did you enjoy the film?
5 What time did the film start?
6 When did it finish?
7 Where did you go after the film?
8 What did you do after that?

Unit 34

Exercise 34A

(i)

1 was standing   6 singing
2 were having   7 was sitting
3 was wearing   8 was playing
4 was wearing   9 was barking
5 was listening   10 were watching

(ii)

Example answers:
I was having breakfast at 8.00 in the morning. I was working at 11.00 in the morning. I was playing basketball at 3.00 in the afternoon. I was watching TV at 10.00 last night.

Exercise 34B

1 What was he doing when it started to rain? – He was hanging out his washing.
What did he do when it started to rain? – He took the washing inside.
2 What was he doing when his car broke down? – He was driving into town.
What did he do when his car broke down? – He phoned a garage.
3 What was he doing when the dog ran in front of him? – He was cycling along the street.
What did he do when the dog ran in front of him? – He fell off his bicycle.
4 What was he doing when he saw the shark? – He was swimming in the sea.
What did he do when he saw the shark? – He got out of the water.

Unit 35

Exercise 35A

Exercise 35B

(i)
1 've lived; since
2 've worked; for
3 've been; since
4 's worked; for
5 've had; since

(ii)
Example answers:
1 How long have you worked for the sports magazine?
2 How long have you and Theo been married?
3 How long have you lived in London?
4 How long have you had your flat?
5 How long has Theo worked in the bank?

Exercise 35C

(i)
1 I've eaten Chinese food. *or* I haven't eaten Chinese food.
2 I've ridden a camel. *or* I haven't ridden a camel.
3 I've been sailing. *or* I haven't been sailing.
4 I've climbed a mountain. *or* I haven't climbed a mountain.
5 I've flown in a helicopter. *or* I haven't flown in a helicopter.
6 I've seen a UFO. *or* I haven't seen a UFO.

(ii)
1 Have you ever eaten Chinese food?
2 Have you ever ridden a camel?
3 Have you ever been sailing?
4 Have you ever climbed a mountain?
5 Have you ever flown in a helicopter?
6 Have you ever seen a UFO?

Exercise 35D

Jane has had a haircut.
Keith has grown a moustache.
Keith and Jane have had an argument.
Monica and David have got engaged.
David has shaved off his beard.
Jack has broken his arm.

Exercise 35E

Example answers:
1 He's just done the washing up.
2 They've just arrived.
3 She's just dropped some plates.
4 He's just woken up.
5 She's just received some good news.
6 They've just had breakfast.

Exercise 35F

(i)
Have they collected the plane tickets yet? – Yes, they have.
Have they packed the suitcases yet? – No, they haven't.
Have they bought a film for the camera yet? – Yes, they have.
Have they collected the traveller's cheques yet? – Yes, they have.
Have they ordered a taxi to the airport yet? – Yes, they have.
Have they found the passports yet? – No, they haven't.
Have they taken the cat to the cattery yet? – No, they haven't.

(ii)
They've already collected the plane tickets. They haven't packed the suitcases yet. They have already bought a film for the camera. They have already collected the traveller's cheques. They have already ordered a taxi to the airport. They haven't found the passports yet. They haven't taken the cat to the cattery yet.

Unit 36

Exercise 36A

(i)
1 has been
2 was
3 made
4 was
5 has made
6 has taken
7 has been
8 visited
9 have been
10 bought
11 have lived

(ii)
Example answers:
1 has David been
2 did he make
3 has he made
4 Has he been
5 did he go
6 did; get
7 have they lived

Exercise 36B

Example answers:
I've been to New York. I went there in 1990. I've been to Africa. I went there in 1987. I've been to Mexico. I went there in 1985. I've been to Amsterdam. I went there in 1984.

Unit 37

Exercise 37A

(i)
1 played
2 went
3 was
4 were
5 posted
6 watched

(ii)
1 She didn't play tennis last Saturday. Did she play tennis last Saturday?
2 He didn't go to the cinema last week. Did he go to the cinema last week?
3 The train wasn't late yesterday. Was the train late yesterday?
4 They weren't at home last night. Were they at home last night?
5 She didn't post the letter yesterday. Did she post the letter yesterday?
6 You didn't watch TV last night. Did you watch TV last night?

Exercise 37B

1 It was raining when I got up this morning.
2 When I got up, I had a shower.
3 We were going home when we saw the accident.
4 When we saw the accident, we phoned the police.
5 John was riding on his bike when he fell off.
6 He broke his leg when he fell off.
7 I was getting undressed when I heard a strange noise outside my bedroom window.
8 When I heard the noise, I went over to the window and looked outside.

Exercise 37C

1 She hasn't arrived. Has she arrived?
2 They haven't gone out. Have they gone out?
3 The train hasn't left. Has the train left?
4 We haven't finished. Have we finished?

Exercise 37D

(i)

Infinitive	Past tense	Past participle
be	was/were	been
break	broke	broken
do	did	done
eat	ate	eaten
go	went	gone
have	had	had
know	knew	known
live	lived	lived

(ii)
Example answers:
1 Did; go
2 Have; been
3 went
4 did; go
5 has gone
6 've had
7 had
8 Did; have
9 have; lived
10 did; live

Exercise 37E

1 I had
2 I've had
3 We were
4 left
5 did you get
6 I've been
7 for

Unit 38

Exercise 38A

(i)
1 Where is Diana going?
2 Where is she flying from?
3 When is she leaving?
4 How long is she staying in Milan?
5 Which hotel is she staying at?
6 When is she coming back to England?
7 What time is she arriving in London?

(ii)
1 She's going to Milan.
2 She's flying from Heathrow Airport.
3 She's leaving on Monday morning.
4 She's staying in Milan for three days.
5 She's staying at the Hotel Mediterraneo.

6 She's coming back to England on Wednesday.

7 She's arriving in London at 8 o'clock in the evening.

Exercise 38B

1 I'm going out this evening. *or* I'm not going out this evening.

2 I'm having an English lesson tomorrow. *or* I'm not having an English lesson tomorrow.

3 I'm meeting a friend tomorrow evening. *or* I'm not meeting a friend tomorrow evening.

4 I'm going to the doctor's this week. *or* I'm not going to the doctor's this week.

5 I'm playing tennis next weekend. *or* I'm not playing tennis next weekend.

6 I'm going away on holiday next month. *or* I'm not going away on holiday next month.

Exercise 38C

(i)

1 Are you going out on Friday evening?

2 What are you doing on Saturday afternoon?

3 Are you going out on Saturday evening?

4 Are you doing anything on Sunday morning?

5 Are you staying at home on Sunday evening?

(ii)

Example answers:

1 Yes, I am. I'm going to the cinema. *or* No, I'm not.

2 I'm meeting some friends.

3 Yes, I am. I'm going to a party. *or* No, I'm not. I'm staying at home.

4 Yes, I am. I'm going swimming. *or* No, I'm not.

5 Yes, I am. *or* No, I'm not. I'm going out.

Unit 39

Exercise 39A

(i)

1 ✓

2 The children aren't going to play golf. They're going to play tennis.

3 ✓

4 The motorcyclist isn't going to turn right. He's going to turn left.

5 ✓

6 The young couple aren't going to see a play. They're going to see a film.

(ii)

1 Is the motorcyclist going to turn right? – No, he isn't. He's going to turn left.

2 How many children are going to play tennis? – Three.

3 Are the young women going to cross the road? – Yes, they are.

4 Is the old man going to make a phone call? – Yes, he is.

5 Which film are the young couple going to see? – LA Story.

6 How many letters is the old woman going to post? – Three.

Exercise 39B

(i)

1 I'm going to watch TV. *or* I'm not going to watch TV.

2 I'm going to read a book. *or* I'm not going to read a book.

3 I'm going to cook dinner. *or* I'm not going to cook dinner.

4 I'm going to wash my hair. *or* I'm not going to wash my hair.

5 I'm going to go to bed early. *or* I'm not going to go to bed early.

(ii)

1 Are you going to watch TV this evening?

2 Are you going to read a book?

3 Are you going to cook dinner?

4 Are you going to wash your hair?

5 Are you going to go to bed early?

Unit 40

Exercise 40A

1 I think I'll open a window.

2 I think I'll get something to eat.

3 I think I'll tidy it.

4 I think I'll go to the post office.

5 I think I'll go to the optician's.

6 I think I'll turn on the heating.

7 I think I'll take a taxi home.

8 I think I'll watch it.

9 I think I'll buy a new one.

Exercise 40B

(i)

1 Will children go to school in 100 years?

2 Will people watch more TV than they do now?

3 Will people read fewer books?

4 Will people live longer?

5 Will everyone speak the same language?

6 Will the world's climate be different?

7 Will life be better?

(ii)

1 Children will go to school in 100 years. *or* Children won't go to school in 100 years.

2 People will watch more TV than they do now. *or* People won't watch more TV than they do now.

3 People will read fewer books. *or* People won't read fewer books.

4 People will live longer. *or* People won't live longer.

5 Everyone will speak the same language. *or* Everyone won't speak the same language.

6 The world's climate will be different. *or* The world's climate won't be different.

7 Life will be better. *or* Life won't be better.

Exercise 40C

Example answers:

1 I think I'll learn a new language. *or* Perhaps I'll learn a new language. *or* I don't think I'll learn a new language.

2 I think I'll travel a lot. *or* Perhaps I'll travel a lot. *or* I don't think I'll travel a lot.

3 I think I'll move to a different country. *or* Perhaps I'll move to a different country. *or* I don't think I'll move to a different country.

4 I think I'll learn a musical instrument. *or* Perhaps I'll learn a musical instrument. *or* I don't think I'll learn a musical instrument.

5 I think I'll be richer. *or* Perhaps I'll be richer. *or* I don't think I'll be richer.

Unit 41

Exercise 41A

(i)

Example answers:

1 I'll clean 2 I'll post 3 I'll make 4 I'll take

(ii)

Example answers:

1 I'm going to make some spaghetti.

2 I'm going to clean my room.

3 I'm going to take a taxi.

4 I'm going to post a letter.

Exercise 41B

1 'll or will   5 is going to

2 is going to   6 'll or will

3 're going to   7 'll or will

4 's going to   8 'm going to

Unit 42

Exercise 42A

Mistakes:

2, 4, 6, 7

Example corrections:

2 I think it *will snow* soon. *or* I think it *is going to snow* soon.

4 Perhaps *I'll visit* New York one day.

6 Who *will win* the next World Cup? *or* Who *is going to win* the next World Cup?

7 I'm sure you *won't fail* the exam next week. *or* I'm sure you *aren't going to* fail the exam next week.

Exercise 42B

1 It'll bite   3 You'll look

2 I'll go   4 I'm going to move

Exercise 42C

1 You won't be at home tonight. Will you be at home tonight?

2 I'm not going to see you tomorrow. Am I going to see you tomorrow?

3 He isn't working next Saturday. Is he working next Saturday?

4 It won't rain tomorrow. Will it rain tomorrow?

5 They aren't coming next week. Are they coming next week?

6 She isn't going to be late tonight. Is she going to be late tonight?

7 We won't be here tomorrow. Will we be here tomorrow?

Unit 43

Exercise 43A

(i)

1 He can swim. He can't windsurf.

2 He can play tennis. He can't play golf.

3 He can ski. He can't ice-skate.

(ii)

1 I can swim. *or* I can't swim. I can windsurf. *or* I can't windsurf.

2 I can play tennis. *or* I can't play tennis. I can play golf. *or* I can't play golf.

3 I can ski. *or* I can't ski. I can ice-skate. *or* I can't ice-skate.

Exercise 43B

(i)

1 Can you play the piano?

2 Can you dance the tango?

3 Can you type?

4 Can you touch your toes?

5 Can you whistle?

6 Can you stand on your head?

(ii)

1 Yes, I can. *or* No, I can't.
2 Yes, I can. *or* No, I can't.
3 Yes, I can. *or* No, I can't.
4 Yes, I can. *or* No, I can't.
5 Yes, I can. *or* No, I can't.
6 Yes, I can. *or* No, I can't.

Exercise 43C

You can buy flowers in a florist's. You can buy medicine in a chemist's. You can buy bread and cakes in a baker's. You can wash your clothes in a launderette. You can buy meat in a butcher's.

Exercise 43D

Example answers:
You can play tennis. You can go to the cinema. You can go to a disco. You can play golf. You can go to the beach. You can go swimming. You can go windsurfing.

Unit 44

Exercise 44A

(i)

Example answers:
1 He could swim when he was four.
2 He could ride a bicycle when he was six.
3 He could use a computer when he was seven.
4 He could play chess when he was eight.

(ii)

Example answers:
1 I could swim when I was four. *or* I couldn't swim when I was four.
2 I could ride a bicycle when I was six. *or* I couldn't ride a bicycle when I was six.
3 I could use a computer when I was seven. *or* I couldn't use a computer when I was seven.
4 I could play chess when I was eight. *or* I couldn't play chess when I was eight.

Exercise 44B

(i)

1 Could you read when you were six?
2 Could you write?
3 Could you cook?
4 Could you use a calculator?
5 Could you speak English?

(ii)

1 Yes, I could. *or* No, I couldn't.
2 Yes, I could. *or* No, I couldn't.
3 Yes, I could. *or* No, I couldn't.
4 Yes, I could. *or* No, I couldn't.
5 Yes, I could. *or* No, I couldn't.

Unit 45

Exercise 45A

1 You must do your homework.
2 You mustn't play with matches.
3 You must eat your vegetables.
4 You mustn't touch my camera.
5 You mustn't wake the baby.
6 You must go to sleep.

Exercise 45B

1 You must see the doctor.
2 I must have a drink.
3 You mustn't go near it.
4 I must go to the optician's.
5 We mustn't forget to send him a card.
6 I must tidy it.
7 I must hurry.
8 We mustn't make any noise.
9 I must go to bed.
10 You must come.

Exercise 45C

(i)

1 I must lose
2 I mustn't eat
3 I must buy
4 I must have

(ii)

Example answers:
I must stop smoking. I must study harder. I mustn't spend so much money on clothes. I must take more exercise. I mustn't watch so much TV. I must get more sleep. I must go to bed earlier.

Unit 46

Exercise 46A

(i)

1 She has to get up a 6.30.
2 She has to take the Underground to work.
3 She has to stand all day.
4 She has to be polite to all the customers.

(ii)

1 She doesn't have to get up at 6.30.
2 She doesn't have to take the Underground to work.
3 She doesn't have to stand all day.
4 She doesn't have to be polite to all the customers.

Exercise 46B

1 I have to get up early. *or* I usually have to get up early. *or* I don't have to get up early. *or* I don't usually have to get up early.
2 I have to start work before 9.00. *or* I usually

have to start work before 9.00. *or* I don't have to start work before 9.00. *or* I don't usually have to start work before 9.00.
3 I have to work hard. *or* I usually have to work hard. *or* I don't have to work hard. *or* I don't usually have to work hard.
4 I have to work in the evenings. *or* I usually have to work in the evenings. *or* I don't have to work in the evenings. *or* I don't usually have to work in the evenings.

Exercise 46C

(i)

1 have to	3 has to	5 have to	7 has to
2 has to	4 have to	6 have to	8 have to

(ii)

Example answers:
Children have to start school when they are six. Everyone has to stay at school until the age of sixteen. All men have to do military service. You have to be sixteen to get married. You don't have to have your parents' permission to get married before you are eighteen. You have to be eighteen to vote. Everyone with a job has to pay taxes. You have to have a licence for a TV.

Exercise 46D

(i)

1 do; have to	5 Do; have to
2 Do; have to	6 Do; have to
3 Does; have to	7 do; have to
4 do; have to	8 Does; have to

(ii)

Example answers:
1 You have to be eighteen.
2 Yes, you do.
3 Yes, everyone has to.
4 You have to be sixteen.
5 Yes, you do.
6 No, you don't.
7 You have to be fifteen.
8 Yes, everyone has to.

Exercise 46E

1 You mustn't smoke.
2 You don't have to pay to park.
3 You mustn't light fires.
4 You don't have to pay cash.
5 You mustn't turn right.
6 You mustn't drink the water.

Exercise 46F

(i)

1 Did you have to get up early yesterday?
2 Did you have to do a lot of housework last weekend?

3 Did you have to take an exam last week?
4 Did you have to go to the dentist's last month?
5 Did you have to go into hospital last year?

(ii)

1 I had to get up early yesterday. *or* I didn't have to get up early yesterday.
2 I had to do a lot of housework last weekend. *or* I didn't have to do a lot of housework last weekend.
3 I had to take an exam last week. *or* I didn't have to take an exam last week.
4 I had to go to the dentist's last month. *or* I didn't have to go to the dentist's last month.
5 I had to go into hospital last year. *or* I didn't have to go into hospital last year.

Unit 47

Exercise 47A

Example answers:
1 The girl may cut herself. *or* The girl might cut herself.
2 The boys may fall into the river. *or* The boys might fall into the river.
3 The dog may bite the girl. *or* The dog might bite the girl.
4 The man may shoot himself. *or* The man might shoot himself.
5 The old man may drop the boxes. *or* The old man might drop the boxes.
6 The boy and girl may wake up the baby. *or* The boy and girl might wake up the baby.
7 The woman may miss the bus. *or* The woman might miss the bus.
8 The boy and girl may start a fire. *or* The girl and boy may start a fire.

Exercise 47B

(i)

1 It might rain tomorrow.
2 A friend may visit me next weekend.
3 I may buy a new computer next month.
4 I might change my job next year.
5 I might not go to work tomorrow.
6 We may not have a holiday next summer.

(ii)

Example answers:
It might be sunny tomorrow. My brother and I may play golf next weekend. I may go swimming next week. I might buy some new clothes next month. I may visit the United States next summer. I might buy a new car next year.

Unit 48

Exercise 48A

1 You should try it on first.
2 You shouldn't swim straight after a meal.
3 You should go out more.
4 You shouldn't get up today.
5 You should wear walking boots.

Exercise 48B

1 I think people should watch less TV. *or* I don't think people should watch less TV.
2 I think boys and girls should go to the same schools. *or* I don't think boys and girls should go to the same schools.
3 I think men and women should get the same pay for the same job. *or* I don't think men and women should get the same pay for the same job.
4 I think people should be free to smoke in public places. *or* I don't think people should be free to smoke in public places.
5 I think we should stop testing medicine on animals. *or* I don't think we should stop testing medicine on animals.
6 I think we should destroy nuclear weapons. *or* I don't think we should destroy nuclear weapons.

Exercise 48C

1 When do you think I should visit your country?
2 Do you think I should go in the summer?
3 How do you think I should travel when I'm there?
4 Do you think I should hire a car?
5 Which places do you think I should visit?
6 Do you think I should stay in hotels?
7 Do you think I should take traveller's cheques?

Unit 49

Exercise 49A

1 Can I have a menu, please? *or* Could I have a menu, please? *or* May I have a menu, please?
2 Can I have a glass of water, please? *or* Could I have a glass of water, please? *or* May I have a glass of water, please?
3 Can I have a burger with French fries, please? *or* Could I have a burger with French fries, please? *or* May I have a burger with French fries, please?
4 Can I have some coffee, please? *or* Could I have some coffee, please? *or* May I have some coffee, please?

5 Can I have the bill, please? *or* Could I have the bill, please? *or* May I have the bill, please?

Exercise 49B

1 Can I put my bag there?
2 May I borrow £10?
3 Can I try on these trousers?
4 Could I see your driving licence, sir?

Exercise 49C

1 Can you help me move this table?
2 Could you fill in this form, please?
3 Could you open your suitcase, please?
4 Can you answer the phone?

Exercise 49D

(i)

1 Can you change some money for me? *or* Could you change some money for me?
2 Can you repair my car today? *or* Could you repair my car today?
3 Can I have a stamp, please? *or* Could I have a stamp, please? *or* May I have a stamp, please?
4 Can you cut my hair very short? *or* Could you cut my hair very short?
5 Can I have ten roses, please? *or* Could I have ten roses, please? *or* May I have ten roses, please?
6 Can I have a room with a shower? *or* Could I have a room with a shower? *or* May I have a room with a shower?

(ii)

Example answers:
May I ask a question, please? Could you spell that word, please? Could you write that on the board, please? May I have a book, please? Can you repeat that, please? Could you explain that again? Could you pronounce this word? May I leave the room? Could I open the window? Could you help me with this, please?

Unit 50

Exercise 50A

Example answers:
1 Would you like a cup of tea? *or* Would you like some tea?
2 Would you like some ice cream?
3 Would you like a sandwich?
4 Would you like an aspirin? *or* Would you like some aspirins?

Exercise 50B

1 Would you like to go to a disco this evening?
2 Would you like to go to the cinema on Saturday?
3 Would you like to play tennis this weekend?
4 Would you like to see a football match tomorrow?

Exercise 50C

1 I'll lend you mine.
2 I'll get you a ticket, then.
3 I'll show you on the map.
4 I'll help you clean it.
5 I'll close the window.
6 I'll look it up in my dictionary.

Exercise 50D

Example answers:
1 Shall I do the washing up?
2 Shall I clean the windows?
3 Shall I do the ironing?
4 Shall I clean the car?
5 Shall I empty the rubbish bin?

Exercise 50E

(i)

1 Would you like me to fill up
2 Would you like me to check
3 Would you like me to clean
4 Would you like me to check

(ii)

Example answers:
Would you like me to type this letter? Would you like me to file that report? Would you like me to send a fax message? Would you like me to answer this memo?

Unit 51

Exercise 51A

Example answers:
1 Let's have
2 How about playing
3 Shall we go
4 Why don't we see
5 Let's go
6 Why don't we go

Exercise 51B

You: What shall we do this evening?
Friend: Let's go out somewhere.
You: All right. Where shall we go?
Friend: Why don't we go out for a meal?
You: Okay. Shall we go to Pizza Hut?
Friend: We went there last Saturday. Let's go somewhere different this evening.

You: All right. How about trying that new Chinese restaurant in East Street?
Friend: Okay. Good idea. Let's do that.

Exercise 51C

1 shall we
2 Let's
3 Why don't we *or* Shall we
4 Let's
5 How about
6 Let's
7 shall we
8 How about
9 shall we
10 Why don't we *or* Shall we

Unit 52

Exercise 52A

1 I can't cook.
2 My grandmother couldn't ski.
3 We mustn't stop now.
4 The letter may not arrive tomorrow.
5 He might not be here next week.
6 You shouldn't buy that car.
7 They can't speak French.
8 She might not remember you.
9 You mustn't go out today.
10 I don't have to work late tomorrow.
11 She doesn't have to get up early.
12 They didn't have to walk home yesterday.

Exercise 52B

1 Should we ask for help?
2 Can you come to the concert?
3 Could he ride a horse?
4 Should I go to the police?
5 Can she dance the tango?
6 Should he see the doctor?
7 Do I have to pay for the ticket?
8 Does she have to work on Saturdays?
9 Did they have to sell their car?

Exercise 52C

(i)

(b) I *had to* clean my room yesterday.

(ii)

1 (a) and (c)   2 (b)   3 (d)

Exercise 52D

1 (b)   2 (a) and (c)

Exercise 52E

1 (b)   2 (a)

Exercise 52F

Example answers:

1 **Asking for something**
   Can I have a cup of coffee, please?
   Could I have some bananas, please?
   May I have the bill, please?
2 **Asking for permission**
   Can I see your driving licence?
   Could I use your pen?
   May I ask you a question?
3 **Asking someone to do something**
   Can you help me?
   Could you lend me some money?
4 **Offering something**
   Would you like some coffee?
5 **Inviting someone**
   Would you like to go to a concert tomorrow?
6 **Offering to do something**
   I'll lend you some money.
   Shall I do the washing up?
   Would you like me to help you?
7 **Asking for a suggestion**
   What shall we do this evening?
8 **Making a suggestion**
   Shall we stay at home?
   Let's go out.
   Why don't we go to a restaurant?
   How about going to a concert?

Unit 53

Exercise 53A

What? – A book.
Who? – Diana.
Whose? – My friend's.
How? – By car.
Where? – At school.
When? – Today.
Why? – Because it's late.

Exercise 53B

1 What	4 Where	7 How	10 What
2 How	5 How	8 What	11 Why
3 Where	6 When	9 Who	

Exercise 53C

1 What   2 Which   3 Who   4 Which

Exercise 53D

1 When *or* What time
2 What
3 Who
4 How
5 When *or* What time
6 How much
7 Where
8 How often
9 How many
10 When *or* What time

Exercise 53E

1 Where	4 Who	7 What
2 When	5 How	8 How long
3 Where	6 Where	9 What

Unit 54

Exercise 54A

(i)
Reading about the people

(ii)
1 Who is sitting next to Oscar?
2 Who is Oscar talking to?
3 Who is standing next to Ella?
4 Who is Ella talking to?
5 Who is playing table tennis with Carmen?
6 Who is Rob waving to?
7 Who is looking at Marty?
8 Who is Marty looking at?

(iii)
Gina is sitting next to Oscar. Oscar is talking to Nancy. Bernie is standing next to Ella. Ella is talking to James. Franco is playing table tennis with Carmen. Rob is waving to Yoshiko. Judy is looking at Marty. Marty is looking at himself in the mirror!

Exercise 54B

(i)
Reading about who likes who

(ii)
Who likes Sammy the best? – Lisa.
Who does Sammy like the best? – Cindy.
Who likes Cindy the best? – Sammy.
Who does Cindy like the best? – Dizzy.
Who likes Dizzy the best? – Cindy.
Who does Dizzy like the best? – Lisa.
Who likes Lisa the best? – Dizzy.
Who does Lisa like the best? – Sammy.

Exercise 54C

(i)
Reading the facts

(ii)
Example answers:
1 Who wrote *Frankenstein*? What did Mary Shelley write? When did she write it?
2 Who invented the radio? What did Guglielmo Marconi invent? When did he invent it?
3 Who invented the vacuum cleaner? What did Hubert Booth invent? When did he invent it?
4 Who invented the razor? What did King Camp Gillette invent? When did he invent it?
5 Who produced the first cheap car? What did Henry Ford produce? When did he produce it?
6 Who built the first windsurfer? What did Peter Chilvers build? When did he build it?

Unit 55

Exercise 55A

(i)
Reading about Martha Miller

(ii)
1 haven't you?	6 weren't you?
2 didn't you?	7 don't you?
3 aren't you?	8 aren't you?
4 weren't you?	9 is he?
5 did you?	10 haven't you?

Unit 56

Exercise 56A

1 What	8 How
2 What	9 How old
3 Which	10 How tall
4 Whose	11 How many
5 Where	12 How much
6 When	13 How often
7 Why	14 How long

Exercise 56B

1 Who is Jack waiting for?
2 Who is waiting for Jack?
3 What is happening?
4 Who has got the money?
5 Who does Carmen want to see?
6 Who wants to see Carmen?
7 What does Carmen want to see?
8 Who did Steven smile at?
9 Who smiled at Steven?
10 What did Steven smile at?
11 What happened?

Exercise 56C

1 Smoking is bad for you, isn't it?
2 Money isn't everything, is it?
3 Computers are very useful, aren't they?
4 Some people watch too much TV, don't they?
5 People didn't have TV 100 years ago, did they?
6 Life was better 100 years ago, wasn't it?
7 We can all make mistakes, can't we?
8 Parents shouldn't hit their children, should they?

Exercise 56D

1 What is Tony writing?
2 What does Julia want to do?
3 Who wants a cup of tea?
4 Who killed President John F Kennedy?
5 Who invented the telephone?
6 Who is your favourite actor?
7 Whose is this coat?
8 Which hand do you write with?
9 Arthur is 21, isn't he?
10 You're a student, aren't you?
11 They live in Milan, don't they?
12 Does Diana like golf? *or* Diana likes golf, doesn't she?

Unit 57

Exercise 57A

1 listening
2 cooking *or* to cook
3 speak
4 learning *or* to learn
5 to learn
6 gardening
7 jogging
8 to swim
9 going *or* to go
10 drawing
11 play
12 getting *or* to get
13 to travel
14 to move
15 move
16 to have
17 to be
18 getting
19 to learn; to fly
20 to be
21 to be
22 answering

Exercise 57B

Example answers:
1 play	10 to learn
2 playing	11 learn
3 to play	12 learning
4 playing	13 sail
5 going *or* to go	14 to sail
6 go	15 wearing *or* to wear
7 to go	16 to swim
8 going *or* to go	17 swimming
9 learning *or* to learn	18 getting

251

Answers to the exercises

Exercise 57C

1 to come	6 offering	11 afford
2 cleaning	7 do	12 to go
3 to do	8 go	13 going
4 helping	9 go	14 do
5 clean *or* to clean	10 going	

Exercise 57D

1 to open the bottle.
2 him to open the bottle.
3 to play chess.
4 her to play chess.
5 him to drive.
6 them to close the door.
7 him to open his mouth.
8 her to go to a concert.

Unit 58

Exercise 58A

(i)

1 They went to the supermarket to do some shopping.
2 They went to the park to play tennis.
3 They went to the cafe to have lunch.
4 They went to the library to borrow some books.
5 They went to the cinema to see a film.

(ii)

Example answers:
I went to the cinema to see a film. I went to a restaurant to have a meal. I went to town to do some shopping. I went to the Sports Centre to play basketball. I went to my bank to get some money.

Exercise 58B

1 You go to a baker's to buy bread and cakes.
2 You go to a hairdresser's for a haircut.
3 You go to a restaurant for a meal.
4 You go to a petrol station for petrol.
5 You go to a disco to dance.
6 You go to a launderette to wash your clothes.

Exercise 58C

1 for cutting metal.
2 for cleaning carpets.
3 for putting rubbish in.
4 for mixing food.
5 for holding things.
6 for putting out fires.

Unit 59

Exercise 59A

(i)

1 I **would like** (*to* infinitive).
2 You **can** (infinitive without *to*).
3 You're good **at** (*-ing* form).
4 I **love** (*-ing* form or *to* infinitive).
5 **Teach** me (*to* infinitive).

(ii)

1 **Word + infinitive without** *to*
  eg can, could, may, might, must, shall, should, will, let's, why don't we, help
2 **Word +** *to* **infinitive**
  eg (can) afford, decide, expect, hope, learn, promise, want, would like, help, easy, difficult, important, possible, expensive, stupid
3 **Word + object +** *to* **infinitive**
  eg ask, expect, invite, teach, tell, want, would like, help
4 **Word +** *-ing* **form**
  eg enjoy, finish, mind, go, about, at, in, of, for
5 **Word +** *-ing* **form or** *to* **infinitive**
  eg begin, hate, like, love, start

Exercise 59B

1 We must *go* now.
2 ✓
3 Do you enjoy *playing* chess?
4 They want *to get* married next year.
5 ✓
6 Do you mind *working* at weekends?
7 How about *going* to the cinema?
8 ✓
9 I finished *writing* the report yesterday.
10 Tony phoned Julia before *leaving* work.
11 They went to the park *to play* tennis.
12 ✓
13 Did you go out *to do* some shopping?
14 ✓
15 I must go to the bank *to get* some money.
16 I'd like *you to come* to the party.
17 We don't want *you to* worry.

Unit 60

Exercise 60A

1 tall woman 4 old women
2 short man   5 clean shirts
3 young boy   6 dirty shirt

1 She's tall.   4 They're old.
2 He's short.   5 They're clean.
3 He's young.   6 It's dirty.

Exercise 60B

1 She looks rich.   4 They look sad.
2 He looks poor.   5 She looks cold.
3 They look happy. 6 He looks hot.

Unit 61

Exercise 61A

1 Edith teaches French in Paris.
2 I go shopping in town on Saturdays.
3 We play volleyball at the beach at weekends.
4 They have lunch in the school canteen at 1 o'clock.
5 Mr Wilson watches TV in his room in the evenings.

Exercise 61B

Example answers:
1 I always work hard.
2 I'm always polite.
3 I sometimes get angry.
4 I'm sometimes nervous.
5 I rarely feel bored.
6 I'm usually happy.

Exercise 61C

Example answers:
I clean my bedroom once a week. I brush my teeth twice a day. I eat in a restaurant twice a week. I have a haircut once a month. I go on holiday three times a year.

Exercise 61D

1 Do you usually speak English every day?
2 Are you sometimes tired in the mornings?
3 Do you usually watch TV every evening?
4 Are you always in bed before 12.00?
5 Do you often go to the cinema at weekends?

Unit 62

Exercise 62A

1

stronger	– strongest
faster	– fastest
smaller	– smallest
louder	– loudest
quicker	– quickest
colder	– coldest

2

larger	– largest
nicer	– nicest
whiter	– whitest

3

sadder	– saddest
hotter	– hottest
slimmer	– slimmest

4

heavier	– heaviest
friendlier	– friendliest
sunnier	– sunniest

Exercise 62B

Example answers:
1 George is taller than Frank.
2 Frank looks friendlier than George.
3 Frank is older than George.
4 George is slimmer than Frank.
5 George looks more serious than Frank.
6 George looks fitter than Frank.
7 Frank looks more relaxed than George.
8 George is better-looking than Frank.

Exercise 62C

(i)

1 the youngest	6 the most serious
2 the oldest	7 the nicest
3 the tallest	8 the best-looking
4 the shortest	9 the most intelligent
5 the funniest	

(ii)

1 My sister is the youngest.
2 My grandfather is the oldest.
3 My father is the tallest.
4 My sister is the shortest.
5 My grandfather is the funniest.
6 My father is the most serious.
7 My mother is the nicest.
8 My mother is the best-looking.
9 I'm the most intelligent!

Exercise 62D

1 A cheetah isn't as big as a lion. A lion isn't as fast as a cheetah.
2 An elephant isn't as tall as a giraffe. A giraffe isn't as heavy as an elephant.
3 A duck isn't as strong as a swan. A duck isn't as beautiful as a swan.
4 A whale isn't as dangerous as a shark. A shark isn't as big as a whale.

Unit 63

Exercise 63A

1 He's walking slowly.
2 She's running fast.
3 She's shouting angrily.
4 He's working hard.
5 She's waving sadly.
6 They're laughing happily.

Exercise 63B

1 well 3 well 5 strong 7 fast
2 good 4 quickly 6 hard 8 carefully

Exercise 63C

1 You play the guitar very well.
2 My sister speaks Spanish fluently.
3 I play chess very badly.
4 Mark drives his father's car very carefully.

Unit 64

Exercise 64A

(i)

1 was too dirty.
2 wasn't windy enough.
3 wasn't big enough.
4 wasn't sunny enough.
5 was too dangerous.
6 were too bumpy.

(ii)

1 The beach was too dirty to lie on.
2 It wasn't windy enough to windsurf.
3 The swimming pool wasn't big enough to swim in.
4 It wasn't sunny enough to sunbathe.
5 The river was too dangerous to swim in.
6 The tennis courts were too bumpy to play on.

Unit 65

Exercise 65A

1 New York is a very interesting city.
2 That's a very good film.
3 Julia is wearing a green jacket.
4 I meet my friends in town every Saturday.
5 We usually go to the cinema once a week.
6 Mr Bird always arrives at work at 8.30.
7 Mr Bird is never late for work.
8 I like windsurfing very much.
9 You speak English very well.
10 Sue isn't old enough to get married.

Exercise 65B

Example answers:
I'm taller than my friend. She's more serious than I am. She isn't as friendly as I am. I'm older than she is. I'm slimmer than she is. She's quieter than I am. She's more nervous than I am. She's better-looking than I am. I'm more intelligent than she is!

Exercise 65C

1 There are two *young* girls outside.
2 ✓
3 Which is the *largest* city in the world?
4 Mike is the *youngest* student in his class.
5 ✓
6 Diana can sing very *well*.
7 I'm *older than* Maria, but she's taller *than* me.
8 Boxing is much more dangerous *than* judo.
9 Loretta is a very *hard* worker.
10 My father always drives very *carefully*.

Exercise 65D

1 too heavy 3 old enough
2 windy enough 4 too late

Unit 66

Exercise 66A

1 on 3 in 5 at 7 at 9 in
2 in 4 at 6 in *or* at 8 on 10 on

Exercise 66B

(i)

1 in 2 in 3 at 4 on

(ii)

Example answer:
I live in Zurich. I live in Winterthurerstrasse. I live at 70 Winterthurerstrasse. My flat is on the third floor.

Unit 67

Exercise 67A

1 in 3 at 5 on 7 in 9 on
2 at; in 4 at 6 in 8 on

Exercise 67B

in	on
in the morning	on Friday
in March	on Tuesday
in the afternoon	on 1st March
in 1980	on Monday morning
in the summer	on my birthday
in July	on Friday night
in 1804	on 4th July
in the spring	on New Year's Day

at	without a preposition
at 2 o'clock	last Friday
at night	next Tuesday
at the weekend	this morning
at 8.15	every summer
at weekends	tomorrow evening
at Christmas	yesterday afternoon

Unit 68

Exercise 68A

(i)

1 under 7 past 13 round
2 next to 8 in front of 14 from
3 opposite 9 behind 15 at
4 out of 10 across 16 near
5 into 11 to 17 onto
6 along 12 on 18 off

(ii)

1 into 7 in 13 on
2 through 8 on 14 between
3 up 9 next to 15 Under
4 in 10 In front of 16 On
5 on 11 off 17 near
6 behind 12 onto

(iii)

Example answers:
The woman is climbing out of the house. The man is walking down the stairs. The briefcase is under the chair. The camera is on the desk, next to the photograph. The key is behind the phone. The cat is jumping onto the desk. The large picture is on the floor, between the chair and the box.

Exercise 68B

1 down 4 to
2 over 5 in front of
3 out of 6 off

Unit 69

Exercise 69A

(i)

1 Diana went to Italy a week ago.
2 The London train left ten minutes ago.
3 Tim bought a new car two months ago.

(ii)

Example answers:
1 I started learning English two years ago.
2 I had my last holiday three months ago.
3 I first met my best friend eight years ago.

Exercise 69B

(i)

1 since 4 since 7 since 10 since
2 for 5 since 8 for
3 for 6 for 9 for

(ii)

Example answers:
1 I've lived in Madrid for ten years.
2 I've had my watch since 1991.
3 I've been at this school for two months.
4 I've known my girlfriend since last summer.

Exercise 69C

1 for 2 for 3 since 4 ago 5 ago 6 since

Unit 70

Exercise 70A

(i)

1 on 2 on 3 on

(ii)

1 in 5 at 9 at
2 in 6 at 10 in
3 on 7 in *or* at 11 in
4 on 8 at 12 at

Exercise 70B

in

in the morning, in the afternoon, in the evening, in January, in February, in 1930, in 1992, in 2001, in the summer, in the winter

on

on Monday, on Tuesday, on Monday morning, on Tuesday afternoon, on 1st May, on 7th June

at

at ten o'clock, at 2.15, at night, at the weekend, at weekends, at Christmas, at Easter

Exercise 70C

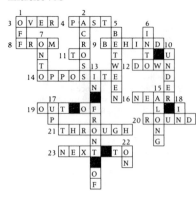

Exercise 70D

1 two years ago   4 for five years
2 left   5 since two o'clock
3 four weeks ago

Unit 71

Exercise 71A

1 I can windsurf, but I can't water-ski.
2 I play volleyball and basketball.
3 I've got a cat, but I haven't got a dog.
4 I go swimming and I do yoga.
5 Are you left-handed or right-handed?
6 I can't speak Italian, but I can speak Spanish.
7 I've got two brothers and two sisters.
8 Are you married or single?
9 I enjoy watching TV and listening to music.
10 I like playing tennis, but I don't enjoy watching it.

Exercise 71B

1 I was late for work because my car broke down.
2 I was late for work, so I hurried.
3 I was late for work, so I took a taxi.
4 I was late for work because my alarm clock didn't go off.
5 I was late for work because I overslept.
6 I was late for work, so I didn't have time for breakfast.
7 I was late for work, so I apologised to my boss.

Unit 72

Exercise 72A

1 When he wakes up, he'll have a shower.
2 When he's dressed, he'll have breakfast.
3 When he finishes breakfast, he'll do the washing up.
4 When he finishes the washing up, he'll go to work.

Exercise 72B

1 If she sunbathes for too long, she'll get sunburnt.
2 If he doesn't take an umbrella, he'll get wet.
3 If he eats all that ice cream, he'll be sick.
4 If she touches that broken glass, she'll cut herself.

Exercise 72C

Example answers:
1 When I finish this exercise, I'll go for a walk.
2 When I get up tomorrow, I'll have a shower.
3 If I feel ill tomorrow, I'll see the doctor.
4 If it rains this weekend, I'll stay at home.

Unit 73

Exercise 73A

1 but   2 and   3 or   4 and   5 but

Exercise 73B

Example answers:
1 my car broke down.
2 I took a taxi.
3 it is raining.
4 I don't know the time.
5 I felt tired.
6 we went for a walk.

Exercise 73C

1 when   2 if   3 when   4 If   5 When

Exercise 73D

1 When I go, I'll post   4 When I finish, I'll go
2 If I stay, I'll watch   5 If it is, I'll go
3 If I sell, I'll buy

Unit 74

Exercise 74A

Monday, Tuesday, Wednesday, Thursday, Friday, Saturday, Sunday

Exercise 74B

January, February, March, April, May, June, July, August, September, October, November, December

Exercise 74C

1 four hundred and twenty
2 a hundred and ten *or* one hundred and ten
3 nine hundred and four
4 seven hundred and twenty-eight
5 eight hundred and ninety-two
6 a thousand, two hundred and one *or* one thousand, two hundred and one
7 a million *or* one million

Exercise 74D

1 two six double nine oh two
2 four two eight oh nine five
3 seven three seven six nine three
4 five double one four eight one
5 double oh double six double three

Exercise 74E

January is the first month, February is the second month, March is the third month, April is the fourth month, May is the fifth month, June is the sixth month, July is the seventh month, August is the eighth month, September is the ninth month, October is the tenth month, November is the eleventh month, December is the twelfth month

Exercise 74F

1 the ninth of March nineteen eighty *or* March the ninth nineteen eighty
2 the tenth of February nineteen fifty *or* February the tenth nineteen fifty
3 the thirty-first of May nineteen forty-one *or* May the thirty-first nineteen forty-one
4 the nineteenth of August nineteen sixty-three *or* August the nineteenth nineteen sixty-three
5 the seventh of July nineteen seventy-seven *or* July the seventh nineteen seventy-seven
6 the twenty-first of September nineteen ninety-two *or* September the twenty-first nineteen ninety-two
7 the third of June nineteen eleven *or* June the third nineteen eleven
8 the second of November nineteen twenty-five *or* November the second nineteen twenty-five
9 the thirteenth of January nineteen thirty *or* January the thirteenth nineteen thirty
10 the thirtieth of October nineteen oh eight *or* October the thirtieth nineteen oh eight

Unit 75

Exercise 75A

1 It's four o'clock.
2 It's one o'clock.
3 It's half past two. *or* It's two thirty.
4 It's quarter past eleven. *or* It's a quarter past eleven. *or* It's eleven fifteen.
5 It's twelve o'clock.
6 It's quarter to four. *or* It's a quarter to four. *or* It's three forty-five.

Exercise 75B

1) 6.05 — half past six
2) 6.10 — ten to seven
3) 6.15 — ten past six
4) 6.20 — a quarter to seven
5) 6.25 — a quarter past six
6) 6.30 — five past six
7) 6.35 — five to seven
8) 6.40 — twenty-five past six
9) 6.45 — twenty-five to seven
10) 6.50 — twenty past six
11) 6.55 — twenty to seven

Exercise 75C

1 It's quarter past three. *or* It's a quarter past three. *or* It's three fifteen.
2 It's half past one. *or* It's one thirty.
3 It's twenty past four. *or* It's four twenty.
4 It's seventeen minutes past eight. *or* It's eight seventeen.
5 It's quarter to six. *or* It's a quarter to six. *or* It's five forty-five.
6 It's twenty-five past ten. *or* It's ten twenty-five.
7 It's two o'clock.
8 It's five past nine. *or* It's nine oh five.
9 It's three minutes past seven. *or* It's seven oh three.

Answers to the progress tests

1 Singular and plural nouns
1 chairs	5 eyes	9 countries
2 pens	6 men	10 houses
3 churches	7 lives	11 foxes
4 students	8 children	12 people

2 A, an
1 a 2 an 3 / 4 one 5 a 6 one

3 Possessive 's
1 Diana's office
2 Bruce's wife
3 the corner of the room
4 my parents' house
5 Mike's sister
6 the end of Delaware Street

4 Countable and uncountable nouns
1 hair	3 are	5 spaghetti; is
2 furniture	4 is; bread	6 is; some; news

5 A, an, the
1 My car has got *a* radio.
2 Can you switch off *the* radio, please?
3 There isn't *a* telephone box near here.
4 Who is *the* woman outside?
5 Astrid is *a* secretary in *an* office in Zurich.
6 My parents have got *a* cat and *a* dog. *The* cat's name is Ziggy and *the* dog's name is Barry.

6 Talking in general
1 / 2 the 3 / 4 the 5 /;/

7 Proper nouns
1 Tahiti is in *the* Pacific Ocean.
2 Rome is on *the* River Tiber.
3 *Greece* is in *Europe*.
4 The British Museum is in *London*.
5 Sicily is in *the* Mediterranean.
6 *Peter's* birthday is in *November*.
7 *Sam* is a student at the University of Bristol.
8 *Diana* speaks *French* and *German*.
9 My sister is a student at *Oxford University*.
10 *The* Odeon Cinema is between *the* Park Hotel and *the* Playhouse Theatre in Shelley Street.

8 Expressions with and without *the*
1 the	3 /	5 /	7 /	9 /;/
2 /	4 the	6 the	8 the	10 the; the

9 Some, any, no
1 some	6 any
2 some ('any' is also possible)	7 no
3 any	8 any
4 any	9 some
5 any	10 some ('any' is also possible)

10 Much, many, a lot of, a little, a few, enough
1 C ('B' is also possible, but not so usual)
2 A
3 B
4 C ('A' is also possible, but not usual)
5 B
6 C
7 C

11 Subject pronouns
1 He	3 I	5 you	7 They
2 She	4 We	6 They	8 It

12 Possessive adjectives
1 Their	3 his	5 its
2 her	4 My	6 Our; your

13 Subject and object pronouns
1 her	3 him	5 them
2 He	4 me	6 We; them

14 Possessive adjectives and pronouns
1 mine	3 yours	5 their
2 her	4 your	6 ours

15 This, that, these, those
1 this 2 those 3 these 4 that

16 One, ones
1 one (one = a cup of coffee)
2 ones (ones = trousers)
3 one; one (one = girl)

17 Something, anything, somebody, anybody, etc
1 something ('anything' is also possible)
2 anything
3 Nobody *or* No one
4 somebody *or* someone ('anybody' *or* 'anyone' is also possible)
5 Everybody *or* Everyone
6 everything
7 nothing
8 anybody *or* anyone
9 Everywhere
10 anywhere
11 somewhere
12 nowhere

18 Reflexive pronouns
1 himself	3 yourselves	5 ourselves
2 herself	4 myself	6 themselves

19 Present tense of the verb *be*
(i)
1 is	4 are	7 is	10 is
2 am	5 is	8 is	
3 is	6 are	9 is	
(ii)
1 I'm not tired.   3 Mike isn't married.
2 You aren't late.   4 We aren't hungry.
(iii)
1 What is your name?
2 Are you a student?
3 Is your teacher English?
4 What are your parents' names?

20 There is, there are
1 There is	6 there are
2 Is there	7 They are
3 there is	8 are there
4 It is	9 There are
5 Are there	10 They are

21 Have got
1 have ('ve) got; haven't got
2 hasn't got; has ('s) got
3 Have you got; haven't
4 Has your car got; has
5 Have your parents got; have ('ve) got

22 Imperative
1 Close	3 Switch	5 Don't forget
2 Don't sit	4 Hurry	

23 Present simple
1 starts; finishes
2 don't come; come
3 opens; does it close
4 gets up; doesn't get up
5 speak; don't speak; do you speak

24 Present continuous
1 am ('m) writing
2 are ('re) playing
3 is wearing
4 Is she talking
5 are ('re) painting
6 are you eating
7 am ('m) not reading
8 isn't raining; is shining

25 Present continuous and present simple
(i)
1 B 2 C 3 B 4 C 5 A
(ii)
1 Are you working; am
2 Do you work; do
3 Does Pete usually walk; doesn't

26 Verbs not normally used in the continuous
1 Mmm! *I like* this ice cream.
2 *I don't understand* this sentence.
3 ✓
4 Michael *has* black hair and brown eyes.
5 ✓
6 *Do you think* Julia Roberts is a good actress?
7 *Do you know* those people?

27 Past tense of the verb *be*
1 Were; were	3 Were; was	5 Were; were
2 Was; was	4 Was; was	

28 Past simple
1 did you go	9 was
2 went	10 didn't have
3 Did you go	11 rained
4 didn't	12 was
5 went	13 Did you have
6 drove	14 did
7 did you stay	15 enjoyed
8 stayed	

29 Past continuous
1 was	7 was carrying
2 were sitting	8 came
3 stopped	9 was carrying
4 were	10 got
5 got	11 rode
6 ran	12 arrived

30 Present perfect simple
1 has lived	4 Have you ever been
2 have ('ve) visited	5 has just arrived
3 has Diana had	6 Have you seen

31 Present perfect simple and past simple
(i)
1 have ('ve) lived	4 have ('ve) worked
2 was	5 worked
3 lived	6 worked
(ii)
1 How long have you lived in London?
2 How long did you live in Liverpool?
3 How long have you worked for the travel company?
4 How long did you work for the export company?
(iii)
1 a) started   3 a) have you had
   b) has started   b) did you have
2 a) Did you go
   b) Have you been

32 Present continuous for the future
(i)
1 are you doing   3 Are you doing
2 Are you going
(ii)
1 I'm going to evening class.
2 I'm having dinner with Andrew.
3 I'm visiting Jenny and Karen.

33 *Going to*
1 am ('m) going to watch
2 am ('m) going to buy
3 is ('s) going to be
4 is she going to live?
5 are you going to do?

34 *Will*
Example answers:
1 will you be   2 won't be   3 'll
clean   4 'll do

35 *Will* and *going to*
1 is going to leave   3 he's going to start
2 You'll enjoy   4 I'll lend

36 *Can*
1 can   2 can   3 can't   4 Can you

37 *Can, could*
1 I *could* play chess when I was eight.
2 Mike is a good runner. He *can* run very fast.
3 ✓
4 When I was younger I *couldn't* swim.
5 *Could you ski* when you were ten?

38 *Must*
1 must drive   3 must tidy
2 mustn't make   4 mustn't forget

39 *Must, have to*
(i)
1 have to *or* must   4 have to *or* must
2 has to *or* must   5 have to
3 had to   6 have to
(ii)
1 don't have to   3 doesn't have to
2 mustn't   4 mustn't

40 *May, might*
1 may go *or* might go; may stay *or* might stay;
   may watch *or* might watch
2 may play *or* might play; may rain *or* might
   rain

41 *Should*
1 should wear   3 should help
2 shouldn't go   4 should do

42 Requests: *can, could, may*
(i)
1 Could we have two coffees, please?
2 May I have a new cheque book, please?
3 Can I try on these jeans?
4 Could you check the oil, please?
(ii)
a clothes shop – 3
a bank – 2
a petrol station – 4
a cafe – 1

43 Offers and invitations: *would like, will, shall*
1 Would you like something to eat?
2 Would you like to go with me?
3 Shall I switch on the central heating?
4 I'll lend you mine if you like.
5 Would you like me to help you carry them?

44 Suggestions: *shall, let's, why don't we, how about*
1 shall   6 go   11 don't
2 do   7 How   12 go
3 Shall   8 about   13 Let's
4 stay   9 having   14 stay
5 Let's   10 Why

45 Question words
1 Who   4 How old   7 How   10 How often
2 What   5 Where   8 Why
3 Which   6 When   9 Whose

46 Subject and object questions
1 Who is helping you?
2 What are you reading?
3 Who wants to see Jim?
4 What does Jim want to say?
5 Who phoned you?
6 Who did you phone?
7 What did Diana give you?

47 Question tags
1 haven't you?   6 was he?
2 isn't she?   7 don't you?
3 are you?   8 does she?
4 can't you?   9 didn't you?
5 aren't I?

48 Word + infinitive or *-ing* form
1 use   10 sailing
2 to ride   11 to have
3 buying   12 listening *or* to listen
4 going   13 to listen
5 go   14 do *or* to do
6 to pass   15 closing
7 going   16 to play
8 go   17 reading
9 to post   18 learning *or* to learn

49 Purpose: *to . . .* and *for . . .*
1 to   2 for   3 for   4 to

50 Adjectives
1 ✓
2 I've got some *yellow* pyjamas.
3 Mrs Kent has got two *young* children.
4 ✓

51 Word order with adverbs and adverbial phrases
1 We have breakfast in the garden in the summer.
2 I usually go to the disco once a week.
3 Julia often visits her parents at the weekends.
4 The roads are always very busy in the mornings.

52 Comparison of adjectives
1 a) the tallest   3 a) the most interesting
   b) tall as   b) interesting as
   c) taller than   c) more interesting than
2 a) good as
   b) better than
   c) the best

53 Adjectives and adverbs
(i)
1 good   3 heavily   5 hard
2 well   4 heavy   6 hard
(ii)
1 You must read the letter carefully.
2 I don't play the guitar very well.

54 *Too* and *enough* with adjectives and adverbs
1 old enough   2 too cold   3 very

55 Place: *in, on, at*
1 on; in   4 at; in
2 at; in; at   5 in; on
3 at *or* in; in   6 in; at

56 Time: *in, on, at*
1 at; in   3 at; in   5 at; /   7 on; in
2 at; /   4 on; on   6 at; in

57 Place and movement
(i)
1 out of; into   3 off; onto   5 to; from
2 under; over   4 up; down
(ii)
1 behind   6 across
2 in front of   7 through
3 opposite   8 round
4 between   9 next to
5 along   10 past

58 Time: *ago, for, since*
1 We've been married *for* twenty years.
2 ✓
3 Diana bought her flat two years *ago*.
4 ✓
5 *I started* learning Italian five years ago.

59 *And, but, or, because, so*
1 or   2 and   3 but   4 so   5 because

60 *When, if*
1 when   2 If   3 When   4 when   5 If

61 Days, months, numbers
(i)
Monday
Tuesday
Wednesday
Thursday
Friday
Saturday
Sunday
(ii)
1 C   2 A   3 C   4 B
(iii)
1 six three one five oh eight
2 four one seven double eight three
3 double two oh five six nine
4 one oh three seven one oh
5 double oh one four three six
6 double seven double four nine oh
(iv)
1 the eighth of February nineteen ninety-one
   or February the eighth nineteen ninety-one
2 the eleventh of March nineteen sixty-six *or*
   March the eleventh nineteen sixty-six
3 the fourth of October nineteen fifty-nine *or*
   October the fourth nineteen fifty-nine
4 the twenty-fifth of August nineteen ninety-
   two *or* August the twenty-fifth nineteen
   ninety-two
5 the sixteenth of May nineteen seventy-
   eight *or* May the sixteenth nineteen
   seventy-eight
6 the twelfth of December nineteen twelve *or*
   December the twelfth nineteen twelve
(v)
1 Our holiday is *in* April.
2 The next meeting is *on* Monday.
3 Diana's birthday is on *the sixteenth of* April.
4 I have ten *thousand* dollars.
5 You have *a* hundred pounds.
6 There's a concert *on the first of* January.

62 The time
1 eight o'clock
2 half past eight *or* eight thirty
3 quarter to eight *or* a quarter to eight *or*
   seven forty-five
4 quarter past eight *or* a quarter past eight *or*
   eight fifteen
5 five to eight *or* seven fifty-five
6 twenty-five past eight *or* eight twenty-five
7 three minutes past eight
8 twenty to eight *or* seven forty